Language Wars and Linguistic Politics

LOUIS-JEAN CALVET

Translated by
Michel Petheram

OXFORD UNIVERSITY PRESS
1998

Oxford University Press, Great Clarendon Street, Oxford OX2 6DP

Oxford New York
Athens Auckland Bangkok Bogota Bombay
Buenos Aires Calcutta Cape Town Dar es Salaam
Delhi Florence Hong Kong Istanbul Karachi
Kuala Lumpur Madras Madrid Melbourne
Mexico City Nairobi Paris Singapore
Taipei Tokyo Toronto Warsaw

and associated companies in
Berlin Ibadan

Oxford is a trade mark of Oxford University Press

Published in the United States
by Oxford University Press Inc., New York

British Library Cataloguing in Publication Data
Data available

Library of Congress Cataloging in Publication Data
[Guerre des langues et les politiques linguistiques. English]
Language wars and linguistic politics/Louis-Jean
Calvet; translated by Michel Petheram.
Includes bibliographical references and index.
1. Language and languages. 2. Language policy. 3. Language planning. I. Title.
P106.C27813 1997 306.44'9–dc21 97-39157

ISBN 0-19-823598-4
ISBN 0-19-870021-0 (pbk.)
10 9 8 7 6 5 4 3 2 1

Typeset by Best-set Typesetter Ltd., Hong Kong
Printed in Great Britain on acid-free paper by
Bookcraft (Bath) Ltd., Midsomer Norton

Contents

To the English Reader   ix

Introduction   xiii

PART I.   The Origins of Conflict   1

1. The Question of Origins   3

2. Religions and Language   17

3. A Multilingual World   26
     Bilingualism and Diglossia   26
     French as a Touchstone   31
     Writing   38

4. Ideologists of Superiority   41
     Greeks, Barbarians, and Others   41
     Du Bellay and his 'Defence'   44
     Rivarol and the Universality of French   47
     Ideologists of the Wars   50

PART II.   The Battlefield   53

5. Lingua Francas and Vernaculars   55
     The Tendency to a Vernacular   55
     The Tendency to a Lingua Franca   56
     The Example of Gavot   57
     Pygmalion and Dominici   59
     Mauritius   61
     Language and Belonging   63

6. The Family as a Battlefield   67
     The Case of Senegal   67
     Mother Tongue or Father Tongue?   69
     From Mother Tongue to National Language   72
     The Family Versus Society   73

7. Markets and Languages   76
     The Markets of Canton (China)   77

The Markets of Brazzaville (Congo)   80
The Little Market of Niamey (Niger)   84
Markets and Multilingualism   88

8. Lingua Francas   90
   The Example of Quechua   90
   Factors in the Spread of Lingua Francas   94
   And Yet They Do Communicate   98

9. The Death of Languages   100
   We Speak Dead Languages   100
   The Disappearance of Languages   103
   The Quechua of Cochabamba   104
   The Death of Languages   107
   Linguistics and Sociolinguistics   109

PART III.   Among the Administrators   111

10. Language Policy and Planning: First Approach   113

11. Case Studies: The Management of Multilingualism   119
    The Case of China   119
    The Case of India   125
    The Case of Guinea   128
    Discussion   134

12. Case Studies: Language Planning and Nationalism   137
    The Case of Norway   137
    The Case of Turkey   140
    Discussion   142

13. Case Study: The Language Struggle of the Jivaro of Ecuador   146

14. The War of Writing   153
    The Mandingo Alphabets   153
    The Soviet Example   155
    The Chinese Example   158
    Discussion   163

15. The War of Words   166
    First Approach   166
    The Example of Bambara   167
    Neologisms and Ideology   170

16. Trench Warfare: The Case of French   175
    The Growth of French   175
    The Reasons for the Growth and Subsequent
       Decline of French   177

Skirmishes in Quebec 179
The 'Defence' of French 182
Between Ineffectiveness and Chauvinism 184
French in the World 187

17. The Pacifist Illusion and Esperanto 194
Historic Landmarks 194
The Ideology of Esperanto 198
The Sociolinguistic Approach 200

Conclusion 202

Bibliography 204
Index 209

To the English Reader

This book, published in French in 1987, stands at the halfway point in research started at the very beginning of the 1970s and which continues today. For this reason I would like to give a brief account of the enterprise of which it is part, an enterprise which started in 1974 with the publication of *Linguistique et colonialisme*.[1] In that book I showed how a brutal 'war of languages' took place in the colonial period. The linguistic theories of previous centuries had constructed a model of the relations between peoples, which was founded on the principle of inequality. The peoples of the 'civilized' West were superior to the 'savage' peoples, and their languages ('clearer', 'more logical', 'more developed') were, in the same way, superior to the languages of those who had been colonized. In practice, this theory of inequality gave birth to an organization of the relations between languages that was based on dominance, the dominance of one people by another, of course, but at the same time, dominance of one culture by another, and of one language by another. Whether it was the establishing of European states or the colonizing of African countries, in both cases the language of those in power was considered to be legitimately dominant and this dominance, this process of 'linguistic cannibalism' was justified by ideology. For the one and indivisible Republic, there must be one, indivisible language—this was the proclamation of the French Revolution and the model was then exported to Africa, using partly 'scientific' arguments: a false distinction between languages, dialects, and patois, or the ideological use of classification (e.g. agglutinative, isolating, flexional languages, etc.). This process, which I described primarily from a French point of view, is not specifically French, and a similar description of English practices can be found in the work of Robert Phillipson.[2] 'Linguistic cannibalism', then, is a process inherent in any colonial dominance, and can be read at different levels: how languages are

---

[1] *Linguistique et colonialisme, petit traité de glottophagie* (Paris: Payot, 1979 and 1988). Translations into Italian, German, Serbo-Croat, Spanish, Galician.

[2] Robert Phillipson, *Linguistic Imperialism* (Oxford University Press, 1992).

described, how social communication is organized, the system of word-borrowings, the names people give each other, feelings of guilt at using native languages, and so on.

The analysis of postcolonial situations gradually led me to work, on the one hand, on the large-scale developments of lingua francas, on the way in which speakers coped with social multilingualism *in vivo*[3] and, on the other hand, on intervention *in vitro* into this multilingualism.* In the first case this was done by treating linguistic communication as a self-regulating homoeostatic machine, and in the second case by observing interference with this machine from outside, by those in power.

Along the way a methodological problem arose: how to measure the spread of lingua francas, and to understand their emergence? They appeared where they were needed, along tracks, railways, rivers, in towns, in markets. For this reason I undertook sociolinguistic research into multilingual markets, research which will be alluded to in Chapter 7 of this book and on which I have published several books and articles, alone or in collaboration. It is at this point in the enterprise that this book, *Language Wars and Linguistic Politics*, stands.

Since then, in part influenced by William Labov's position, which is that sociolinguistics is linguistics, all of linguistics, I have attempted to broaden my aims and, especially, to work on the linguistic counterpart of urban phenomena.[4] From my point of view all this research has a continuity, in which two or three books are stepping-stones; *Language Wars and Linguistic Politics* is one of these. The anecdotal history behind the book is that I conceived its structure in 1985, while working in China, and while reading *The Art of War* by Sun-Zi. In my files I had all the material of what was not yet a book, but the initial metaphor which gave me my plan came from this Chinese author. I have, of course, continued to work on the problem of language policy and I have gone more deeply into some matters.[5] But this book, which is just one stage in a research project, is still of current interest for me. This is why I am glad that through this translation it can reach English-speaking researchers who do not read

---

[3] *Les Langues véhiculaires* (Paris: Presses Universitaires de France, 1981).

* The terms 'lingua franca' and 'vernacular (language)' have been chosen as the translations for, respectively, *langue véhiculaire* and *langue grégaire*. Neither is an exact translation of the French, but each is the closest commonly-used English term. Lingua franca is to be understood in the sense of 'language of wider communication', and vernacular in the sense of 'the language of a particular class or group of people'.

[4] *Les Voix de la Ville, introduction à la sociolinguistique urbaine* (Paris: Payot, 1994).

[5] See e.g. *La Politique linguistique* (Paris: Presses Universitaires de France, 1996).

French. It only remains for me to apologize for having spoken a little too much of myself, for having used the word 'I', but it appeared to me important to give a brief description of the course I have followed.

Louis-Jean Calvet

Introduction

There is a distinction current both in linguistics and in ordinary usage, which contrasts *living languages* with *dead languages*, and these two adjectives, *living* and *dead*, applied to languages, suggest the metaphor of a *life of language*, as several works have in fact proclaimed in their titles, ever since W. Whitney published *The Life and Growth of Language* in 1867. These titles suggest that languages are born, live, and die like living organisms, like biological substances. But, perhaps because these works were written when formal linguistics, or structuralism, was beginning, for the most part they looked for the causes of this life of language in language alone.

Without over-insisting on these biological metaphors, it can nevertheless be noted that languages have always changed (and so one speaks of *old* French, of *old* German, of *classical* Arabic, etc.), that some have absorbed others (today the French speak Latin, but a Latin that is two thousand years old and which is influenced by a German substratum, by the speech of 'our Gaulish ancestors'), that some have merged (such as French and Saxon to produce English) and some, finally, have disappeared or are on their way to disappearing.

These changes, which anyone with a little education knows something about, are not properly speaking linguistic phenomena: to consider them as such is to be condemned to not understanding them. They are the linguistic translation of deeper social movements. This is the case with the expansion of Latin in Europe and of Arabic in the Maghreb; they can of course be treated in terms of formal linguistics, but at the cost of losing important information. The laws of phonetics explain, for example, that the Latin stressed open *o* regularly becomes the dipthong *uo* in Italian, *ue* in Spanish, and *eu* in French (for the sake of simplicity I here use the classical alphabetic notation): *foco* in Latin, *fuoco* in Spanish, and *feu* in French. If we were to multiply these examples a thousandfold, we would obtain a reliable picture of the phonetic transformations of these languages. But in doing this we remain on the surface of things, we see only the form of the change and not its deep social roots. This is obviously more clear-cut with regard to semantic or lexical changes. For example, when Antoine Meillet, who was without doubt the French linguist most aware of the relationship between language and society, studied the way in which the Latin word *captivus* had passed from the sense of 'prisoner' to 'wretched, bad', he insisted on the importance of paradigms in maintaining the sense of words and on the fact that terms cut off from their paradigm (or, put another way, from words of the same root) acquire a much greater freedom and evolve more easily.

In Latin, the word *captivus* 'prisoner' was closely associated with *capere*, 'to take', *captus*, 'taken', etc. and the sense of 'captive' could not consequently be ignored; but *capere* has partly disappeared, and partly survives with particular meanings, and it is words derived from *prehendere* which express the idea of 'prendre' in Romance languages; since then *captivus* has been at the mercy of outside influence and the word has taken the sense of 'wretched, bad' in the Italian *cattivo*, in the French *chétif* ('Comment les mots changent de sens', in *L'année sociologique*, 1905–6).

If it is true that the paradigm of *capere* anchors *captivus* semantically, this formal analysis does not explain why the word, freed of its links, has evolved into this particular sense and not in another: it shows us what made the change possible but does not tell us why it took place in one direction rather than another. It is clear that a prisoner can be considered from two points of view: there is the prisoner that we have taken, the enemy we have captured, and he is hated, considered to be wicked, bad; then there is the prisoner that the enemy has taken from us, and he is considered to be unfortunate, wretched. Hence the two senses of the word, each evidence of a different usage, denoting the same status (that of a prisoner) but connoting a different attitude to this status. The semantic development of the term consists in the connotation turning into the denotation. It can be seen that this explanation, which complements the previous one, takes into account factors of social practice, and of linguistic function, and so makes it possible to explain the change by the interaction between analysis of language and analysis of society.

A comparison will provide a better explanation of the relationship between the formal and the social point of view. Faced with the question how and why does a boat float and move? it is of course possible to reply in terms of Archimedes' principle, of hydrostatics and hydrodynamics, of the force of the wind and of the combustion engine, etc. But this would give us only part of the answer, for the question cannot be separated from another: Why did man at a given moment in his history feel the need to invent the boat? What has maritime transport brought to society? What has been its influence on exploration, on commerce, on war? This shows that the history of the boat cannot be separated from the history of its uses, that there is a dialectic relationship between the two.

It is just the same with language. In describing it from a strictly formal point of view, one is describing a code, a structure that can be compared to a boat at moorings or in dry dock. But in the same way that boats are linked to the history of man, language is directly involved in the world and linguistics should take this into account.

If there is a history of languages, it is a chapter in the history of society, or rather, the linguistic aspect of the history of society. If one considers the hardly original idea that violence is the great midwife of history, then this violence also affects the history of language. It is in this sense that the title of the book, *Language Wars*, should be understood, and as we shall see when it comes to examples such as Greece, Turkey, India, or Norway, this is not a metaphor.

We shall begin, then, by devoting the first part to a study of the origins of conflict. Modern linguistics is built on a refusal, a refusal to take into account the problems raised by the origins of language. The childhood of human communication, of which we know little, is nevertheless of obvious interest and, at the same time, it rightfully belongs within the domain of linguistics. Without pretending to bring definitive knowledge to bear on this point, far from it, I have tried out a number of hypotheses at the beginning of this book, to see how far they can help us to understand the genesis of our subject. For if there have been language wars, this is because multilingualism exists; a world with only one language would have no knowledge of this kind of conflict, hence the pacifist illusion to which we shall return, which has led some to invent artificial languages like Esperanto. Of course, the prehistory of this multilingualism, which Christian myth dates back to Babel and treats as a punishment, is obscure and lacking in reliable evidence, but we shall still look into it for factors to explain our history.

We shall then proceed to an analysis, based on a number of research enquiries that I have carried out or directed, of the large-scale development of lingua francas and their impact on smaller groups. This part, which constitutes the second third of the book (*The Battlefield*) is therefore an *in vivo* study of language wars, as waged on the ground by speakers for centuries. We shall show how and why the history of humanity can be read in the history of their languages, how the conflicts of human beings can be seen from a linguistic point of view.

Finally we shall tackle the critical study of a discipline which has been fashionable for thirty years, that is, language planning. This last third of the book (*Among the Administrators*) is an analysis of the *in vitro* aspect of language wars as directed by planning specialists, language commissions, academies, in a word, the administrators.

For if people and their languages have always been involved in vast conflicts, man today attempts to intervene directly in this area, 'in the laboratory', as it were. The relationship between the *in vivo* and the *in vitro* will allow us to grasp what is at stake in language planning, what its aims are and the extent to which it conforms to what actually takes place in society.

PART I

The Origins of Conflict

1

The Question of Origins

The reason why animals do not speak is because they have nothing to say. This first sentence, presented as a witticism, is of course only an approximation. Although animals do not **speak**, which is obvious, they do sometimes communicate, even though, as far as we know, the content of this communication is very limited. Among the many studies dedicated to animal communication, the two examples that have been quoted most frequently are the dance of bees[1] and the acquisition of signs by chimpanzees.[2] It should be noted here that these two examples, the best known within the subject, are not to be classed together. The bees' dance described by von Frisch, is an endogenous system, that is, produced by the bees themselves, which enables them to indicate the existence of the food source in a certain direction and at a certain distance, while the signs of chimpanzees are exogenous: they are taught to apes by humans, in order to communicate a content introduced by humans. Although it is noticeable that the careful inverted commas of von Frisch's first texts (in a German article of 1923, 'Über die «sprache» der Bienen', the word for language, *Sprache*, is put in inverted commas) disappeared thereafter (in 1974 for example, in an article in English, 'Decoding the Language of the Bee'), we should not come to the conclusion that there is a close parallel between the semiological behaviour of human beings and that of animals. This does not mean that chimpanzees, for example, cannot 'communicate' (the continuing studies of this issue have produced and will continue to produce interesting material) but simply this: animal species, among which of course human beings are to be classified, have developed various means of communication directly linked to what they have to communicate. Bees, for example, indicate the distance and direction of the nourishment they have located through their dance, and perhaps also its concentration of sugar: the distance is given by the tempo of the patterns

[1] See e.g. K. von Frisch, 'Decoding the Language of the Bee', *Science*, no. 185 (1974).
[2] A survey of the problem can be found in Roger Fouts and Randall Rigby, 'Man–Chimpanzee Communication', in Thomas Sebeok (ed.), *How Animals Communicate* (Bloomington, Ind., 1976).

danced by the bees and the direction by the angle of its figures-of-eight. So the bee will dance a dozen patterns in fifteen seconds to indicate that the food source is a hundred metres away, seven patterns in fifteen seconds if the food source is two hundred metres, two if it is six kilometres off, while the dance's angle of inclination in relation to the horizontal indicates the direction where the nourishment is to be found.

This may seem extraordinary, especially if one compares the weight and volume of the brain of a bee with that of man; or it may, on the contrary, seem a minor matter. But that is not the point: it is neither extraordinary nor insignificant, it simply is. The bee has put into practice a system that responds to its needs. It does not speak of philosophy or politics, it communicates a fact necessary to its survival. I cannot do better here than to quote the conclusion of a famous article by Emile Benveniste:

As a whole these observations bring out the difference between the processes of communication discovered in bees and our language. This difference can be summed up in a term which seems to me the most appropriate for defining the method of communication used by bees; it is not a language, it is a code of signals. All its characteristics flow from this: the fixity of content, the invariability of the message, the reference to a single situation, the irreducibility of the statement.[3]

This brings me back to the sentence which opened this chapter, slightly modified: animals do not have much to say. But Benveniste adds, a few lines later: 'It nevertheless remains significant that this code, the only form of "language" it has been possible to discover among animals until now, should be appropriate for insects living in a society. It is society which is the condition of language.'

This emphasizes a fundamental characteristic of communication, that is, its social character.

It will be understood that this brief incursion into the field of zoösemiotics and ethology aims only to establish a principle that will serve as a guide throughout this chapter: there is a close relation between the communication needs of a group (what there is to be said, to use a trival expression) and the means of communication the group employs (the way in which it is said). On this basis, there is no reason for giving separate consideration to the human species, to treat it as different from other animal species, and it is this view, treating communication as a social fact,

---

[3] E. Benveniste, 'Animal Communication and Human Language', *Diogène*, I (1952), reprinted in *Problèmes de linguistique générale* (Paris: Gallimard, 1966). The quotation is on p. 62.

that we shall adopt in order to examine the question of the origins of human communication.

In 1866, when the Société de Linguistique de Paris was established, article 2 of its statute stipulated that 'the Society does not allow any communication concerning either the origin of language, or the creation of a universal language'. In other words, the first and last chapter of this book are, in the eyes of the Society, outside the law. We can understand the reasons for such a taboo in a period when linguistics was trying to establish itself as a science: a fear of metaphysics, of charlatanism, and so on. I think, however, that the venerable founders of the SLP were wrong, for nothing that has to do with linguistics should be alien to linguists, and the question of origins, of why and how language emerged, quite rightfully concerns us.

The first linguist to oppose the terms of this taboo was, without doubt, Otto Jespersen who, at the beginning of the 1920s, loudly declared of these questions that 'as they *can* be treated in a scientific spirit, [they] should not be left exclusively to dilettanti'.[4]

Jespersen, who showed a lot of nerve considering the time at which he was writing, devoted a chapter of his book to the problem. He began by declaring that the worst way of posing it was to ask: 'how would it be possible for men or manlike beings, hitherto unfurnished with speech, to acquire speech as a means of communication of thought?'.[5] For him there were three possible approaches to developing an inductive argument: first of all, child language, if one admits that the development or the acquisition of language by a child is evidence for the linguistic history of mankind; then, the language of primitive tribes, considered to represent an archaic state of language; finally, the history of language, which appeared to him to be the main route for going back step by step through evolution, to the very origins.

It is true that the tendency common to both child language and the history of languages, which consists in systematically imposing order on what is irregular, can give us some lines of thought to pursue. It enables us to postulate a historical law and to project it into the past. This law is a simple one: languages have a systematic tendency towards regularization and simplification.

From this point of view it is necessary to put an end to the myth of the 'beautiful' ancient languages, Latin, Greek, Hebrew, or classical Arabic,

[4] O. Jespersen, *Language: Its Nature, Development and Origin* (Allen & Unwin, 1922), 96.
[5] Ibid. 413.

which, with their declensions and irregularities are in fact enormously complicated. We can see clearly, in old French or old English for example, how case-marking and declensions were gradually replaced by prepositions and the syntactic use of a fixed word order, in a word, how language 'simplified', which is a crude way of saying that it became more systematic. If we do project this law into the past, we can formulate a first historical hypothesis according to which the first codes had no regularity. In fact they were not codes but nomenclatures. This is to say that in the course of history languages have not become more complicated, as certain racist theories would have it ('primitive', limited languages, gradually becoming more refined as cultures evolve), nor have they become simpler, but they were codified: codes were created at the beginning of rudimentary communication, and our problem is therefore to discover how this rudimentary communication appeared and how this codification occurred.

Certainly we can take chance into account (a cry or gesture is received in a certain way, when repeated it leads to the same behaviour, and gradually it is adopted with this 'sense') as well as necessity (the beginning of certain social activities making a means of communication necessary). But these two approaches are not in fact contradictory, as we shall see later. To begin with, however, we shall refrain from constructing theories, preferring rather to examine the records in our possession.

What are these records?

They are not linguistic, obviously: the first languages were not written down and so have left no trace. On the other hand, we do have fossils and objects which are the materials of two sciences that we can examine: craniology and prehistory.

In 1861 the surgeon Pierre-Paul Broca demonstrated that certain lesions of the brain led to loss of speech, and located the centre of language in the third frontal convolution. Since then, we have come a long way in our knowledge of the topography of the brain, and specialists distinguish between aphasia (the inability to emit sounds), linked to disorders in area 44 of the brain, verbal deafness (the inability to identify sounds received) linked to disorders in areas 41 and 42, agraphia (the inability to write) linked to lesions of the lower part of the second frontal convolution, area 9, and alexia (the inability to read) linked to lesions of the preoccipital visual area (19). Such technical exactitude will probably not make much sense to the reader, but the important point here is that the study of fossil skulls has established two things that directly concern us: first, the fact that the development of these areas of the brain is directly linked to the upright posture of bipeds; and, secondly, the fact that this development runs parallel to the appearance of manual activity.

In other words, there is a close link between the hand and the face and mimicry, language, and manual skill could have developed simultaneously. As Leroi-Gourhan has emphasized:

Bipedal posture and a free hand automatically imply a brain equipped for speech and, consequently, a brain box with a good deal of free space beneath the central convexity. We must, I believe, infer that the physical potential for organizing sounds and gestures was already present in the first known anthropoid.[6]

But there is a gulf between having the 'physical potential' to communicate and putting this potential into practice: craniology tells us when man could have begun to speak, but not at all when nor how he began.

If we venture here onto the terrain of a palaeontology of language, it is not in an attempt to reconstruct the form taken by prehistoric languages, for example, their phonology or their syntax (for these languages we cannot—so far?—carry out the reconstruction carried out in the last century for Indo-European), but in an attempt to understand the social facts at the origins of language. To return to the universally acknowledged link between manual activity and language, between the hand and the face, this enables us to risk certain hypotheses based on the prehistoric traces in our possession, especially those which, like tools or graphic signs, are evidence for the manual skill of early hominids. If communication and tools are the first characteristics of man, and if these characteristics are chronologically and neurologically linked, then we can say that man communicates in the same way that he uses his hands. The question 'how did man speak?' becomes the same as the question 'what could man do with his fingers?', with the difference that for the second question we have some elements of an answer in his manufacture of stone tools and production of graphic signs.

The period that interests us covers the Upper Quaternary (what geologists call the Pleistocene) between *Piltdown man* and *Cro-Magnon man*, that is, the *Chellean* and the *Magdalenian*. It seems clear that Cro-Magnon man could speak, or at least possessed a means of communication, but when did this begin? Let us consider, solely to concentrate our thoughts, the chronological table (Table 1.1).

The righthand column indicates the type of chipped stone to be found in different periods of the Palaeolithic Age. At the beginning came

---

[6] *La Geste et la parole* (Paris, 1964), i. 127.

TABLE 1.1.

Eras	Cultures	Man	Fauna	Tools
Lower quaternary			Mastodon Rhinoceros Hippopotamus	
Upper quaternary (Pleistocene)	Chelean	Piltdown	Rhinoceros	Choppers (40 cm) Bifaces (2 m)
	Acheulean			Bifaces (5 m)
		Mauer		
	Mousterian	Neanderthal		
	Aurignacian			
	Solutrean			Splinters from cores (10 m)
		Cro-Magnon		
	Magdalenian		Reindeer	Microliths (50 m)
(Holocene)	Azilian	Present races		(100 m)

choppers, made from a single movement, a single blow, then bifaces, which have been struck in several places. Then one observes a revolution in the technique of obtaining tools: the core which was originally used as a tool becomes a source of tools, from which splinters can be struck. A good way of quantifying this development is to measure the length of cutting edge obtained in the different periods per kilo of worked stone, and it can be seen that in the period of the first choppers Piltdown man obtained 40 centimetres of useful cutting edge for each kilo of stone, while Cro-magnon man obtained 50 centimetres. To this we can add the information we have on the production of graphic signs in the Palaeolithic Age (Table 1.2).

The oldest graphic signs, incisions on bones, were not, as one might have thought, naive attempts at representing their environment but rather abstract symbols in which some believe they can see a rhythm transcribed. Then animal heads appear, generally associated with sexual symbols (this is style I, between 30,000 and 22,000 BC, then complete animals (style II), compositions which group together oxen and horses, or bison and horses

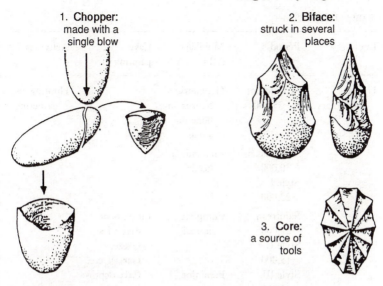

1. **Chopper:**
made with a
single blow

2. **Biface:**
struck in several
places

3. **Core:**
a source of
tools

Fig. 1.1
Source: A. Leroi-Gourhan, *Le Geste et la parole*, pp. 131 and 144

(style III), and finally animals following each other, herds of horses (style IV).

All this evidence, though valuable, does not make for much progress. If we adopt the hypothesis of a close relationship between the hand and the face, between manual skill and communication, we can postulate a 'chopper' language, a 'biface' language, etc. in the same way that we can imagine a parallel between the development in drawing from single animals (Aurignacian) to processions of animals (Magdalenian) and linguistic development, leading from a single sign to the sentence. This would lead us to saying that signs appeared around 35,000 BC and that sentences were constructed around 10,000 BC. It is obviously impossible to declare these hypotheses false, for how could we know? But it is clear that they are tempting by their simplicity (which is a fault as much as a virtue) and also open to criticism for taking a mechanistic view.

In fact, prehistoric man as we have been able to discern him in the preceding pages is only a means of fabricating tools and drawing graphic signs. This is a quite inadequate definition, and will not take us very far in the analysis of how he was able to communicate. There is an important

TABLE 1.2.

Era	Period	Mobiliary ART	Cave painting	Activities
Upper quaternary	Mousterian *c.* −35,000	Geometric figures on bone or stone		Hunting and gathering
	Aurignacian −30,000 Style I −22,000	First animal heads		
	Solutrean −22,000 Style II −15,000	Complete animals	Lit parts of caves: La Grèze, Gargas, etc.	
	Style III −13,000	Feminine statuettes	Cave depths: Lascaux, Altamira	
	Magdalenian −13,000 Style IV −9,000	Decorated assegais and harpoons, stone and wood with reindeer	Cap Blanc, La Magdeleine, Arcy-sur-Cure	Agriculture and stock breeding

dimension regarding communication missing here: how did prehistoric man live in a group, how did he nourish himself, in short, what was his social organization?

From the preceding pages it will be understood that we are suggesting that the origin of language should be sought at the point where biological development (at what point in the evolution of the morphology of the skull and brain was it possible for the linguistic function, the possibility of communication, to emerge?) intersects with sociological development (at what point in the evolution of social relations did some form of communication become necessary?) In other words, with regard to the possibility of communication, which was brought about by the skull's geography, the form of the brain, the appearance of which we can date from fossil skulls, there are social activities which we shall call producers of language, activities which made communication necessary. The evolution of the skull, of teeth, of the face made language possible, but it was social relations that gave birth to it.

We must here refer to a chapter of *Dialectic of Nature*[7] in which Engels puts forward the idea that the hand is not only the organ of work (i.e. it makes work possible) but it is also produced by work (i.e. it appears to be a necessity created by the need for work); the developing biped would have reached the point in his evolution when he needed his hand. But, writes Engels, 'the hand was not alone'. Charles Darwin, in the first chapter of his *Origin of Species* defines what he calls 'correlated variation': white cats with blue eyes are deaf, animals with cloven hoofs have multiple stomachs, etc.

Engels concluded from this that the hand's evolution must have produced, by correlation, other variations. Above all, he continues, work which appeared slowly and modified mankind's relationship to nature, created another need: 'humans' developed at the moment when they had something to say to each other, at the moment when they needed to communicate. It should be noted here that Engels did not know Broca's work, and in the long correspondence between Marx and Engels[8] he is not quoted once, but Engels came to the same conclusion by another route.

So we have two kinds of possible response to the problem of the origin of language. The one suggested by Engels consists in saying that man began to speak when, socially, he felt the need to communicate. The second, in the tradition of Broca's work, consists in saying that man began to speak when the geography of his brain made it possible. But, besides the fact that these two approaches can be easily integrated into a Darwinian view of correlated variation, they are not at all paradoxical and complement each other perfectly.

Let us return to the problem of the social organization of prehistoric man. The first thing to be noted is the obvious fact that the size of a group has always been linked to the density of food sources in the territory it occupies and the way in which the group exploits it. Hunting, as well as gathering, existed from the Mousterian culture (around 35,000 BC) and they both continued as the main activities until the end of the Palaeolithic,

---

[7] 'The role of work in the transformation of ape into man', certainly written in 1876. See *Marxisme et linguistique* (Paris: Payot, 1977).

[8] Darwin, on the other hand, is often quoted. In particular, in a letter to Engels on 19 Dec. 1860, Marx writes on the subject of *The Origin of Species*, 'Despite its English heaviness, this is the book that contains the natural basis of our theory.'

which saw the appearance of stock rearing and agriculture. So it is within this social activity that we must seek to understand the appearance of language, at the level of subsistence units centred on self-sufficiency, as well as at the level of contact between different subsistence units.

One can imagine that rudimentary language, whether it was gestural and/or oral, would have stabilized within a group, constituting a sort of proto-code peculiar to the subsistence unit, a proto-code which must have then encountered other proto-codes, used by other groups, with perhaps a sort of multilingualism (or multicodism). Babel was not the end of the journey, but the point of departure and when one thinks of the multitude of rudimentary codes that marked the beginning of humanity, one is struck not by the plurality of languages but by their relatively low number: basically the appearance of a proto-code only needed two people. The plurality of subsistence units each with its own proto-code, as I have just described it, obviously supports the hypothesis of an original 'multilingualism' or, if one prefers, a polygenesis of language. But we must examine this problem more closely, because it is clearly relevant to the central subject of this book.

If we start with the simple declaration that, for a dozen Romance languages, there is only one Latin, that for a dozen Arab dialects, there is only one classical Arabic, that for several dozen Indo-European languages there is only one Indo-European, in short that 'families of languages' imply mother tongues we can, by projecting this historical knowledge on a vaster scale, infer two things: first, languages tend to multiply, and secondly, that by working back from mother tongue to mother tongue we ought to reach an original language. I think that both these assertions are false.

Let us consider first the problem of the multiplication of languages. It is well known that this is the result of dialect formation, itself linked to the geographic dispersal of populations. So it was the expansion of the Roman empire that lay at the origin of the Romance languages, that is, the fragmentation of Latin; and it was the expansion of Han power that lay at the origin of the fragmentation of proto-Chinese into seven different languages today, and there are many other examples. But there are two counter influences to this tendency to multiplication. There is the fact that if languages are born, others die, that the expansion of one language often implies the disappearance of others, and the history of the Romance languages is a good example of this. Secondly, geographic dispersal as a factor in multiplication (or diversification) is increasingly neutralized by the multiplication of modern communications. Radio, television, satellite communications, etc. mean that American English and British English will never become different languages, nor will the French of France and Quebec French. Six or seven centuries ago, with comparable conditions of geographic separation, things would have turned out very differently.

If, then, languages continue to change, even to the point of some being replaced by others, we have every reason to suppose that the great tendency to multiplication which has marked the linguistic history of the world through several dozen centuries has been halted by modern conditions of communication.

As for the problem of monogenesis, this must be approached differently. Let us imagine the scenario of the emergence of a human semiology. Someone is ill, and groans; this instinctive cry brings his fellow-creatures to see what the matter is with him or to look after him. He will use this groan again each time that he is ill, with the same result, and will end up by using it when he is not really ill but wants to draw attention to himself. This passage from instinct to convention must have occurred in different fields, giving birth to conventional cries expressing pain, a summons, fear, hunger, desire, etc. To this can be added the advent of imitation, in hunting for example, so as to attract animals, to cause fear as well, and then perhaps just to amuse; we now have an image of the way the first men who communicated coined their proto-codes. But there is no reason to suppose that, in the different subsistence units spread over the surface of the globe, that were transforming themselves in this way into communication units, the proto-codes bore any similarity; this rudimentary communication gave birth to a multitude of different proto-codes.

This is not, however, the view of Maurice Swadesh, until recently the only linguist to have followed Jespersen's lead into the subject of the palaeontology of language. In a book published in 1967,[9] he proposed distinctions between the Eoglottic, the Palaeoglottic, and the Neoglottic, following the model of the vocabulary of prehistoric science, and asserted with great optimism: 'We do not yet know how far we may be able to penetrate into the millenia of the past, but there is no doubt that with the hard work of a good number of experts, we shall be able to cast light on the Upper Palaeoglottic, let us say, on a past fifty to a hundred thousand years old'.[10]

He summed up his vision of the 'stages of language' in the following table.

[9] *El languaje y la vida humana*, which I quote in its French translation, *Le Langage et la vie humaine* (Paris: Payot, 1986).
[10] Ibid. 31.

1. Lower palaeoglottic: more than a million years ago
   - spontaneous exclamations, imitative sounds
   - a few demonstratives with internal inflections
   - rare occurrence of simple combinations
   - relative uniformity of language
2. Upper palaeoglottic: about 100,000 years ago
   - spontaneous exclamations, imitative cries
   - increase of demonstratives
   - several hundred associated terms derived from imitation
   - increase in inflection
   - combinations more frequent
   - languages differentiated by large areas
3. Neoglottic: about 10,000 years ago
   - spontaneous exclamations, imitative sounds
   - reduction of demonstratives
   - reduction of internal inflection, beginning of external inflection
   - about 300 different elements
   - internal and external combinations
   - numerous distinct languages.[11]

It can be seen that Swadesh has cast himself in the role of defender of monogenesis. His argument is simple: as conventional language began from a base of intuitive language, it comes from a single origin. And he adds: *'Perhaps it was a million years later that regional spoken languages became formalized, and were still for the most part mutually intelligible'*.[12] But on this point he is not very convincing. For we know that what is not conventional in modern languages, or at least what is considered not to be so, onomatopeia for example, does not point in this direction. If the French take a cockerel to be saying cocorico, then the Spanish take it as quiquiriqui, the English as cock a doodle doo, and the differences between these imitations are more important than the similarities, not only in the example we have just given but for all languages and for all 'onomatopeia'.

Since the preceding material is not as well ordered as it might be, I think it will be useful to conclude the chapter with a summary of the different hypotheses we have touched on:

1. Tools and communication appeared at about the same time and evolved in parallel ('man speaks in the same way that he uses his hands'). Whether it was a million years ago, as Swadesh thinks, or

---

[11] *El languaje y la vida humana*, which I quote in its French translation, *Le Langage et la vie humaine* (Paris: Payot, 1986), 42.   [12] Ibid. 45.

more recently, this communication began with isolated cries (by gestures too, of course, but a cry quickly showed its superiority in darkness), that were imitative and instinctive.

2. This 'language' was slowly transformed through the influence of social needs: collective hunting, power relations, narratives, etc. And this evolved from nomenclatures (isolated signs, without links between them) towards codes (irregular proto-codes becoming simpler, forming into paradigms) and from extreme plurality (the different subsistence units each possessing its own nomenclature) towards unification (neighbouring groups being led through contact with each other to harmonize their means of communication).

3. At the dawn of human communication, multilingualism reigned, despite the opinion of Morris Swadesh and despite the Genesis stories provided by some religions (we shall return to this in the following chapter).

The hypothesis maintained here, then, is of a world that has been multilingual ever since the beginning of communication. But what has communication brought to the human species?

For one thing, language has enabled humans to do all that cannot be done without language. This, of course, includes the transmission of techniques, from the moment that gestures alone were no longer adequate to convey the complexity of manual skills (no longer 'watch how I strike this flint' but 'listen to my explanation'). We have here one of the driving forces of the evolution of language, one of the producers of language which I mentioned above. Narratives also become possible, and therefore collective memory, as can be seen in societies with an oral tradition. Finally, there is the conditional threat: without language one cannot say 'if you do or don't do this, I will or will not do that', language being the first weapon of blackmailers, of terrorists, of hostage takers, and of great powers discussing disarmament, for example. In other words, ever since its origins language has been linked to power relations, to power and negotiation, and so it is not impossible to suppose a relation between these forms of power and the evolution of languages themselves (the appearance of the grammatical possibilities of the conditional, of the imperative, etc. is doubtlessly linked to power relations). But that is another story.

What concerns us here is that rudimentary communication placed human beings in a situation of continual semiological conflict. Unceasingly confronted by the language of others, the first groups that could communicate were confronted by semiological difference, by problems of comprehension and non-comprehension, by multilingualism and by contempt for the linguistic forms of others. As they took power in turns, one over another, they had to deal with these fluctuations and differences. The example of the Greeks who complacently declared that all those who did not speak Greek, did not speak at all, but at best produced mumbles, and were therefore barbarians, is far from being an isolated case. Whether they involved pejorative ideologies about the language of others or the temptation to 'linguistic cannibalism',[13] language wars have been part of the history of humanity ever since humanity transformed its first cries and gestures into signs.

[13] Cf. L.-J. Calvet, *Linguistique et colonialisme, petit traité de glottophagie* (Paris: Payot, 1974).

2

Religions and Language: the Myths of a Single Source and of Superiority

This much is obvious: the language wars that will be discussed throughout this book would not have occurred in a world with only one language. At the origin of the conflict lies the multilingualism of the planet. It is not the only reason for the war but it is a necessary condition.

If we examine a map of the world and look for populations and their languages under states and frontiers, we find ourselves faced with a vast jigsaw puzzle. This puzzle works on several levels, with first of all a layer of very local linguistic forms, vernacular forms (we shall define this term in a later chapter, but for the moment we shall content ourselves with recording it), on which are superimposed other layers: regional forms, then national forms, and finally lingua francas on the supranational level (the term *lingua franca* will also be discussed later), the whole making up a complex and changing web of language. This is, generally speaking, the planet's situation and can be confirmed anywhere on human territory: there is no monolingual country and it is the destiny of humanity to be confronted not by one language but by several.

It is possible to examine this plurality, its origin and its consequences, as we have in the previous chapter, but we can also study the ideological explanations that human culture has given for this phenomenon. We can begin with the explanations provided by certain religions: here we shall discuss two, Christianity and Islam, through their fundamental books, the *Bible* and the *Koran*.

The problem of language appears in several passages of the Bible. The most interesting is, of course, the description of the myth of the tower of Babel in Genesis. Here, first of all, is the text:

1. Once upon a time all the world spoke a single language and used the same words.
2. As men journeyed in the east, they came upon a plain in the land of Shinar and settled there.
3. They said to one another, 'Come, let us make bricks and bake them hard'; they used bricks for stone and bitumen for mortar.

4. 'Come,' they said, 'let us build ourselves a city and a tower with its top in the heavens, and make a name for ourselves; or we shall be dispersed all over the earth.'
5. Then the Lord came down to see the city and tower which mortal men had built,
6. and he said, 'Here they are, one people with a single language, and now they have started to do this; henceforward nothing they have a mind to do will be beyond their reach.
7. Come, let us go down there and confuse their speech, so that they will not understand what they say to one another.'
8. So the Lord dispersed them from there all over the earth, and they left off building the city.
9. That is why it is called Babel, because the Lord there made a babble of the language of all the world; from that place the Lord scattered men all over the face of the earth.[1]

Taking this text literally, several things can be observed:

– Obviously, an assertion of a primordial monolingualism (verse 1), which follows logically from chapter 1 (God naming the heavens and the earth, etc.) and from chapter 2 (Adam naming the animals) of Genesis.
– A description of a method of construction (verses 3, 4, and 5), which commentators agree to be how the ziggurats of Babylon were built, pyramidical towers with several floors, made out of brick and bitumen (in Palestine a different method of construction was used: stone and mortar).
– The picture of a relatively homogeneous and organized society, whose organization (verse 6) actually seems to annoy the Eternal Being.
– The notion of divine punishment (verses 7 and 8).
– Finally, at verse 9, a hint of linguistics: 'That is why it is called Babel', the passage relying on an approximate pun (or on false etymology) linking babel with the verb *bâlal*, in Hebrew, 'he made a babble of', although the word should in fact be related to *bâbili*, 'gate of God' (hence Babylon).

What is most interesting here is, of course, the 'confusion of languages' which constitutes, according to the Bible, the beginning of multi-lingualism. The text suggests that there were pre- and post-Babel periods, a time when 'all the world spoke a single language and used the same words', which was followed by the time when the Lord 'made a

---

[1]   Genesis 11: 1–9, translation from New English Bible.

babble of the language of all the world; from that place the Lord scattered men all over the face of the earth'. The tower, as often illustrated by engravers and painters, has also remained a complex symbol in the popular imagination, in common usage. It combines human pretension (how could man dare raise himself to the heavens?) with divine punishment of this pretension, as well as an anecdote relating to the origin of the multiplicity of languages with a value-judgement that has entered common usage, which treats this multilingualism as a punishment.

This first reading, keeping close to the text, is the one most current. There is another reading that sees in this confusion and dispersion of languages not a divine response to the arrogance of man, but rather the necessary condition for the carrying out of man's destiny. Claude Hagège, for example, emphasizes that it is possible to link this passage to another in Genesis (1: 28), 'Be fruitful and increase, fill the earth and subdue it': 'the singleness of language, far from being a blessing that is suddenly taken away from man, is the major handicap to his vocation, the obstacle to the carrying out of his destiny . . . this is why it had to be followed by social dispersion, which is here inseparable from linguistic dispersion'.[2] But these are exegetes's quarrels.

What we must keep in mind is that, for a large part of the world, multilingualism is experienced, with reference to the myth of Babel, as a punishment, even as a curse. The neologism 'babelization', which means the multiplication of languages on a particular territory, is the linguistic equivalent of the term 'balkanization' for states. In both cases, multiplicity is seen as a bad thing, and a good-sized monolingual state properly circumscribed within political and linguistic frontiers is much to be preferred. The trouble is that this scenario is very rare, not to say, non-existent, and so we end up back at Babel.

One of the consequences of this ideological view of multilingualism, which I have discussed in another work, is the controversy that began in the Renaissance concerning 'pre-Babel' language. In the conflict that flourished in the sixteenth century in Europe, Hebrew was generally considered as *the* language of Babel, the language that came before punishment, but everyone tried to show that their own language (Italian, French, German, etc.) was the one closest to the language of the Golden Age.[3]

---

[2] Claude Hagège, 'Babel, du temps mythique au temps de langage', *Revue philosophique*, no. 4 (1978), 469–70.

[3] See Louis-Jean Calvet, *Linguistique et colonialisme* (Paris: Payot, 1974), 17–20.

Thus one of the first ways of dealing with multilingualism was to convert difference into inequality: for the Athenians strangers, people who did not speak Greek, were *barbarians*, and history is full of expressions showing that the language of others is not highly esteemed: *speak white*, don't talk *gibberish*, what is this *double-Dutch*, this *pidgin English*?

Of course, these mythologies should not be taken too seriously, even if they are religious. But nor should it be forgotten that, being ready-made ideas, they govern us, they have affected dozens of generations of human beings in their perception of their social experience, and will continue to do so for a long time. This is why the idea of multilingualism as a divine punishment, even if it does not always agree with serious exegesis of the sacred texts, seems to me important, for it throws a special light on the way that human beings have analysed their linguistic relations, and the way they have dealt with their differences.

Furthermore, the Bible is not the only founding text that carries this linguistic lesson. The Koran's second sura (The Cow) takes up the essence of the scenario from Genesis: God created the heaven and the earth (2: 27), then created Adam who named the animals (2: 31). In what follows, without coming down on one side or the other of the problem of the origin of multilingualism (Babel does not appear in the book), the Koran is full of references to Arabic which can be reduced to two major ideas.

First, there is the idea that the language of the Koran, the language in which the text was dictated to the prophet, is 'pure Arabic'. In fact, the language in which the book was drafted poses a certain number of philosophical problems, given the tradition that claims that Mahomet received the text in the Qoraich dialect, that is, the spoken language of Mecca, while specialists, on the other hand, incline towards a koine. So this vague notion of a 'pure Arabic' is not satisfactory,[4] but it remains the case that this idea is central in the consciousness of Muslims, which leads us to the second point.

This is the idea that the style of the Koran is inimitable. The claim appears in many passages:

And if you are in doubt concerning that We have
sent down on Our servant, then bring a sura
like it. (2: 21)

Or do they say, 'Why, he has forged it'?
Say: 'Then produce a sura like it.' (10: 39)

[4] Cf. e.g. Régis Blachère, *Introduction au Coran* (Paris, 1959), 156–69.

Or do they say, 'He has forged it'? Say:
'Then bring you ten suras the like of it.' (11: 16)[5]

This type of argument, frequent in the Koran, is generally considered to be decisive. The evidence that the text was not invented by Mahomet but was indeed dictated by God is that no one is capable of producing anything similar. The assertion that Arabic was the language of Adam and of paradise can be found in both the so-called 'apocalyptic' literature and in common Islamic usage. 'The language of Adam is Arabic; it is also the language of paradise. When Adam disobeyed his God, He made him speak Syriac', wrote Al Gazairi,[6] inventing the supreme punishment: depriving sinful man of Arabic. But, above all, one finds in common Islamic usage the idea that no other language can surpass Arabic in eloquence or poetry. For the theory of *i'jaz al Qur'an*, of the inimitability of the Koran, goes well beyond the argument I have just described, which aims at showing the truth of the divine origin of the text.

If the first Arabic teachers of rhetoric took it upon themselves, generally speaking, to prove the authenticity of the Koran and its divine origin by linguistic arguments, this aim very quickly transcended its initial religious framework to take on secular and social importance. The stages of this development are quite clear. First, it is 'demonstrated' that the text must be divine because it is inimitable: as we have seen this argument is already contained in the Koran. Secondly, it is shown that, on the one hand, this divine eloquence is linked to Arabic, and the sacred text makes best use of its possibilities: 'in a clear, Arab tongue' (26: 195) and, on the other hand, that no one can claim, in any language whatever, to be able to do what the Arabs themselves have failed to do, which is to surpass the Koran in eloquence. Consequently, the superiority of the Arabic language flows from the inimitability of the holy text itself. If the most eloquent Arab cannot rival THE text (in Arabic, of course), this leaves the other languages of the world and their speakers a long way behind. It has often been said that one of the differences between Christianity and Islam was that the latter does not invoke miracles as evidence of its truth. This is a mistake for, as will have been understood, the text of the Koran is considered a true miracle, a prodigy of eloquence, and there are many anecdotes which tell of people being converted simply by hearing it (the caliph Omar, for example). The truth of this is shown by the fact that, since the time of the

[5] The translation used is by A. J. Arberry, *The Koran Interpreted* (Allen & Unwin, 1955).
[6] *Al nur al-mubin fi qisas a-'arbiya* (Beirut, 1978). Quotation provided by Abdallah Bounfour.

prophet, unbelievers have centred their criticisms on the doctrine of *i'jaz al Qur'an*, on this inimitability, and this movement has been going on a long time:

In the course of history, there are, from time to time, heretics like Ibn ar'Rawandi . . . sceptics like the rationalist theologian, Isa ibn Cabin and, it is said, the poet philosopher al-Ma'arri . . . who claimed that the style of the Koran contained nothing exceptional that a good writer could not also lay claim to. Taking their boldness further, some even went so far as to pastiche it.[7]

But this has not prevented a theory becoming established: that eloquence is a 'distinctive trait of Arabs'. Being the language of God, Arabic is the perfect language; speaking the language of God, Arabs are the chosen people, and their eloquence is surpassed only by God's. The Arab is the prince of eloquence and poetry.[8]

So the Bible and the Koran, though very different in their history and historical impact, have some significant points in common. In Genesis, first of all, as in the sura of the Cow, which largely borrows from it, we find the claim that God created and named the world. Only the Bible clearly proposes the monogenesis of language, a linguistic uniqueness which ended at the time of Babel, and we have seen that this divine punishment resulted in multilingualism being largely experienced as a curse. But the Koran is most often interpreted in the same sense: a single language at the beginning, Arabic as the language of God, of Adam, of paradise.

In both cases, then, we have an original misfortune. This misfortune, in the Bible, concerns the human species as a whole, the orphan of monolingualism. In the Koran, it concerns only a portion of humanity, the portion which is not fortunate enough to speak Arabic. This multilingualism, which was the will of God, reappears in the Bible several times after Babel, in different ways. In the Acts of the Apostles, of course, during Pentecost: 'And there appeared to them tongues like flames of fire, dispersed among them and resting on each one. And they were all filled with the Holy Spirit and began to talk in other tongues, as the Spirit gave them power of utterance' (2: 3–4).

In this passage one has the impression that the Holy Spirit is dealing with the difficult inheritance of multilingualism, that the legacy of Babel is an obstacle to the evangelizing mission of the apostles, and so they must

[7] Blachère, *Introduction au Coran*, 170.
[8] Cf. the thesis of Abdallah Bounfour, under the supervision of Roland Barthes, *Théories et méthodologies des grandes écoles de rhétorique arabe*, mimeograph, École Pratique des Hautes Études, 6th section.

be given the gift of languages, a gift made necessary by the confusion of languages that was spread abroad at the beginning. But at bottom this was a peace mission, and the warlike legacy of Babel is also present in the Bible. This appears in the passage in Judges which relates that the people of the tribe of Galaad defeated the tribe of Ephraim and occupied the banks of the Jordan, that is, the ford by which the Ephraimites could escape:

The Gileadites seized the fords of the Jordan and held them against Ephraim. When any Ephraimite who had escaped begged leave to cross, the men of Gilead asked him, 'Are you an Ephraimite?', and if he said, 'No', they would retort, 'Say Shibboleth.' He would say 'Sibboleth', and because he could not pronounce the word properly, they seized him and killed him at the fords of the Jordan. At that time forty-two thousand men of Ephraim lost their lives. (Judges 11: 5–6)

The passage clearly requires some explanation. The Hebrew word *schibboleth*, which means 'ear of corn' has, as its spelling shows, a 'sh', a palato-alveolar fricative at the beginning. But the people of Ephraim employed a sibilant in that position and pronounced it *sibboleth*, and this phonetic deviation was enough to expose them and be their death-sentence. In this way, in the Bible itself, a linguistic difference, even though a minimal one (for it is after all only a dialectal variation) becomes the place where hate of the Other is embodied, where discrimination occurs.

Here, as in many other fields, the Bible has established a tradition. We shall give just two examples, from different moments of history. First of all, from the thirteenth century, at the time of the famous 'Sicilian vespers': on 31 March 1282, in Palermo, while the bells were ringing for vespers, a revolt erupted against the French occupation, and in order to identify the fugitives fleeing in panic through the streets, the plotters made them pronounce the Sicilian word that means 'chickpea' with the same palato-alveolar fricative at the beginning, and which they were unable to say. The Sicilian singer Benito Merlino tells this story in his song *Li vespiri*.

> 'di ciciri
> —sisiri
> —a morti!' (Say ciciri, sisiri, die!)

The refrain succinctly sums up the issue (life or death) that can depend on a linguistic criterion.

We have, nearer to our own day, another example of this practice, when the Dominican dictator Trujillo wanted to expel Haitian workers. Some say that, in order to distinguish between Dominican blacks (who spoke Spanish) and Haitian blacks (who spoke Creole and French), the police quite simply required them to pronounce Trujillo's name, in which the *jota* was a problem for anyone who did not speak Spanish. Others give a somewhat different version, but it relies on the same principle:

You know that blacks who speak French have difficulty in pronouncing the 'r'; this is also the case with Haitians. On the other hand, the blacks of San Domingo, speaking Spanish, manage it perfectly. So perfectly that with his characteristic sadism, Trujillo ordered that all detainees should pronounce the word 'perro', which means 'dog' in Spanish. All those who said 'pego' were shot.[9]

The use of Shibboleth has entered history to the extent that the Hebrew word has become part of ordinary French and English usage: 'decisive test that judges the ability of a person' according to one dictionary. But if the linguistic reference has disappeared from this definition, the facts remind us, from Judges to the story from contemporary San Domingo, that one can die on account of a phoneme, on account of a difference of pronunciation. Here phonology has become lethal: once again, a language war.

Even though the Bible and the Koran agree on this point, on the idea of monogenesis, of the single origin of language, they nevertheless differ on another point, which is just as important, that is, the value they give to the original language, the divine language. For the holy text on which Christianity is built is not linked to a sacred language. It was without doubt originally written in Aramaic, and then very soon translated into Hebrew, Greek, Syriac, Coptic, Gothic, Latin, Slav, etc., without causing any problems. We should not be deluded by the controversy that has taken place in the second half of the twentieth century among Catholics between partisans of the mass in Latin and of the mass in the vernacular; for Christians there is no sacred language.

It is of course very different for Muslims, who consider the Koran to be untranslatable and its language as God's. If, therefore, Christianity has a pre-Babel period, and it is considered preferable to the post-Babel period, this is not for linguistic reasons. The misfortune lies not in the loss of a perfect language but in the divine punishment that is the consequence of human arrogance. For Islam, on the other hand, Arabic is THE language par excellence, the language of poetry and eloquence, and this gives its speakers a linguistic superiority over others. No one has ever claimed that it is possible to fall into ecstasy while listening to the Bible, while I have

---

[9] Jean Contenté, *L'Aigle des Caraïbes* (Paris, 1978), 94.

noted that Islamic tradition abounds in anecdotes of this kind, relating of course to the Koran. The form of the text is here as important as its content, and this is the whole lesson of the theory of *i'jaz al Qur'an*.

The myths established by the two religions, or at least by the reading that some make of them, the myth of a single source of languages and the myth of the superiority of one language over others, carry ideological arguments that are likely to fuel linguistic conflict. In the previous chapter we saw that there is no scientific argument in favour of a scenario portraying monogenesis, and that it is much more likely that the human being's capacity for language was slowly embodied through thousands of different proto-codes, evolving slowly under the pressure of social needs towards the first languages, and we shall not insult the reader by demonstrating here that there are no superior or inferior languages. In both cases it is not the scientific aspect of the Bible or the Koran that attracts our interest (the texts studied contain myths and not science), but their ideological aspect, their ideological and secular consequences. It was through a specific reading of the Bible that it was possible in the sixteenth century to subordinate reflection on language to nationalist conflicts, by trying to show that one's own language was closer to the pre-Babel language. It was through a specific reading of the Koran that it was possible to develop a racist theory aimed at showing the superiority of Arabic over other languages.

3

A Multilingual World

So human beings are confronted by languages.

Wherever they are, whatever the first language they understood or learnt, they meet other people every day, understand them or not, recognize them or not, like them or not, are dominated by them or dominate them. It is a fact that the world is multilingual. Linguistic history, which is one aspect of the history of the world, is to a great extent constituted by how this multilingualism is managed.

Contrary to what some might think, this multiplicity of languages does not define particular situations or continents, it is not especially the prerogative of the Third World, of the developing countries that are easily imagined as torn between their 'patois' or 'dialects' and our 'languages'. It is a fate common to all, even if it manifests itself differently in different cases. In this chapter we shall attempt to describe these different situations, to sketch a typology of multilingualisms.

Bilingualism and Diglossia

It was in 1959 that the American linguist Charles Ferguson launched a term borrowed from Greek into the literature of linguistics, the term 'diglossia'.[1] Although the word means simply 'bilingualism' in Greek, in Ferguson's work it has a much more restricted sense. Drawing on four situations that he took to be 'defining' instances (German Switzerland, Egypt, Haiti, and Greece), the author described diglossia as a stable relationship between two linguistic varieties, one called 'High' and the other 'Low', genetically related (classical Arabic and spoken Arabic, demotic Greek and 'purified' Greek). The usage of these varieties can be given a functional distribution, shown in Table 3.1.

The example of Haiti was taken as an illustration of this table: French was used in school, in church, in political speeches, and the like, while Creole was used in daily life, in relations with 'inferiors', etc. (we should

---

[1] C. Ferguson, 'Diglossia', *Word* (1959).

TABLE 3.1.

Situation	'High' variety	'Low' variety
Sermons, worship	+	
Instruction to workmen, servants		+
Personal letters	+	
Political speeches	+	
University lectures	+	
Private conversations		+
News broadcasts	+	
'Soap operas'		+
Cartoon captions		+
Poetry	+	
Folk literature		+

remember that the article in question dates from 1959: the situation in Haiti has changed somewhat since then). According to Ferguson diglossia brings together two varieties of a single language, where one has prestige, is standardized, and is the vehicle of a respected body of literature, but spoken by a minority, while the other is believed to be inferior, but is spoken by most people.

What is most interesting in the situations described by Ferguson is the interplay between what is the same and what is different. On the one hand, 'similar' linguistic forms, in the sense that they derive from the same model, in a standard variety and a popular variety (even if the example of Haiti does not appear to fall into this category); on the other hand, 'different' in the sense that it is possible to have control of one without controlling the other. From the tension between these two poles, and from the relationship that speakers maintain with one or other of these linguistic forms, there naturally results behaviour that one can try to approach either in psycholinguistic terms (individual linguistic attitudes towards these two forms) or in sociolinguistic terms (the social significance of diglossia, the groups differentiated by it). This duality, which leads to both the richness and to the limitations of Ferguson's essay, is the reason for the proposals of another American linguist, Joshua Fishman, put forward in 1967.[2] Contrasting bilingualism (an individual's capacity to use several languages), which comes under psycholinguistics, with

[2] J. Fishman, 'Bilingualism with and without Diglossia, Diglossia with and without Bilingualism', *Journal of Social Issues*, no. 32 (1967).

diglossia (the use of several languages in a society) which comes under sociolinguistics, Fishman modified Ferguson's theory in two crucial ways. First, he places much less emphasis on the presence of two codes (there can be more, although he thinks that usually the situation comes down to an opposition between High and Low varieties). Secondly, he suggests that diglossia emerges as soon as there is a functional difference between two languages, whatever the degree of difference, from the very subtle to the very radical: it is not necessary for the two languages to be related.

The author sums up his thought in Table 3.2, which is a perfect illustration of the title of his article ('Bilingualism with and without diglossia, diglossia with and without bilingualism').

These four theoretical possibilities correspond to the following situations:

1. Paraguay, where everyone speaks Spanish and Guarani, Spanish being functionally the High form and Guarani the Low form.
2. Certain unstable situations where there are many bilingual individuals but no social bilingualism (the German-speaking area in Belgium, where French is slowly replacing German).
3. Tsarist Russia, where the nobles spoke only French and the people only Russian.
4. The rare situation where a small community has a single linguisitic variety.

Taken as a whole, these two texts require comment. What seems to me to be lacking above all in Ferguson's definition, with its insistence above all on the notions of functions and prestige, is of course any reference to power. It is not enough to analyse the differences between the linguistic forms involved in terms of prestige (for example the claim that French has

TABLE 3.2.

	Diglossia	
	+	−
Bilingualism +	1. Diglossia and bilingualism	2. Bilingualism without diglossia
−	3. Diglossia without bilingualism	4. Neither diglossia nor bilingualism

more prestige than Creole in Haiti) and functions (the claim that French has functions not shared by Creole). If French has that prestige and those functions, this is for historic and sociological reasons which result from the form of power and the organization of society, all of which are matters that Ferguson hardly touches upon. On the other hand the notion of diglossia is useful (even if it should be sometimes refined: triglossia, etc.) insofar as it is in fact opposed to the notion of bilingualism, a point stressed by Fishman. It is extremely useful to be able to distinguish between individual bilingualism and social bilingualism (which we shall therefore call diglossia), and thus to emphasize the sociological implications of language differences.

This being the case, matters are often more complex than these two texts seem to suggest, and I would like to mention a few examples in order to quickly demonstrate (we shall return to this later) the plurality of situations to be encountered in the world.

1. For one thing, despite its etymology, 'diglossia' can bring together more than two languages, as Fishman has already admitted. But it does not indicate the possibility of what I would call overlapping diglossia, which can often be found in former colonies. In Tanzania, for example, there was at first diglossia between the language inherited from colonialism, English, and the national language, Swahili. But there was also a second period when there was a diglossia between this same Swahili, which is the mother tongue of only a minority of the population, and the other African languages. The same situation can be found in Mali (French/Bambara/other African languages), in Senegal (French/Wolof/other African languages), and so on. In all these cases, access to power depends on mastery of the official language (English or French) inherited from colonialism, but mastery of the dominant African language (whether or not it is viewed by the law as the only 'natural' language) confers another power. In other words, English is in Tanzania a High form with regard to Swahili, which is itself a High form with regard to the other languages: a case of overlapping diglossia.

2. As for the definition of diglossia adopted by Ferguson, the notion that the languages involved must be related is, as Fishman has noted, extremely limiting. This poses another problem: should we distinguish diglossia from the relationship that holds between a standard language and its dialects (its local or social forms)? Everyone knows, for example, that there is a socially acceptable way of speaking English, and that certain pronunciations of the language (Cockney, for example) can be

a social handicap. But is this strictly comparable to the situation in Tanzania, where English is contrasted with Swahili? Evidently not, although for Fishman the most subtle differences can generate as much diglossia as the most radical differences. It is not, however, the difference between the Queen's English and Cockney which creates diglossia, but the social usage of this difference, and it is history not nature that endows one of these forms with more prestige than the other. If the barbarians gain power anywhere, their language, which was previously considered to be inferior, can become the prestige language.

So if the concept of diglossia can be used to define multilingual societies, we must however be quite explicit that these situations should be analysed according to their social relationships and not their language relationships. For example, In Mali, Bambara can be experienced as a language of liberation (compared to French) but also as a language of oppression for the Songhaï of Timbuctoo or the Tamasheq of the North.

3. Finally, Ferguson's typology (he insists on the 'stable' factor in situations of diglossia) even when revised by Fishman, errs through its lack of a dynamic vision. Take for example the situation of second-generation emigrants, whether they be the children of Portuguese- or Arab-speakers in France, the children of Chinese in America, the children of Turks in Germany, or similar. The parents are, of course, bilingual and they experience, within their micro-society, in their relations with speakers of the offical language, a situation of diglossia: this is Fishman's case 1. On the other hand, the children are often monolingual, even though this monolingualism is relative; these 'monolingual' children often demonstrate a psychological rejection of the language of their parents, which they understand but do not wish to speak, out of desire for assimilation, for example, and so find themselves, when together, in Fishman's case 4 (neither diglossia nor bilingualism). But the children do not always remain together, they live with their parents, in society, and this overall situation, permeated by history, raises the problem of the transmission of bilingualism or of diglossia from one generation to another, at the same time as presenting us with a sort of mixing (in the cinematic sense) of Fishman's categories. In parts of Paris inhabited by migrant workers, like Belleville, one can in fact find a macro-situation of diglossia (between French on the one hand and Arabic, Berber, Vietnamese, and Chinese on the other), micro-situations of bilingualism, and situations of

monolingualism (people who speak only French, but also women who speak only Arabic, etc.), bearing in mind that the monolingualism of a Frenchman is not comparable to the monolingualism of the son of an Algerian or Cantonese.

In other words, the typology we would like to sketch cannot be satisfied with a view that we shall call, metaphorically, 'photographic'; instead, it should incorporate a cinematic vision. That society is permeated by history is obvious, but this is something that sociolinguistics has not always understood, and it is one of the points on which the notion of diglossia needs to be modified.

French as a Touchstone

We shall retain the notion of diglossia in its broadest sense, which is the one most useful for a sociolinguistic approach (that is, to describe functional and social relations between different languages or varieties of languages) and we shall now go on to work out a typology of different 'diglossia', using French as a touchstone. In other words, we shall begin by reviewing the situations in which French is involved (we could of course just as well give an account of English or Russian), working from the hypothesis that they provide us with a more or less complete panorama of the different possibilities for multilingualism.

But first of all, a preliminary comment: if we examine these different situations, whether a European country (France, Belgium, Switzerland, Italy), black Africa (more than a dozen countries), the Mahgreb (Tunisia, Algeria, Morocco), North America (Canada, Louisiana), the Creole-speaking islands (Guadeloupe, Martinique, Réunion), or any other, we find that nowhere is there any correspondence between political frontier (a state), nation, and language. If French is officially present in several countries and involves a significant number of speakers, it coexists everywhere with other languages, and it is the modalities of this coexistence that I would like to study.

This non-correspondence between state, nation, and language leads us to a first criterion for classification: the relationship between official language and mother tongue. Taking the countries mentioned above as a whole, there is not one of which it can be said that all speakers have as their first language (the one learnt in the home, most often called the mother tongue) the official language. Let us leave to one side for the moment countries such as Switzerland or Belgium which have several official languages. But in France itself, where the majority of inhabitants have

French as their first language, a significant proportion of the population have, before acquiring the school language, French, learnt another tongue, which may be Alsatian, Corsican Arabic, Portuguese, Soninke, etc.

An example: Gaillon

Gaillon is a small town of 6,000 inhabitants in the department of the Eure. The population includes 21% foreign workers (the national average is around 8%), a percentage which becomes larger in school since families from North Africa and black Africa tend to have more children than French families. An investigation carried out in 1985 into the 109 pupils of a primary school in the town, the École Louise-Michel, revealed first of all that, besides French, there were three languages (Arabic, Spanish, Portuguese), from five countries (Tunisia, Algeria, Morocco, Portugal, Chile) involving 41 pupils, that is 34% of the whole. Of these 41 pupils, 27 spoke their parent's language, 9 did not speak it all, 5 spoke it a little.[3] We have then, in this microcosm of a school, a population with 66% speaking French alone and 34% from families not speaking French and experiencing or not a diglossia situation. Here French is clearly THE functional language of the school, yet its population is in large part bilingual, a situation which is not rare in France, even if in this case it is statistically 'abnormal'.

What, however, is characteristic of France is that the official language is clearly dominant and that there is no alternative. The possible introduction of bilingualism into schools (French/Breton, French/Provençal, etc.) may be discussed, and there may be thoughts of introducing the languages of children of migrant workers (Portuguese, Spanish, Arabic, etc.), but within the country there is no language that can aspire to replace French. So we have here a situation characterized by a dispersed multilingualism (it should be possible to list a good thirty minority languages spoken in France), appearing in one place as diglossia in the strict sense of the word (Corsica, Catalonia, Alsace), in another in the form of a diaspora (e.g. the Polish and Armenian communities), confronted by a dominant language which has been established by history as the state language and is spoken by practically the whole population. As we have seen, this first type is in no way monolingual, but nor is it a case of a confrontation between two languages, where one might aspire to the

[3] L.-J. Calvet, 'Le Plurilingualisme à l'école primaire', *Migrants formation*, no. 63 (1985).

functions of the other. We shall call this situation multilingualism with a single dominant language. The dominant language (which in the case of France is the national language) is spoken by everyone, or almost everyone and is, moreover, the mother tongue of the majority of the population. But we shall see later, when we discuss some of the countries of black Africa, that the single dominant language may not fill the official functions carried out by French in France. In other words, there may be no correspondence between the dominant language and the national (or official) language.

The countries of North Africa present us with a quite different situation. Three languages are in use everywhere and two of the countries (Algeria and Morocco) are distinguished by the presence of four languages with very varied functions. Gilbert Grandguillaume, in his work *Arabisation et politique linguistique au Maghreb*, defined these languages as follows:

In today's North Africa, three languages are used: Arabic, French, and the mother tongue. The first two are languages of culture, of writing. French is also used as a language for conversation. Nevertheless, the mother tongue, actually spoken in daily life, is always a dialect, Arabic or Berber. The mother tongue, save for some very rare exceptions, is never written down.[4]

These languages each have a very different status, of course. French, the language inherited from colonialism, was for a long time the only official language, and has been relegated to the status of a foreign language since the policy of Arabization. Yet it remains the prerogative of the middle classes, a language of cultural reference, an important asset for social success, compared to Arabic, the national language. Arabic, which is difficult to define linguistically, owes its status (primarily) to the fact that it is simultaneously the language of religion, the language of the Koran, and the language for unification of the Arabic world. The language of the Koran, the Arabic known as classical Arabic, is primarily a written language, which can also be used for preaching or for some teaching, as was Latin in some countries of Europe in the Middle Ages. It is also, therefore, like Latin, a dead language. On the other hand, the form promoted to the status of national language (what is called modern Arabic, middle Arabic, or as I prefer to call it, official Arabic), which has developed out of classical Arabic through enrichment and modernization of the vocabulary, is most widely used in the media and in public life. There remain the mother tongues, usually called, in official terms, dia-

---

[4] G. Grandguillaume, *Arabisation et politique linguistique au Maghreb* (Paris: Maisonneuve et Larose, 1983).

lects: spoken Arabic or Berber. Of course, the former types are related genetically to classical Arabic, the latter are not, but in both cases they are the only real vehicles for day-to-day communication. So, contrary to the first type of multilingualism that we distinguished (multilingualism with a single dominant language), the situation in North Africa provides us with a specific model which requires us first of all to give a better definition of what we understand by 'dominant language'. In the case of France, French can be considered as a dominant language from two points of view: from a statistical point of view (French is, by a long way, the language spoken the most) and from a sociological point of view (French is the language of political and cultural power). In Tunisia, a country in which the Berber language is hardly spoken at all (according to estimates, around 1%), the statistically dominant language is, without question, Tunisian Arabic while official Arabic is sociopolitically dominant and shares cultural domination with French. In Algeria and Morocco, things are a little different: Berber is statistically dominant in Morocco (50%, 60%?), and is spoken by a large minority in Algeria (30%), while official Arabic and French occupy almost the same positions as in Tunisia. In other words, we have here a second type of multilingualism, which we shall name multilingualism with minority dominant languages, in which the languages that are statistically dominant are in fact languages that are politically and culturally subordinate. This type is to be defined primarily by two things: the fact that we have used the plural, dominant languages, and the fact that the people's systems of communication and expression are not represented in state structures.

The part of black Africa that is called 'francophone' Africa presents us with yet another situation. In general, in these countries we find a distinction between the official language (French) and one or several national languages (the African languages). The status of official language is relatively clear: the languages used for the functioning of the state, of schools, of the media, etc. On the other hand, the status of national language varies greatly from one country to another.

Table 3.3 shows that some countries, like Burkina Faso, consider all their languages to be national languages, while others, like the Central African Republic, have chosen one, while yet others, like Zaire or Guinea, have chosen a limited number, and while yet more, like Chad, do not consider any of their languages to be national languages. In these different situations, the notion of national language takes on, therefore, different meanings. A single national language can, in the case of Burundi or the Central African Republic, be the language of education and administra-

TABLE 3.3. *Official and national languages in French-speaking Africa*

Country	Number of languages spoken	Official languages	National languages
Burkina Faso	70	French	70
Burundi	1	French and Kirundi	Kirundi
Central African Republic	65	French	Sango
Chad	100	French	0
Guinea	20	French	8
Zaire	250	French	4

tion, and replace French in its functions. A limited number of national languages (Zaire, Guinea) can be regional languages, with the official language serving as a link between the different regions. On the other hand, when all the languages of a country are considered to be national, then these several national languages have no possibility of achieving any real status. In one case, the status of national language is practical, and may allow for an alternative language policy; in another, it is symbolic and makes no difference to the sociolinguistic situation. But in all cases it is the official language that is the language of power, the language that makes bettering oneself possible, in short, the social key. Whether French is confronted with two, four, eight, or seventy national languages, it remains THE dominant language, but, unlike the French situation, this language with its political and cultural dominance is in statistical terms a minority language (the number of real speakers of French in francophone Africa is estimated at 10%). And, unlike the situation in North Africa, this dominant language does not share power (except in the case of Burundi, which we shall therefore classify as the second type). After multilingualism with a single dominant language, and multilingualism with minority dominant languages, we therefore have a third type of situation, multilingualism with a minority dominant language which, like the previous one, is defined by the fact that the people's systems of communication are not represented in the state's structures, but unlike the previous one, presents us with a single dominant language. It is, however, necessary to introduce here a subdivision, to distinguish between the countries where a statistically dominant language might aspire to replace French (Wolof in Senegal, Bambara in Mali) and those where this alternative does not exist (Cameroon, Gabon, etc.).

Let us now turn to the situation in the Creole-speaking territories (Réunion, Martinique, Guadeloupe, Guyana) that normally illustrate diglossia in the strict sense defined by Ferguson. The genetic kinship which is the basis for the definition will not detain us long, for it is clear that French plays a very definite role in the history of Creole. It is equally clear that the relationship between French and Creole is not the same kind of relationship as between demotic Greek and *katharevousa*. In one case we have two languages which are not mutually intelligible, and in the other two varieties of the same language. We shall give no more credit to theories of 'de-creolization' which argue that, in the same way that people who speak 'badly' aim to speak 'well', so Creole has a tendency to converge with French (I am speaking here only of French-based Creoles; the same thing could of course be said for Creoles based on English or Portuguese). In all of this, there are traces of a pejorative discourse which shall be described in the following chapter and so does not concern us for the moment.

In the overview that we are carrying out here, Creole-speaking countries can be defined by the following characteristics:

- Creole is the first language (the mother tongue), widely dominant from the statistical point of view, even if it coexists with other first languages (French, of course, but also Chinese, some Indian languages, etc.).
- Creole, on the other hand, is not a 'prestige' language, but this does not in any way imply that it does not convey a culture, a hypothesis which would be absurd (all languages convey a culture), only that this culture is not 'recognized'.
- French is the official language, the dominant language from the socio-economic point of view, as in the African situation we have just described. Here again state structures do not take the organization of popular communication into account.
- But French is statistically less of a minority language than in Africa. Education (which is almost general in France's dominions and overseas territories) is increasingly spreading it more as a second language (of course things are different in a country like Haiti).

We have here, then, multilingualism with an alternative dominant language, a situation in which it is completely possible that French might be replaced in its official functions by another language (further on in the book we shall see what conditions are required for a subordinate language to rise to the status of a dominant language; it comes under language work and planning), a situation which can also be found in French Polynesia, where Tahitian is replacing Creole.

TABLE 3.4.

	German	French	Italian	Romansch	Others
1910 (in %)	72.7	22.1	3.9	1.2	0.1
1941	73.9	20.9	3.9	1.1	0.2
1960	74.4	20.2	4.1	1	0.3
1970	74.5	20.1	4	1	0.4
1980	73.6	20	4.5	0.9	1

Switzerland and Belgium present us with another type of situation. It is well known that in Belgium there is an official bilingualism of French and Flemish, these two languages forming the boundary of different parts of the country (with the exception of Brussels, which is officially bilingual) and that in Switzerland there are four official languages, distributed statistically as shown in Table 3.4. These figures relate only to the population with Swiss nationality.[5]

The Swiss constitution lays down that the country has four national languages (German, French, Italian, Romansch) and three official languages (German, French, Italian), and it can be seen that the relationship between these two notions is very different from that encountered in Africa. Romansch is a national language and as such has a legal right to existence in the region where it is spoken, but it is not an official language, that is, it is not recognized in confederal proceedings.[6] As for Belgium, an attempt is being made, not without causing conflict, to give the two languages involved an equal part in the life of the state. So we are here confronted with a situation of multilingualism with dominant regional languages: French coexists with Flemish or with German, each language normally marking out the boundaries of a well-defined territory.

Of course, French is spoken in other parts of the world, in the Seychelles, in Mauritius, in Louisiana, in Canada, in the Val d'Aoste, in Madagascar, etc., but these situations may be reduced to one of the types we have been examining. This typology under five headings (multilingualism with a single dominant language, with dominant minority languages, with one dominant minority language, with alternative dominant languages, and with regional dominant languages), which

---

[5] Table 3.4 taken from R. Schläpfer, *La Suisse aux quatre langues* (Geneva, 1985), 259.
[6] Cf. L.-J. Calvet, *La Tradition orale* (Paris, 1984).

illustrates almost all imaginable situations, is nevertheless open to criticism. We have analysed multilingualism by taking the situations in which the French language is involved as a touchstone, but we have at the same time taken these situations as pre-defined from the point of view of the state. In practice we have spoken only of the 'country'. Now, taking Europe alone into consideration, French-speaking territory transcends frontiers: French is spoken in France, Italy, Switzerland, Belgium, but at the same time not only French is spoken in these countries, and the same situation can be found everywhere. Bambara, the dominant language of Mali, is also spoken in Senegal (where Wolof is dominant), in Burkina Faso, on the Ivory Coast, and elsewhere; Quechua is spoken in Colombia, in Ecuador, in Peru, in Chile, and so on.

The political map and the linguistic map do not correspond, and this general characteristic is as important in our typology of multilingualisms as the five major situations which we have briefly described. The world would appear to be a vast linguistic mosaic in three dimensions, with geographic differentiations (horizontal) in two dimensions, and social differentiations (vertical) in the third. In the horizontal plane will be found, for example, differences between local languages (in France: French, Corsican, Alsatian, etc.) or local varieties (the French of Paris, Marseilles, Grenoble, etc.) and in the vertical plane the social function of these differences, whether these are relationships between regional forms of French or relationships between languages opposing each other. From this point of view, this three-dimensional linguistic mosaic cannot be reduced to the single notion of diglossia; the multilingual world presents us with much more varied, much richer situations, and it is only through isolating arbitrarily this or that situation that it can be reduced to a pre-established framework.

Writing

The multiplicity of language situations is, furthermore, cut across by another criterion of differentiation which will be covered in less detail: the way in which different cultures manage the problem of their social memory, the problem of the transmission of their ancestral knowledge, in other words, their relationship to writing.

Throughout the world there are civilizations of the spoken word and civilizations of the written word which are to be distinguished by the way in which they preserve the memory of human experience and knowledge, rather than by the formal presence of a system of transcribing language.

From this point of view, it is possible to distinguish between four types of situation:

- Societies with a long tradition of writing, in which the written language is a transcription of the linguistic form spoken every day. This is the case with French; knowledge is passed on primarily by books.
- Societies with a long tradition of writing, in which the written language is not the form spoken but a prestige language. This is the case with Arabic. Some knowledge is passed on by books, in a language which is not the language spoken by the people; other knowledge is passed on through the channel of orality.
- Societies in which the alphabet has recently been introduced. This is the case with certain postcolonial situations where languages which until recently were not written down have been endowed with an alphabet. We are here speaking of writing, which does not yet act as a vehicle for knowledge.
- Societies with an oral tradition in which social memory does not rely on writing but on *griots* and storytellers, etc.

These differences share some of the characteristics of our cursory description of the multilingual world, not only in themselves but also because, as we shall see later, the presence or absence of writing in a culture has often been used to dignify or disparage this culture, as part of an ideological vision which treats written transcription as a support of knowledge. Societies with an oral tradition are generally regarded as societies without writing and therefore deprived, which is a very reductive way of defining them and, at the same time, a way of disparaging them in comparison with Western societies.

But literacy and orality often coexist, and this coexistence has some characteristics in common with the different kinds of multilingualism which we have just described. Our typology of the situations in which French played a role has so far taken into account the status of subordinate or dominant languages only from the sociological or statistical point of view. But the fact that these languages are written down or not, transmit a literature or not, have a literary tradition or not, must be integrated into this typology, and has a considerable influence on the way language situations develop.

If, for example, we compare Algeria and Mali, two colonies that gained independence at the same time (1962), we can see that the relationship between the languages involved, which was much the same at the beginning (in both cases French was the one official language), changed considerably. The status of French has practically not changed in Mali, where the teaching of African languages in school has barely begun; it has been overturned in Algeria where Arabic has replaced French for almost all official uses.

There are many explanations for this different development. In particular, of course, there are the different choices in language policy made by the governments of Algeria and Mali, but the fact that one of the alternative dominant languages, Arabic, has long existed in written form, while the other, Bambara, has only been written down recently, has played an important role. In these two cases the struggle for cultural decolonization was not at the beginning equipped with the same weapons. We shall see the same reasons operating in other cases, where the speakers of subordinate written languages take refuge, in some periods, in literature (this was the case with Provençal and Breton, for example), a recourse which was obviously not available to the speakers of subordinate languages that were not written down. So the relationship to writing, insofar as it has been perceived through the filter of Western cultures, which are spread by written languages, has played a fundamental part in determining the power relationships of language and continues to do so. The reader will recall that, in the examples of diglossia given by Ferguson, the High varieties were all written while only some of the Low varieties were ('dialect' Arabic is not written, but demotic Greek is). This is yet another point where the notion has to be adapted. The three-dimensional linguistic mosaic to which I referred above is also affected by the coexistence of languages from an oral tradition and languages from a written tradition.

As I wrote at the beginning of this chapter, human beings are confronted by languages. It is from the plurality of situation which we have described, from this richness, that the problem which lies at the centre of this book emerges: the war of languages has its roots in multilingualism and in the way in which human cultures have analysed it. For, as we shall see in the following chapter, before dealing with multilingualism, human beings began by first giving it an ideological interpretation.

4

Ideologists of Superiority

It is easy to imagine that, when confronted by linguistic differences, human beings have always had a tendency to laugh at the customs of others, to consider their own language the most beautiful, the most effective, the most precise, in other words to convert the difference of other languages (for of course it is always the other person or language that is different) into inferiority. *La Guerre du feu* (*Quest for fire*, 1981), a film which had worldwide success some years ago, showed 'tribes' speaking different languages, and could also have portrayed this kind of language conflict: you do not speak like me, therefore your speech is ridiculous. From all of this it is possible to take a further step and imagine the extension of war studies to prehistoric language wars.

Greeks, Barbarians, and Others

But we are not here to use our imaginations, and even if it seems to me that such conflicts must have taken place, we have to be content with the historic traces of how language difference was dealt with. From this point of view, our sources do not go back very far, and we have to limit ourselves to ancient Greece to see the emergence in etymology of a word still current in modern languages: 'barbarian' (in its English form), a particular way of treating the Other.

This is well known, and I have mentioned it in passing in preceding chapters. The Greeks had found a comfortable way of dividing up the world by placing all those who did not speak Greek and so were 'strangers' into the category of barbarians, '*barbaros*', and from them the Romans borrowed both the word and its meaning: *barbarus*, 'stranger'. But translating *barbaros* by 'stranger' omits an important piece of information, for the barbarians were, etymologically, those who could not speak, since they could not speak Greek, and who could only produce babblings, gabbling, gibberish, in other words something that one attempted to imitate and ridicule by onomatopoeia based on the repetition of a syllable with a childish sound, brbr, barbar(os). It was in this sense that the word entered the Romance languages. As for French, the Littré dictionary gives, for example, this text from the fourteenth century: 'Barbares, tous ceulz qui sont de estrange langue' (Oresme). In Spanish Antonio de Nebrija (*Gramtica de la lengua Castellana*, 1942) has this enlightening passage:

Barbarism is an intolerable mistake in any part of a sentence; and it is called barbarism because the Greeks called all peoples besides themselves barbarian. In turn the Latins called barbarian all other nations save themselves and the Greeks. And because the strangers they called barbarians corrupted their speech when they wanted to speak it, they called barbarism the mistakes they committed in a word. We can call barbarian all those who are strangers to our language, except Greeks and Latins.[1]

In this way, even if the circle of non-barbarians has progressively widened through successive 'legitimations' (after Greek, Latin and then Castilian are admitted among legitimate languages in the text above), the notion of barbarian is clearly in origin the translation of Greek language racism.

Of course, this kind of label cannot help but take root in the popular view of language difference, where a person whom one does not understand and who does not understand us is always considered to be more ridiculous than ourselves. But echoes of this disparagement can also be found among those whom today we would call intellectuals and, insofar as it concerns Greek culture, in the Plato of the *Cratylus*.

The subject of the dialogue is well known. A discussion springs up between two characters, Hermogenes and Cratylus, on the problem of naming. One, Cratylus, maintains that there is 'a correctness of names, belonging naturally to each reality'; this is the doctrine of *physis* (the natural), while the other, Hermogenes, thinks that the 'correctness' of words is a matter of convention, which is the doctrine of *thesis* (the conventional). Socrates, called to the rescue, has a 'maieutic' discussion with each of them, and, as usual, does not reach a decision but shows them the errors in their reasoning. Here we shall only discuss part of the dialogue, where Socrates questions Hermogenes, who upholds the conventionalist view. Socrates gets him to admit that objects are not named in just any fashion but follow a certain logic.

He then gives a series of examples which all come from what linguists call popular etymology (which sees in the word *humus*, humus or leafmould, the root of the word *homme* because God created man from a

---

[1] Quoted by Raul Avila, 'La Langue espagnole et son enseignement: Oppresseurs et opprimés', in *La Crise des langues* (Paris: Robert, 1985), 337.

lemon, or which analyses *parlement*, parliament, as *parle*, speak, and *ment*, lie). Thus, the gods, *theoi*, who were originally stars, the moon and the sun, describing an unending course through the heavens, are named after the verb *thein*, to run. Man is unlike the animals in that he studies, *anathrei*, and sees, *opope* ('he saw'), hence *anathron-ha-opope*, which gives *anthropos*, man. Or again, why is Poseidon, the god of the sea, called Poseidon? Because he walks in the water which slows his stride, hence *posi-desmos*, hindrance to the feet, and *poseidon*.

Naturally, Hermogenes raises the problem of the primitive correctness of syllables and sounds, since for the moment only the basis of composite words has been demonstrated. Socrates responds to this with a theory of imitation by means of the voice. In order to justify the correctness of primitive words, it is necessary to demonstrate the semantic character of sounds and letters: the letter r expresses movement, the letter l gliding/sliding, the letter o roundness, the letter t a halt, etc.

In this 'demonstration' which we have, of course, taken out of context (for Socrates will defend the opposite position against Cratylus, without however abandoning this one) there are two errors.

There is, first of all, an ignorance of the fact that languages, including Greek of course, evolve, and this or that word did not have the same form five or ten centuries before. So the word *parlement* clearly does not come from *parle et ment*, speak and lie, but from the verb *parler*, to speak, derived from the popular Latin *paraulare*, itself derived from the ecclesiastical Latin *parabolare*, and so on. What is lacking here is historical awareness, and the attempt to justify, at a single point in history, the 'correctness' of a name, in the terms that Socrates understands it, is rendered completely futile by the constant evolution of languages.

More importantly, there is an ignorance of other languages, for if one admits what Socrates has Hermogenes admit, this is of course only valid for Greek. The demonstration mentioned above concerning *anthropos* cannot be accepted without immediately concluding that *homo*, for example, is badly formed. But the problem did not arise for, in the ideology of the period, there were no languages other than Greek. Besides this language, there were only, as we have seen, vague noises uttered by barbarians.

Plato's text, which is a stage in the history of reflection on linguistic signs and expresses a point of view that was not radically abandoned until the beginning of the twentieth century, with Ferdinand de Saussure's theory of the arbitrariness of signs, is at the same time an illustration of a stage in the ideology of superiority which gives this chapter its title.

Du Bellay and his 'Defence'

Confronted by language difference, men have always felt the need to demonstrate the excellence of their own language and the inferiority of others. We have just examined a secular version of this temptation, with the Greeks and their barbarians; we saw in Chapter 2 a religious version, with the Koran seeking to justify the superiority of Arabic. In neither case was the ideology based directly on practice, nor did it aim to inspire a policy, unlike the example that follows.

It was in 1549 that Joachim du Bellay, expressing the beliefs of a group known under the collective name of the 'Pleiad', published his *Défense et illustration de la Langue Française*, which I would now like to analyse.[2] First of all, we should remember that some years before, an Italian, Sperone Speroni had published a *Dialogo delle lingue* (Venice, 1542) and the existence of this book has some relevance to du Bellay's. Speroni wished to demonstrate the superiority of his language, Italian, over Latin, and du Bellay had the same goal while drawing sometimes more inspiration from his predecessor than is normally allowed. To begin with (in chapter I of book I: 'The origin of languages') he argues for the equality of all languages, 'since they all come from a single source and origin', and he adds: 'it is true that in the succession of time, some from having been more carefully regulated have become richer than others: but this should not be attributed to the felicity of the said languages but to the sole artifice and industry of men.'

All languages are equal, then, since they all descend from the pre-Babel language, even if some are 'more equal than others', but this superiority does not come from the languages themselves but from their speakers, who have been able to improve them: 'For languages are not born of themselves after the fashion of grasses, roots and trees; some are infirm and weak in their nature; others healthy, robust and more fitted to carry the burden of human conceptions; but all their virtue is born in the world of the desire and will of mortals.' Du Bellay's originality can be appreciated by comparing the passage above with Speroni's text: it is a direct translation.[3]

Be that as it may, in defending the idea of the equality of languages, the

[2] The translation used here is *The Defence and Illustration of the English Language* (Dent, 1939).

[3] 'Dunque non nascono le lingue per se medesme, a guisa di alberi a d'herbe, quale debole & inferma nelle sua specie, quale sana & robusta & atta meglio a portar la soma di nostri humani concetti: ma ogni loro vertu nasce al mondo dal voler de mortali.'

author is here relatively original, for as I have argued elsewhere,[4] the sixteenth century had experienced an intense controversy between the French and the Germans, each wanting to show that their tongue was closest to the pre-Babel language, proximity of course conferring superiority. But we shall see later that this text returned to the dominant discourse, in its second part.

From this equality of origin, du Bellay draws an aggressive argument in favour of the French language:

In this connection, I cannot sufficiently blame the foolish arrogance and temerity of some in our nation who, being in no wise Greeks or Latin, misprize and reject all things written in French; and I cannot sufficiently wonder at the strange opinion of some learned men who think that our vulgar tongue is incapable of good letters and erudition.

In book II, these generalities are abandoned in order to come down to concrete matters, that is, the defence of French, where the author's discussion is almost entirely lexical. First of all there is the theoretical justification: 'No man, unless he be ignorant of everything, nay, deprived of common sense, doubts that first there have been things, then afterwards words were invented to designate them; and consequently on new things it is necessary to impose new words.' Then comes the appeal to lexical creativity: 'Fear not, then, o future poet, to innovate some terms' . . . And, especially, the caution: 'Among other things, let our poet take care not to use the Latin or Greek proper names, a thing as absurd really as if thou shouldst apply a piece of green velvet to a dress of red velvet' (chapter 6).

The tone becomes progressively more inflated, and after having given some syntactical and stylistic advice in chapter 9 ('Use then boldly the infinitive for a noun, as *l'aller, le chanter, le vivre, le mourir*. Use the substantial adjective, as *le liquide des eaux, le vuide de l'air*'—the wetness of the waters, the emptiness of the air), he comes in chapter 12 to an *'Exhortation' to the French to write in their language*. This exhortation, which ends the book, demonstrates first the superiority of France over Italy:

- the gentleness of the air, fertility of the soil, abundance of every kinds of fruits . . .
- so many great rivers, so many fair forests, so many towns . . .
- so many crafts, arts, and sciences which flourish amongst us . . .

---

[4] *Linguistique et colonialisme* (Paris: Payot, 1974).

Then he continues: 'Why then are we so great admirers of others? Why are we so unjust to ourselves? Why do we beg from other tongues as if we were ashamed to use our own?' in order to come to what is, of course, the centre of his argument; 'you should not be ashamed to write in your language'. No one should be able to deny this, neither in du Bellay's time nor today, but on the other hand, the conclusion does sound like a declaration of cultural war and is much more debatable: 'Fear no more those shrill geese, proud Manlius, and the traitor Camillus . . . Attack this lying Greece . . . Pillage without scruple the sacred treasures of the Delphic shrine . . . fear no more this dumb Apollo, his false oracles nor his blunted arrows'.

This text, often referred to by teachers of French but rarely read, often quoted for its title but not for its content, is worth a moment's reflection, for it presents a profound ambiguity in the true sense of the term: it has two meanings. On the one hand, it is part of a movement of cultural liberation, a desire to make the French tongue, along with Latin, a language fit to carry poetry and the sciences. All histories of French literature make this claim and it is this contribution to a 'just war' that has given the work its fame. But even on this point the text does not perhaps have the value which has often been attached to it and the view of Ferdinand Brunot, in his *Histoire de la langue française* is worth considering: 'I would regard the book only as an apology for the language; it must be acknowledged, at the risk of appearing too critical, that the work is almost without interest'.[5]

But much more interesting here is the fact that, in order to 'defend' the French language, du Bellay felt the need to attack other languages to such an extent. From this point of view, his text should be looked at from a political perspective which takes into account not only the debate on the pre-Babel language referred to above (the desire, ultimately shared by du Bellay, to demonstrate the superiority of French over the other languages of Europe) but also the relations between the languages spoken in France itself. In particular it should be remembered that ten years before the *Défence et illustration*, on 15 August 1539, François I issued the Edict of Villers-Cotterets on the administration of justice, in which articles 110 and 111 specifically stated that legal proceedings would henceforth take place in French. The language was replacing Latin of course, but at the same time it was taking precedence over other local languages: as Brunot stresses, from now on there was a 'state language'. It is in this context that

[5] F. Brunot, *Histoire de la langue française* (Paris, 1906), ii. 85.

du Bellay's book should be assessed, in the sense that the author is of course part of a literary movement, along with Ronsard, Baïf, Jodelle, and others, and so the work is in this regard a 'manual of poetry', but it is also part of an ideological campaign in a language war, directed simultaneously inwards (to impose French in France as the state language) and outwards (to demonstrate the superiority of French as against other state languages).

Rivarol and the Universality of French

For reasons that will be explained at the end of the chapter, I should like now to make a leap in history to the end of the eighteenth century, when on 6 June 1782 the Academy of Berlin chose the following question for its annual competition: 'What has made the French language the universal language of Europe? On what grounds does it deserve this privilege? Can it be assumed that French will retain it?'

So, a little more than two centuries after du Bellay sounded the attack, a foreign academy considered that French had a 'universal' status, that it was 'the common language of Europe'. In fact, the Academy of Berlin was not at all original on this point. Montesquieu, after a journey to Vienna in 1728, noted that 'our language is universal there'; the 1762 edition of the Dictionary of the Academy describes it as 'almost as necessary to strangers as their own natural language'; Voltaire, in his *The Century of Louis XIV*, added that French 'has become the language of Europe' and the *Encyclopedie* itself said, in the article 'Language', that 'already all courts are in favour of it, and it is spoken almost as much as at Versailles'. And many more quotations could be brought forward as evidence, in France at least, of a kind of consensus.

In fact, even if it is true that French held a privileged place in literature and diplomacy, even if it is true that it was spoken by the European bourgeoisie and taught in many schools, this idyllic vision must be seen relatively. For, as the *Encyclopedie* said, it was very much a matter of courts, of nobles, of power, and it was very optimistic to postulate the universality of French at a period when it was not even a majority language in France. To be convinced of this one has only to refer to the report presented, some years later, by the Abbé Grégoire to the Convention on Prairial 16, year II (28 May 1794). Here one finds first of all the same tone: 'If our language has been so well received by tyrants and courts, to which monarchical France gave theatres, pompons, fashions and manners, what reception should it not look forward to from the people to whom republican France reveals their rights by opening up the route of liberty?'

In this way the universal language becomes the idiom of liberty. But, a little later, Grégoire writes:

It can be declared without exaggeration that at least six million French people, in the country especially, do not know the national language; the same number of people is almost incapable of maintaining a continuous conversation; and, in the final analysis, the number of those who speak it does not exceed three million, and probably the number of those who can write it correctly is even less.

It can be seen that these figures are quite low for a language presented, in other respects, as universal.

But let us go back to the competition of 1782. The Academy of Berlin received 21 or 22 replies (the sources contradict each other on this point) of which only 18 have been preserved,[6] and shared the prize between two texts, one in German by Jean-Christ Schwab (1773–1821) and the other in French by Antoine Rivarol (1753–1801). His work was the well-known *Discours sur l'universalité de la langue française*. Ferdinand Brunot, who had access to the sixteen manuscript essays preserved in Berlin, gives an analysis[7] of them from which I have drawn the following points.

– Nine of the texts were written in German, seven in French (though French was not the mother tongue for some of these seven, judging by their style). The trace of this 'universality' can be seen here, without forgetting that though the competition was set by Berlin, it concerns the French language, and these two specific facts explain in part the bilingual division of texts.

– Brunot stresses that the general tone of the essays is one of great objectivity and that the candidates attempted to analyse the questions without showing any aggression towards France.

– Some, not many, argued against the notion of universality itself, bringing out that French is without doubt the most widespread European language, but that its expansion had come up against major social and geographical barriers (it was not spoken in Poland or Hungary, and little in Portugal). 'It is impossible to look for the reasons why the French language has become the general language of Europe', wrote one, 'for this would be to look for the causes of something which has not happened'.

---

[6] On this point, see F. Brunot, op. cit. (Paris, 1935), viii. 839 et seq.
[7] Ibid., viii. 912–14.

- Many reasons were given to explain the status of the French language: the influence of French culture and literature, political circumstances, in particular the role of Louis XIV, French travellers abroad, deserters, Huguenot expatriates, etc.
- Finally, the reasons for this 'universality' were sought in the language itself, in its form: the eminent role of the Académie Française and its dictionary was quoted, the ease of learning and pronouncing French was suggested, as well as its elegance. Above all, its clarity was emphasized, often related to the 'natural' order of its syntax. This last point brings us back to Rivarol.

'What is not clear is not French': this expression, which has entered history, is in fact the conclusion of a long argument that can be summarized into two stages.

Rivarol begins by explaining why French has acquired the status of a universal language, and why other languages (German, Spanish, Italian, English) cannot compete, with sometimes surprising and peremptory judgements (English literature from Chaucer through Shakespeare to Milton 'is not worth a glance'). He details the arguments that have worked in favour of the French language, from the genius of its literature to the grandeur of Louis XIV, and explains that it had taken the lead over other languages which then gave it a sort of right of primogeniture (the expression is Rivarol's).

Then, in a second part, he explains why French has been able to retain this advantage: through its own genius. For, he argues, men experience a permanent conflict between logic and the passions. The passions would have us name the object that strikes our senses first, while logic would have us give the subject first, then the verb and lastly, the object, as happens with French syntax. There are, then, languages which follow the order of the sensations, and because of this, their syntax is corrupt, disordered. But the French language respects logical order: 'French, by unique privilege, has alone remained faithful to direct order . . . French syntax is incorruptible. Its admirable clarity results from this and is the eternal basis of our language. What is not clear is not French.'

This notion of a 'logical order' is not new; it can already be found in the seventeenth century, in particular in the *Grammaire générale et raisonée*, the so-called 'Port Royal grammar', and it served as an argument in favour of French for many long years. It is of course difficult to admit that one language can be 'superior' to another, and no one needs to be a specialist in linguistics to see that behind this so-called rationalism lies a sort of linguistic racism: languages that do not possess the syntactical order of French are not 'logical' and this so-called rationalism results in nationalism.

Ideologists of the Wars

I have devoted a chapter to the relationship between 'theory of language and colonialism' in another work, to which the reader may refer,[8] and so in the preceding pages I have simply analysed texts over which I passed too quickly (as with the *Cratylus*) or did not mention there. This is the case with the *Défense et illustration de la langue française* and the *Discours sur l'universalité de la langue française*, which I have also chosen because they occupy a special place in the French collective unconscious and because they have a resonance that is not without interest at a time when many consider the French language to be under threat.

We have gone straight from du Bellay to Rivarol, from the sixteenth to the eighteenth centuries, although between these two texts a profusion of documents can be found, all aiming to prove the superiority of one language over others. But the number of examples does not make much difference if they all teach the same lesson. The comparative method in linguistics, an approach that flourished in the nineteenth century, slowly established itself as a science and enabled us to understand how languages evolved and to carry out some bold reconstructions. It was, in particular, thanks to the comparative method that it was possible to imagine the form of a language of which we have no trace, Indo-European, and to gain knowledge of the phonetic laws that explain how the sounds of a 'parent' language are transformed into the sounds of this or that 'daughter' language. But the comparisons we have just referred to did not have this function at all. They had to do with the pursuit of knowledge and aimed above all at demonstrating that not all languages had the same value, that there were, to put it briefly, inferior and superior languages.

In this way European languages were contrasted with those of the Third World, and this contrast played an important role in colonial ideology. But the European languages have also been contrasted with each other, a contrast which is not unconnected with the different conflicts that have marked the history of the West. In particular the whole debate on the pre-Babel language, that ran through the sixteenth century, is directly linked to the conflict between the Valois and the Hapsburgs.

[8] *Linguistique et colonialisme*, 15–39.

If humanity, then, entered into linguistic communication through multilingualism, it has at the same time dealt with this multilingualism through condemning others. By converting differences into subordination, by considering the language of others as inferior (in general), even as a non-language (as with the Greeks), right from the beginning human beings have laid down the premisses of a war of languages which religious or secular ideologies have then continued. A quite theoretical war, certainly, but one which, as we shall see, developed in different directions and was taken up in less Platonic fashion by the machinery of state. The war of languages, therefore, seems to be linked to multilingualism itself; we tolerate differences badly.

PART II
The Battlefield

5

Lingua Francas and Vernaculars

All the linguistic forms we use, whether they are different languages or different forms of the same language, are distributed over a vast range of functions. At one end of the continuum is the tendency towards a common language, a lingua franca, that is, the forms we choose when we wish to increase communication to as many people as possible; at the other end is the tendency to what might be called a vernacular language, defining the forms we choose when we wish to limit communication to a few people, to register our specificity, to mark a group's frontier. These two tendencies, towards a lingua franca or a vernacular language, can be applied to multi-lingual situations as well as to monolingual ones.

The Tendency to a Vernacular

There is an idea of complicity here: a vernacular is the language of a small group, which therefore limits communication to a few and whose form is characterized by this desire for limitation. This is, of course, the case with cryptic forms, like coded slang for example (such as largonji, in which words are altered by substituting l for the first letter and adding the original first letter and a vowel to the end, so that jargon becomes largonji). With these, changes to the form are intended to limit access to communication, but this is also the case with social registers, with the linguistic forms of age-groups and even family languages. So, for example, taking a multilingual situation, Breton or Corsican can be vernaculars with respect to French, but in a monolingual situation, there could be vernacular forms (family, regional, the slang of age-groups, etc.) within Corsican itself. Similarly, French people living in the USA and working in English will use their own language between themselves in its vernacular function, as against English. But besides this in their own families they may use particular forms of French, still with a vernacular function, and in the same family the children may use particular vernacular forms to differentiate themselves from their parents. No matter how monolingual we are, we are also all more or less multilingual. I mean by this that, even within the framework of a single language, our own, we use different forms of this language, and the choice of one form or another comes down to particular functions. We all have, in our own lexis, words that come from our personal histories and which we only use with a very limited number of people: the sweet nothings of a pair of lovers, the vocabulary of a group or age-group reserved for friends, pet-names and nicknames reserved for the family, children's words, like those mistakes in pronunciation which follow us all our lives, thanks to the formidable memory of our parents, and which reappear at every family reunion.

Here is an example now in the public domain. When Jean-Paul Sartre was a child, his family called him 'Poulou'; later he called Simone de Beauvoir 'Castor' (from an approximate pun on Beauvoir and the English word 'Beaver', which is '*castor*' in French). Their group of friends also had its own language, its own expressions:

'Vous me faites regret' (You give me regret), 'Ca me fait tout poétique' (It makes me all poetic), 'Ça m'a rarement fait si gratuit et si nécessaire' (It has seldom made me so pointless and so necessary), Sartre could write to his 'little flower', his 'charming, little Beaver', developing a vernacular vocabulary which, along with the animal nicknames, would soon become a deeply impenetrable sign of their complicity

comments Annie Cohen-Solal, Sartre's biographer.[1] This famous example is true for all groups, all families. We all have words like this in a corner of our memories, sometimes reremembered from reading an old letter or by meeting a member of the family: the form of language we use registers where we differ and where we belong.

The Tendency to a Lingua Franca

At the other end of the range of functions we find the tendency to a lingua franca which is a response to an exactly contrary problem. Where the vernacular form would limit communication to as few people as possible, to initiates, to close relations, the lingua franca form increases it to as many as possible; where differences were noticed, now we have the opposite desire of bringing registered. This function can give rise to particular kinds of code, like pidgins, which result from contact between speakers of different languages who find themselves in a situation posing a communication problem. Pidgin English, which gave its name to the type, devel-

---

[1] Annie Cohen-Solal, *Sartre 1905–1980* (Paris, 1985), 132. English translation (Heinemann, 1987), 86.

oped from contacts between English and Chinese in commercial situations. It has a Chinese grammatical base and an English vocabulary pronounced as in Chinese (the word pidgin is itself a deformation of the English word 'business', which is good evidence of its original function). Pidgin was used by both communities when they needed to communicate, but of course each of them returned to its own linguistic form (the vernacular form) outside of these limited exchanges. In other places the lingua franca function was embodied not in an *ad hoc* form, as in the case of pidgin, but in the promotion of one of the languages involved to the status of lingua franca. We shall analyse the history of some lingua francas more closely in Chapter 7, in order to determine the different factors involved when this kind of promotion takes place. For the moment my intention is simply to underline the processes of exclusion and inclusion that might be involved in the definition of this functional pair, vernacular language/lingua franca. For language here registers the desire to belong, it becomes a sign, tracing the boundary of the vernacular implied by the communication. By choosing this or that form, this or that variant, the speaker indicates where he places himself, behind which boundary. The choice of a boundary can be manifested in a regional accent, by the introduction of dialect words in the standard form, or by the use of a different language in multilingual situations. There is a whole continuum of possibilities in the range which runs from the vernacular tendency to the tendency to a lingua franca.

The Example of Gavot

One day, when on holiday in the Gordolasque valley, in the country inland from Nice, I started asking an old lady, whose first language was Provençal, what image she had of languages, a topic which linguists call her 'language attitude'. The first interesting thing was this: for her Provençal did not exist, at least not under that name; she thought that she spoke 'lou patois', that is, her vernacular language, and French, the country's lingua franca, relying on a familiar pejorative contrast. But, besides that, she insisted on the unity of French, which she contrasted with the fragmentation of Provençal. For she carefully distinguished her 'patois' from the patois of other people, which she nevertheless understood perfectly. She explained to me that the people of Lantosque were 'Cougourdiais' who spoke Cougourdiais (because they have a reputation for eating marrow, '*cougourdes*', a lot), the people of La Bollène were '*Amouyans*' (dried cherries), the people of Saint-Martin-de-Vésubie '*totchis*' (perhaps from '*tout petits*', very small) and, to conclude, told me that 'others' called the people of her village, Belvédère, '*banes*' (which could mean 'deer woods', 'horns', perhaps 'cuckolds'). These different places could be found within thirty kilometres of each other, but the old lady strongly emphasized the differences between these spoken languages. So, rather than insist on the fact that she communicated in Provençal with all the old people of the region, she preferred to emphasize differences of detail which seemed to her to be of the highest importance: the fact for example that she called a spade '*lou magaï*', while in another village it was called '*lou magaou*'. In the same region I one day heard a discussion in Provençal between a man from Nice and one from Grasse, who were each reproaching the other for their ridiculous name for a broom: one called it '*la scopa*', the other '*la ramassa*'. In both these cases we have vernacular forms overlapping each other, very local forms of Provençal being perceived as different while, with regard to French, they obviously constitute a unique whole, a single language.

All the conditions for a permanent 'war' between linguistic forms are brought together in this relationship between real or imaginary unity and diversity, in this paradoxical tension. For, however 'different' these Gourdiais, these Amouyans, these Totchis and Banes are, they are subsumed by people from Nice under the generic title of '*Gaouatchs*', a term applied to people from the mountains.

More generally, an inhabitant of the mountains is called a '*Gavot*' in Provence. In Languedoc the word refers to someone from the mountains of the Lozère, while in Gascony the word used is '*gavach*' and in Catalonia a '*Gaback*' is a man from the Béarnais. If we are to believe popular etymology the word means 'chick-pea' and indicates poor people through a reference to their daily food. Frédéric Mistral, in his *Tresor dou felibrige* does not give this etymology, but this does not make much difference for he glosses the term as 'coarse, boorish, leprous; nickname often given in Provence to people from the Alps, and in Languedoc to people from the mountains of the Lozère', and he links it to the Spanish '*gago*', meaning leprous, dirty.[2] In this way a term with a geographical origin (the people of a particular place, here the mountains) gradually takes on a social and pejorative sense: the geographical differentiation turns into irony and denigration. The vernacular form of the Other becomes the basis for denigration. This is the basis of French stories about Corsicans and Belgians, of English stories about the Scots and Irish, Brazilian stories

---

[2] Frédéric Mistral, *Lou tresor dou felibrige*, new edn. (1968), ii. 41.

about the Portuguese, and so on. But it is also the basis of certain social classifications and, sometimes, of dramatic difficulties of communication, as the following examples show.

Pygmalion and Dominici

In Bernard Shaw's *Pygmalion*, or in *My Fair Lady*, the film Cukor made from the play, the science of Professor of Phonetics Higgins is particularly instructive. In the first act of the play he begins by asserting the geolinguistic finesse of his ear: 'You can spot an Irishman or a Yorkshireman by his brogue. I can place any man within six miles. I can place him within two miles in London. Sometimes within two streets'.[3]

A sarcastic passer-by takes the opportunity to compare his science to a music-hall skill, but the linguist is not put off, and he moves on quickly to the pejorative side of his linguistic classification: 'A woman who utters such depressing and disgusting sounds has no right to be anywhere, no right to live'.[4]

In the film, a song performed by Rex Harrison is even clearer:

> 'Look at her, a prisoner of the gutter
> Condemned by every syllable she utters
> By right she should be taken out and hung
> For the cold blooded murder of the English tongue . . .
> Hear a Yorkshire man, or worse
> Hear a Cornish man converse
> I'd rather hear a choir singing flat
> Chickens cackling in a barn . . .'[5]

Poor Eliza Doolittle is far from appreciating these cutting remarks, and she makes this clear, but she is given the opportunity of going to Higgins to learn to speak 'better' and in this way enter into 'society', or change her milieu, that is, appear to change social class by modifying her vernacular language. The story, as with most stories, will therefore end happily, but it is not always the same in reality.

In August 1952, three British citizens, Sir Jack Drummond, his wife, and their daughter, were murdered while camping beside a road in Provence, near the farm belonging to the Dominici family. There was a long, contradictory and faltering investigation, which came to an end after 16

[3] G. B. Shaw, *Pygmalion*, Act I.
[4] Ibid.
[5] *My Fair Lady*.

months, in November 1953, with the indictment of the head of the family, Gaston Dominici. During the trial that opened the following year, in November 1954, Dominici denied everything. He had confessed, he said, under police pressure, but he was innocent. In fact, this old man aged 77 seemed to have only a rough knowledge of French; his language was Provençal, '*lou patois*'. So the whole trial appeared as a gigantic misunderstanding between the old man and the court. Roland Barthes quotes this significant passage:

– The President of the court: *Etes-vous allé au pont*? (Did you go to the bridge?) Gaston Dominici: *Allée? Il n'y a pas d'allée, je le sais, j'y suis été* (Alley? There's no alley, I know, I was there).

Roland Barthes comments:

Naturally everyone pretends to believe that it is the official language that is common usage, while Dominici's is only an ethnological variation, picturesque in its poverty. And yet, the language of the president of the court is just as individual . . . Quite simply two particular uses of language have come up against each other. But one of them has the honours, law and force on its side.[6]

For, whether one considers the language of the court, the president, the public prosecutor, as THE lingua franca or as THEIR vernacular language, it is clear that this opposition between two linguistic forms (lingua franca/ vernacular or vernacular 1/vernacular 2) depends on power relationships, and Dominici is on the wrong side. He was, moreover, condemned to death, without any real proof and—this illustrates the general uncertainty—fifteen days later the Minister of Justice ordered the opening of a new investigation. This did not reach a conclusion, and in 1957 René Coty, the President of the Republic, commuted the death penalty to hard labour; finally, in 1960 another President of the Republic, Charles de Gaulle, used his right of mercy to free Gaston Dominici. Barthes, nevertheless, concluded his article: 'We are all potential Dominicis, not murderers, but accused men and women, deprived of our language or, worse, rigged out in that of our accusers, humiliated and condemned by it. To rob a man of his language in the very name of language—this is the first step in all legal murders'.[7]

It is of course difficult to know whether Gaston Dominici was guilty or innocent, but this is not my point. I simply wished to underline here the

---

[6] Roland Barthes, *Mythologies* (Paris, 1957), 54–5.
[7] Ibid. 56.

functioning of language, to show how certain linguistic forms can give power to those who master them.

In the imaginary case of *Pygmalion* the vernacular difference functioned as a social marker. In the first instance it made it possible to place the speaker, to give him or her an origin, and secondly, to reduce this difference to an inferiority which justified Professor Higgins's scorn for the little flower-seller and for anyone like her. But in the real case of Dominici, his linguistic deficiency led to punishment, a punishment that was nearly fatal.

These are, of course, only a few such examples, but they mount up to establish a relevant statistical fact. Certainly Dominici trials do not happen every day, but we can find similar power relationships every day in linguistic exchanges, though in different degrees. Society is continuously troubled by these conflicts. When the lingua franca is on the side of authority, of the law (we shall see in Chapter 7 that this is not always the case), it takes on an additional power that it can exercise over vernacular forms.

Mauritius

After these somewhat anecdotal examples, I would now like to illustrate the vernacular language/lingua franca relationship by referring to a more complex situation, the one in Mauritius. Situated in the Indian Ocean, in the Mascarene group, the island has little more than a million inhabitants but presents an astonishing diversity of languages, races, and cultures. Issa Asgurally[8] has studied the situation and some aspects of his work are extremely revealing. Using questionnaires he, for example, asked his subjects what language should be used for prayer. There were seven religions (Adventists, Buddhists, Catholics, Hindus, Muslims, Protestants, Tamils) and ten languages in his sample. The replies received were characterized by a large dispersion, but with four languages dominating: Creole (25.5%), French (15.4%), Hindi (14.6%), Arabic (7%). As always, it is difficult to interpret this bare breakdown. But if the replies are matched with the religious affiliation of the subjects, it can be seen that there is a link between religion and choice of language. The majority of Catholics replied that prayers should be said 'in French' and secondly 'in Creole'; the Hindus replied first 'in Hindi', then in 'Creole'; the Muslims

---

[8] Issa Asgurally, 'La Situation linguistique de l'ile Maurice', thesis supervised by L.-J. Calvet (Paris, Université René Descartes, 1982).

replied 'in Arabic', then 'in Creole', etc. That is, we find, in each of these sub-groups, a vernacular language, a sign of belonging to a given religion (Arabic, French, Hindi) which was chosen first, and a popular lingua franca, Creole, which appeared as the second choice, while the official language, English, was the one mentioned least.

The relationships between these different forms becomes clearer when we consider the replies to a series of questions of the form 'what language do you speak to . . . ?' as set out in Table 5.1.

Naturally, a reading of Table 5.1 from top to bottom shows the relative importance of different languages in different situations. We can see for example that Creole and Bhojpuri are the languages most frequently spoken within the family, while French is the most common in formal situations. But if we read the table horizontally we find a spread of vernacular and general functions for each language. There are languages which are very much vernacular languages, like Tamil or Gujerati, that are spoken within the family; there are languages much more general, like English or French, that are spoken above all in work situations, and there is one language, Creole, that is used, in different degrees, in all situations.

The figures decrease from left to right for Creole and Bhojpuri, and increase for French and English, thus revealing a quite characteristic distribution of functions. Creole, which was not then the national language is by far the most widespread, while English, the official language, is hardly a vernacular language at all and is not the most general. So we have degrees in the extent to which languages are vernacular languages or

TABLE 5.1. *What language do you speak?*

	To your mother	To old people	To friends	To civil servants	To your boss
Creole	74.5%	81.5%	91.7%	45.5%	33.1%
French	17.8%	18.5%	28.7%	61.2%	59.2%
English	3.8%	3.2%	10%	21.7%	24.2%
Bhojpuri	30.6%	28.7%	21%	3.2%	3.2%
Hindi	5.1%	6.4%	7.6%	1.3%	1.9%
Hindustani	4.5%	4.5%	3.8%	0%	0%
Chinese	6.4%	3.2%	2.5%	0%	0.6%
Urdu	2.6%	1.9%	2.6%	0.6%	0%
Tamil	1.3%	0%	0%	0%	0%
Gujerati	0.6%	0%	0%	0%	0%

lingua francas, and this can be quantified. Overall, it is possible to measure the extent to which a language is a lingua franca by calculating the relation between the total number of speakers of a language and the number of those who have it as a mother tongue. It is also of course possible to measure the extent to which a language is a vernacular: if a hundred people speak a language and it is the mother tongue of fifteen of them, we can say that this language is a lingua franca for 85% of them and a vernacular language for 15%.

But we can also wonder about the reasons for this distribution. The language spoken to old people is perhaps the only language they know or the only one the speaker has in common with them, or is perhaps a language denoting respect; the language spoken to one's mother is obviously the mother tongue; the language spoken to officials would normally be the official language or a lingua franca (but this is not completely the case in Mauritius; French is the former dominant language, dethroned by English from 1810 onwards when the British took possession of the island). And it can reasonably be supposed that the language spoken with friends is the one 'chosen' most frequently, and that this choice is the one which best reveals linguistic attitudes, in that although one does not choose one's mother tongue nor the dominant language, one can choose a language for conviviality (in Illich's sense of the term).

Finally, we can wonder about the truth of the replies. After all, an enquiry by questionnaire does not deliver the 'truth' about linguistic practices but rather what people imagine their practices to be. They may be deceived, and they may also lie, because they believe, for example, that one language has more prestige than another. A 'lie', therefore, is as informative as the 'truth', and the question 'why do people choose to speak one language rather than another?' is as interesting as 'why do people pretend to speak one language rather than another?'

Language and Belonging

To speak a language or a language form, to prefer the use of one form rather than another or to pretend to use one form rather than another, is always something more than simply using an instrument of communication.

Speaking a language always indicates something besides what I am in the process of saying in the language. When, in the situation in question, I have a choice between several languages, my choice will be noticed at the same time as my message. We can say that the form I adopt *denotes* what

I say, the message, and from another point of view, it *connotes*. Connotes what? It is precisely here that the analysis of language attitudes has much to teach us about societies. When civil servants in an African country formerly colonized by France speak French to each other, although they have the same mother tongue, they connote a desire to conform to a Western model, they encode their difference from the people, the fact that they have studied, that they have university degrees, and so on. If, in the same group, a speaker with the same background as the others expresses himself in his mother tongue, he connotes a rejection, both of the colonial language, and of belonging to it. For the conviviality or the sign of belonging which are linked to vernacular languages or language forms can be necessary or contingent. They are necessary when the vernacular form is the only one known to the speaker. In this case his usage certainly indicates his belonging to a group, but this sign is not one that has been chosen. They are contingent when the speaker possesses other forms or other languages. In this case the use of a vernacular form is a clear sign while in the first case it is only a pointer.

This problem of vernacular and general forms leads us to the problem of strategies of communication, of the conscious choices made by speakers and the meaning of these choices. One of the oldest examples in French history is without doubt that of the Strasbourg Oaths. On 14 February 842, two grandsons of Charlemagne, Louis the German and Charles the Bald met in Strasbourg. The previous year they had defeated their brother, Lothair, at Fontanet and decided to swear an alliance. The scene was recorded by the historian Nithardus: Louis swore the oath in the Romance language, Charles in German, that is, each in the language of the other, and then their soldiers swore the oath in turn, and the traditional analysis of the scene would have it that the two brothers used the language that was not their own in order to be understood by the soldiers of the other side, who thus served as witnesses. This is, for example, F Brunot's view in his *Histoire de la langue française*.[9]

R. Balibar, in her *L'Institution du Français*, has recently proposed a very different approach to the event. If the two brothers each swore the oath in the language of the other, it was, she thinks, not in order to be understood by their troops but to acknowledge the existence of a national and territorial entity defined by language:

Each heir abandoned his claims to their father's kingdom in the language bequeathed to the other. The king of eastern France recognized the linguistic

    [9] Ferdinand Brunot, *Histoire de la langue française* (Paris, 1905), i. 142.

frontier between himself and western France, on condition that this was recipro-cated. He recognized the French nationality of those peoples with the Romance language, while the king of western France recognized that the Teutonic nation-ality was defined outside his territory and was the future home of the Germans.[10]

It is clearly impossible to recover what might have taken place inside the heads of the two brothers, and R. Balibar's analysis of the oaths is only a hypothesis. But it does provide us with an interesting notion, the idea of a definition of sovereignty by language. Charles the Bald's troops took the oath in Romance and this language unified them in the same way that German unified Louis's troops, and the two chiefs, swearing the oath in a language which was not their own, encoded the difference, the division of territory. It was the first time that a linguistic argument has been invoked to define the state. We can see that this operation functioned in two complementary directions. It marked out a frontier between German and French (or rather between German and Romance), in short, it separated; and it brought together under a linguistic banner, in short, it unified. These terms, separation and unification, give a good definition of the finality of territorial wars, and also of the relationship between vernacular languages and lingua francas.

Signs of belonging, whether they are contingent or necessary, always come down to a kind of division. This is the case with a monolingual speaker whose phonology or syntax betrays his or her social or geographic origin, as with Eliza Doolittle in *Pygmalion*: tell me how you speak and I will tell you who you are. The sign can then be used for purposes of discrimination, of dominance or of condemnation, as in the Dominici affair or in the 'shibboleth' test to which I referred in Chapter 2. But in this case it is adopted by the 'other', who uses the evidence of the vernacu-lar form as an excuse, first, to classify and, secondly, to draw conclusions from this classification. It was different when Louis and Charles shared out Charlemagne's empire 'linguistically' by using the vernacular form of the other, since they both acted voluntarily through the choice of a language. At bottom the exact content of the oath did not make much difference; what mattered here, was the language in which the oath was sworn. And when a militant supporter of independence in Guadeloupe refuses, before a court judging his case in French, to speak anything but Creole, we have the same kind of practice, a free affirmation of belonging, that is, of difference.

For a long time clothes were the most accurate of social clues. But the

---

[10] Renée Balibar, *L'Institution du français* (Paris, 1985), 45.

cap or blue collar of the working man, the leather oversleeves, the costume of the employee, the top-hat of the capitalist today belong to folklore. Everyone, in Europe, dresses in much the same way; clothing is no longer a sign of belonging to this or that social class. On the other hand a speaker is placed by the linguistic forms he or she uses. We recognize those who are like us from the fact that they speak like us, and we reject those whose vernacular language is very different from our own. Social mobility depends on linguistic adaptation, on submission to a model, to the model of power. Just like an Englishman who cannot aspirate his H's, a Frenchman whose provincial accent is too strong cannot make his way in 'the world'. In order to secure the possibility of social advancement, both will then apply themselves to losing their accent, to conforming to a central norm that is supposed to be common to all, although it is only the group form of power. It is perhaps by these small denials and abjurations that major renunciations begin.

The vernacular form indicates, voluntarily (and sometimes aggressively, in the case of militant supporters of minority languages, for example) or involuntarily, a sense of belonging. It is, accordingly, a sign or indication of a social or geographical location. Each time there is a conflict between these locations, language plays a role and can even itself become the issue. This tension between the vernacular form and the general form can lead to the progressive disappearance of one or the other, when belonging to a sub-group appears less important than belonging to the larger group. The general form, considered as the neutral unmarked form, becomes the point towards which the different vernacular forms tend to converge.

6

The Family as Battlefield

In some cultures, including French culture, married couples are tradition-ally where power with regard to family names is exercised. If a Marie Dupont marries a Jean Dubois she becomes Marie Dubois, while also changing title, from Miss to Mrs. This was long considered to be normal and it took feminist campaigns to do away with the difference between Mrs and Miss in the USA (to be replaced by the neutral Ms), while in France we have seen Marie Dupont marry Jean Dubois and become either Marie Dupont-Dubois or Mme Marie Dupont. But it remains difficult for a Marie Dupont, who has written a book under her married name, and so has become known under the name of Dubois, to return to her maiden name after a divorce, for example. Although the operation is obviously legal, it is socially awkward, so ingrained are the conventionalities. Clearly married couples are where power with regard to family names is exercised, the power of the husband over the wife.

But this is not properly speaking the theme of this chapter. If the family unit is where names are transmitted to the children, it is also where language is transmitted, when the couple is monolingual, or where lan-guages are, when the parents do not have the same mother tongue. So we can wonder whether linguistic conflict first occurs in mixed or bilingual couples: might language wars involve the family unit?

The Case of Senegal

During the academic year 1963–4, the Centre de Linguistique Appliquée de Dakar (CLAD) launched a major enquiry in Senegal's primary schools with the aim of finding out what languages were spoken by the children when they began their schooling. Questions were asked about the ethnic groups of father and mother, the language spoken in the home and the other languages spoken by the child. The results were no surprise to those who knew the situation in Senegal. Wolof stood out easily as the majority language (96.62% of the children spoke it).

On the other hand, close examination of the detail of the enquiry established some surprising results concerning the process by which children acquired a first language in the family. Consider, for example, Table 6.1.

It can be seen from this that although two-thirds of children speaking Wolof as a first language came from parents speaking Wolof, it was different for a significant percentage of homes. Some, 7% of the overall population, learnt the language (Wolof) from their mothers, others (5.59%) from their fathers, and finally 11.82% spoke a language (Wolof again) in the home, which was the first language of neither the mother nor the father. This situation, which might seem paradoxical to a Western mind, was in fact corroborated by other results from other regions of the country. So, in Ziguinchor in the Casamance, a town in the extreme south of the country, far from Wolof's centre of expansion, where Wolof is much in the minority, a town which has a highly multilingual situation, the results shown in Table 6.2 were obtained.

That is, Wolof was spoken as a first language more by children whose parents did not speak it as a first language (14.58%) than by children where both mother and father spoke it as a first language (8.83%). CLAD's researchers concluded: 'It is not, therefore, the family that has

TABLE 6.1. *Conurbation of Dakar: Wolof the first language spoken in the home*

	Wolof father and mother	Wolof mother	Wolof father	Non-Wolof father and mother
72.23% of pupils, of whom have	47.82%	7%	5.59%	11.82%

TABLE 6.2. *Town of Ziguinchor: Wolof the first language spoken in the home*

	Wolof father and mother	Wolof mother	Wolof father	Non-Wolof father and mother
33.93% of pupils, of whom have	8.83%	4.50%	6.02%	14.58%

most influence on pupils, but the *milieu*. We are faced with a case of social assimilation'.[1]

The matter remained paradoxical, however, for even if these children said that they also knew the language or languages of their parents, their 'mother tongue' was a language which their parents spoke, of course, but which was not their own. This phenomenon, involving 15% of the population in the example above, is far from negligible.

I afterwards attempted, through research carried out in a number of African countries with my students, to try to understand this phenomenon of the transmission of mother tongues, in order to see if Senegal's case was an isolated one or was to be found elsewhere.

Mother Tongue or Father Tongue?

In an enquiry by questionnaire carried out at Bamako (Mali) in April 1984, the replies to a question concerning respondents' mother tongues produced the data presented in Tables 6.3–6.6.

It can be seen in Table 6.3 that, out of twenty people born to couples with different languages, nine first learnt the father's language, six the mother's, and five another language. But these figures can only be fully understood in the context of the language in question. It can be seen that whether it is the father's language, the mother's, or another, it is Bambara which largely dominates as 'mother tongue'; and this tendency was confirmed by those people whose parents spoke the same language.

Table 6.4 shows that out of fifty people born of couples linguistically homogeneous, seven did not speak the parents' language as first language. But it presents us with other important facts.

TABLE 6.3. *Parents with different languages: What is the subject's mother tongue?*

Language	Bambara	Songhai	Wolof	Dogon	Malinke	Fulani	TOTAL
Father's	6	1		1		1	9
Mother's	4		1		1		6
Other	4					1	5
TOTAL	14	1	1	1	1	2	20

[1] Maurice Calvet and François Wioland, 'L'Expansion du wolof au Sénégal', *Bulletin de l'IFAN*, no. 3–4 (1967), 617.

TABLE 6.4. *Parents with the same language: What is the subject's mother tongue?*

	Parent's language	Another language	They speak other African languages	which include Bambara
Bambara	12	—	2	—
Fulani	10	—	10	10
Khassonke	1	1	2	2
Bobo	1	1	2	2
Senoufo	—	2	2	2
Dogon	1	1	2	—
Nonanke	1	—	1	1
Bozo	—	1	1	1
Sarakole	2	—	2	2
Jula	—	1	1	—
Songhai	13	—	13	13
Mossi	1	—	1	1
Malinke	1	—	1	1
TOTAL	43	7	40	35

Note: The left-hand column shows the parents' language.

First, in the case of languages with a wide regional (Fulani, Songhai) or national (Bambara) spread, respondents kept the language of their parents as their first language, while half of the respondents whose parents' language was a minority language have acquired another 'mother' tongue. On the other hand, all respondents born into non-Bambara families (38) were multilingual and the great majority of them (35 out of 38) spoke Bambara, the three exceptions being two Dogons, originally from an isolated plateau where the second language was usually Fulani, and a man from the Ivory Coast born of Jula parents. In other words, the dominant language appears as a practically obligatory second language, while the majority (ten out of twelve) of those who speak it as their first language did not feel the need to learn any other African language.

I obtained similar results in the course of an enquiry carried out at Niamey (Niger) in November and December 1983 (see Table 6.5).

Here it can be seen that it is the minority languages which, in otherwise limited cases, are disappearing as mother tongues in favour of the majority languages, Zarma and Hausa. The dominance of these two languages is confirmed when the parents have different languages (see Table 6.6).

TABLE 6.5. *Parents with the same language: What is the subject's mother tongue?*

	The parents'	Another
Zarma	28	—
Hausa	31	—
Fulani	4	2 (Zarma)
Songhai	7	—
Tamachek	—	1 (Hausa)
Gourmantche	1	—
Kotocoli	3	—
Wobe	1	—

TABLE 6.6. *Parents with the same language: What is the subject's mother tongue?*

	The father's	The mother's	Another	Both
Zarma	7	6	2	2
Hausa	12	6	2	—
Fulani	—	2	—	—
Tchad Arabic	—	—	1	—
Kanuri	—	1	—	—
Kotocoli	—	1	—	—

Here again it can be seen that a child's first language may be its father's (19), its mother's (16), both (2), or another language (5), but this other language is in fact most often one of the country's two dominant languages.

In other words, there is a close relationship between the family and society, and in mixed couples the 'mother' tongue, which can also be the 'father' tongue, is most often the language that is dominant outside the household: Wolof in Senegal, Bambara in Mali, Zarma or Hausa in Niger. In the next two chapters we shall examine more closely the status of these dominant languages. For the moment, we shall note this result of our researches: language conflict occurs in multilingual families (a result which will surprise no one) and that they record and reflect the language conflicts of the society around them.

From Mother Tongue to National Language

There are, then, no 'mother' tongues, only 'first' tongues. Nevertheless, the great majority of European cultures use the same image to describe this first language: *langue maternelle* in French, *lengua materna* in Spanish, *idioma materno* in Italian, *Muttersprache* in German, etc., a misuse of language in that it assumes the mother's language is the one which the child will necessarily inherit. This idea of inheritance, of descent is even clearer in Russian: роднйязлк 'mother tongue' refers simultaneously to the idea of 'birth' (родйт, to bring into the world), of 'parents' (роич), and of 'source' (роднйк). And there are many metaphors, in particular in African languages, which describe this first language in terms of milk, the breast, of suckling, etc. On the other hand, in some languages we find the idea that this first language is linked to the earth. This is for example the case with Chinese where the expression *pen guo yu yen*, ¥» Œ»y¤¥mother tongue' means, taking it word by word, 'language of root nation'.

The *Dictionnaire Robert* gives a good summary of this confusion which, as emphasized below, applies to different languages but can be found within one language, in this case French.

Current dictionaries define 'mother tongue' as 'the language of the country of one's birth'. This definition does not cover the majority of cases. For a French person born in Japan, brought up in an environment where French is spoken, the mother tongue is without doubt French. Inversely, a French person whose parents are of foreign origin and now speak only French, might very well consider his or her mother tongue to be a language he does not know, the one spoken by his distant ancestors, if, emotionally, he does not consider himself to be French. The mother tongue can therefore be sometimes the mother's language, sometimes the mother–country's.[2]

But this desire for clarification collapses into a total confusion of points of view. On the one hand the mother tongue is considered to be the language of the family, or even of the ancestors, endowing this metaphor with the classic connotations found in phrases like 'the maternal breast', 'maternal love', 'the maternal instinct', etc., while, on the other hand it is considered to be the language of the territory, the country, the 'father-land'. In one case the line passes through the mother, but in the other, it passes through the father. For the root '*pater*' (father) is to be found in the French '*patrie*' (as also in the Italian and Spanish '*patria*') which means etymologically the 'country of the father', just as in German there is

[2] *Dictionnaire Robert*, iv. 314.

'*vaterland*' and in English 'fatherland' (even though English also uses 'motherland', and in Chinese for example the idea of 'fatherland' is linked neither to the father nor the mother but to the ancestors: *zu guo*, fl" Œ, 'land of the elders').

According to this general view, it seems that the parents take separate roles in what they hand down, the father passing on the land (which here is the land he defends with his weapons rather than the land he cultivates) and the mother passing on the language. What is most striking in this division of responsibilities is that it ignores multilingualism. Between the family unit and the national entity there is something like a continuum for which the main evidence is the language (from the mother) and the land (from the father). In this way fatherland and language are the authority for a mythical unity which represents the group as a microcosm of the whole, and the family as a microcosm of the nation, since the mother tongue and the country's language are but one. The world, which as we have seen, can be defined primarily by its multilingualism, is imagined as a juxtaposition of monolingual units which are produced principally by the language bequeathed by the mother to her children and the land bequeathed by the father. There is an imperceptible progression from the idea of mother tongue to national language.

The Family Versus Society

The examples we have examined, those of Senegal, Mali, and Niger, have shown us, however, that the reality is very different. Nor was there any need to go so far afield. In the town of Gaillon which we discussed in Chapter 3, research into the children of migrants in a primary school produced almost the same results. Out of 41 children interviewed, 27 spoke the language of their parents (Arabic, Portuguese, or Spanish) and French, while the others had French as their first language.[3] In other words, the family unit once again reflects the linguistic conflicts around it. For a child born of Moroccan parents in France, as for a child born of Chinese parents in the USA or of Indian parents in Great Britain, the language of the host country is the language of integration, for bettering oneself, and at the same time the language of conformity to a dominant model outside the family, the language of social prestige. This tension between belonging (being like others) and difference (remaining faithful

---

[3] L.-J. Calvet, 'Le Plurilinguisme à l'école primaire, note sur une enquête à Gaillon (Eure)', *Migrants formation*, no. 63 (1985), 17–21.

to one's origins) can develop into an acceptance of the duality, with the child becoming bilingual, or towards denial, when the child's first language will not be his parents' language. In the case of people from North Africa, the research at Gaillon revealed that the mother frequently did not speak French. Consequently, a child that does not know (or no longer knows) his or her mother tongue (in the strict sense of the word) necessarily finds itself at the centre of a language conflict within the family.

But matters are not always so clear-cut nor so simple. During the research at Gaillon, over and above the filling out of questionnaires, we decided to interview the pupils of the school systematically and so one day I had before me a young boy, whom we shall call Mohammed, whose parents were Moroccan. Mohammed explained to me that he did not speak Arabic, that he was born in France, had never been to Morocco, and that the language was too difficult for him. Then, speaking of one thing and another, we came round to the subject of his mother who, he said, never left the house.

'Not even to go shopping?'

'No', replied Mohammed proudly, 'I do the shopping.'

'Does your mother give you a list of what to buy?'

'No, my mother can't write. She tells me what to buy, that's all.'

I was suddenly suspicious.

'Does your mother speak French?'

'No, she doesn't understand a word.'

'Then in what language do you speak to her?'

'Well, in Arabic', he replied, as if it were obvious.

Why had this 10-year-old child felt the need, both in filling out the questionnaire and in responding to my oral questions, to claim that he did not know Arabic? Here the conflict between French, the prestige language, the language of school and especially of normality, of belonging, and Arabic, the language of difference, was not resolved by its real disappearance, but by an alleged disappearance. In pretending not to speak Arabic, Mohammed asserted that he was the same as other people; he made a symbolic sacrifice of his vernacular language in order to belong to the language that would make him a Frenchman and no longer the son of a Moroccan. Not to speak Arabic was to be assimilated.

It is of course very different for adults. I visited Mohammed's family, who had re-created their council flat as a Moroccan interior with rugs, low furniture, verses of the Koran on the walls, and so on. His mother, dressed in traditional style, remained in the kitchen, preparing dishes that the elder daughter brought to us. The father attempted to speak French and

Mohammed seemed troubled by his strong accent and his mistakes. He did not understand that the Arabized French of his father was as much a sign of belonging as his own French that had no trace of North Africa. 'Sometimes migrants reject French in order to preserve the identity of their origins; others retain a marked accent, as a sign of "distinction" in Bourdieu's sense', writes C. de Heredia,[4] and this behaviour in the end complements that of children rejecting their parents' language.

Whether it is a matter of highly multilingual situations and the mixed couples that these situations bring about, or of migrant couples, linguistically homogeneous but surrounded by a prestige language, the family appears as the site of a language conflict that echoes the conflicts of society. We have known for a long time that a language changes through the influence of children whose phonology, for example, often different to that of their grandparents, gives an idea of what the language will be like in twenty or thirty years' time. The children of these children will certainly not speak like their great-grandparents. It is the same with the relations between languages. When a vernacular language belonging to a small minority is still spoken daily in the family, there is every chance that it will retain this function for a long time (as is, for example, the case with Berber in North Africa or with Corsican in France). But when the children object to speaking a language, gradually forget it or pretend to have forgotten it because they are ashamed of it, its future is much less assured. Young Senegalese, born of Fulani parents, who have acquired Wolof as a first language and speak Fulani only with their grandparents will speak Wolof to their children.

I wrote in the introduction that the history of languages constitutes the linguistic aspect of the history of societies. It can be seen here that the language history of the family is the product of social history. A child who rejects the Arabic of his immigrant parents is the product of surrounding racism, of an ideological devaluing of his language; he brings the language war to an end by abandoning the field. Of course, this is an individual solution which can lead to a language disappearing by degrees. Later we shall see in what conditions a language can disappear collectively.

[4] C. de Heredia, 'Les Parlers français des migrants', in APREF, *J'cause français, non?* (Paris, 1983), 115–16.

7
Markets and Languages

Multilingualism is, as we have seen, the language situation most frequently found in the world, and it naturally poses problems of communication. Every day, everywhere, hundreds of thousands of people meet, and need to communicate but do not have the same language. Now trade is the social activity that encounters this problem the most often: how to buy from and sell to people with a different language? In fact, every time that a person needs to communicate, he or she finds the means. Maurice Delafosse describes, for example, the way in which exchanges were managed in West Africa during the Middle Ages:

The traders unpacked their goods (salt, copper rings, blue pearls). Each placed the goods that belonged to him in small separate bundles on the ground, then all withdrew out of the sight of the indigenous peoples. These now approached and placed a specific quantity of gold powder beside each pile of merchandise before withdrawing. The merchants returned, each taking what he found beside his pile of goods, and then went away again, leaving the goods behind on the ground, beating a drum to announce their departure and the conclusion of the trading. It seems that these mute transactions were carried out very regularly, and without either party afraid of being cheated by the other.[1]

This purchasing of gold by the Arabs was carried on, then, without any linguistic exchange, but this does not mean that there was no communication. In the scene described above, an economist would notice that the 'trading' took place without money, that general equivalent to goods which Marx described (we should not be misled by the fact that gold was one of the items being exchanged: gold here was merchandise and not money). A semiologist would stress that although there was no language, there was clearly a sending of messages (my heap of merchandise = your heap of gold, I beat a drum to show that the trading is over). This mute bartering was characterized, then, by two absences: of language and of money, but also by the fact that, despite these absences, exchange and communication took place. When confronted by linguistic obstacles to

---

[1] Maurice Delafosse, *Haut-Sénégal Niger* (Paris, 1912), ii. 47.

communication, man has always attempted to get round them in his social practice. In the field, *in vivo*, there is the emergence of pidgins, of lingua francas (see Chapter 8), while some have sought the solution in the calm of their studies, *in vitro*, through artificial languages, like Esperanto, or through planning (see the whole of the third part of this book). It is this *in vivo* dealing with multilingualism that I should like to describe here, by beginning with a distinctive setting, that is, multilingual markets.

By the number of languages they sometimes bring together, and by the communication they necessitate (praise of one's goods, calling to the client, asking the price, discussing the price, etc.) markets are in fact very revealing of the social practice of dealing with multilingualism. We can see lingua francas become established, languages which sometimes are only used in markets and which sometimes gain ground elsewhere with functions other than the commercial one. For languages which establish themselves in this setting and this function can become, in society as a whole, the lingua francas of tomorrow.

The Markets of Canton (China)

In the town of Canton, in the south of the People's Republic of China at least two languages coexist. On the one hand, there is Cantonese, a local language spoken throughout the province of Kuang-tung as well as in Hong Kong, and on the other, Putonghua, the 'common language' (which is very close to what is called, in the West, 'Mandarin'), taught in school, broadcast on radio and television, first language in the North but here the second language, to which should be added other Chinese languages (Wu, Hakka, etc.) as well as some 'minority' languages. Between September and November 1985 I carried out a research project with my students from the Institute of Foreign Languages[2] on two markets in the town: the food market of Qing Ping Lu, situated beside the Pearl River, opposite Shamien Island, and the clothing market of Gao Di Jié, in the centre of the town, close to the major shopping area of Beijing Lu.

Before turning to strictly linguistic communication, it is interesting to describe what I observed in a small part of the market of Qing Ping Lu where porcelain and bonzai trees were sold, the only place where foreigners sometimes came to buy. The sellers spoke no Western language. Their competence went generally no further than the 'hello' which they used to

---

[2] Six student researchers took part in this research: Lin Yi, Zeng Ying, Zi Du, Shao Yang, Shi Wang Li, and Zhang Xin Mu.

accost prospective foreign clients and, more rarely, 'how do you do?' If the tourist appeared interested in a piece, the merchant would take out of his pocket a piece of stiff cardboard on which he had written in regular rows the numbers from 1 to 100, usually the first 50 on one side and the second 50 on the other. He would point to a number corresponding to the price in yuans he wanted, and the buyer would in his turn point to the price he wished to pay. In this way the index recovered its etymological function, 'that which indicates' and the negotiation continued through a succession of deictic actions. This very simple practice calls for some comment.

First of all, it is interesting to note that, for these traders, all foreigners speak English. They do not think about what language to use for accosting them (which would be the case for example in the souks of Marrakesh in Morocco, where the sellers have a good eye for 'placing' their clients), 'hello' is more than enough. So across the world there are places of business where the trader knows several languages and can address the client in his language or in an international one (English, French, as is the case in Egypt or Morocco, for example), places where the language inherited from colonialism is spoken to the tourist (this is the case most frequently in Africa), places where the client is expected to speak the trader's language (which is the case in the majority of European countries) and places, like Canton, where an *ad hoc* system of communication has been invented.

Secondly, the piece of cardboard described above is perfectly appropriate as a social response to the need for communication. The only necessary content of communication here is the price and the bargaining, and the code is sufficient for both, with sign language making up for the declarations that are usual when bargaining.

Lastly, the system perfected by the traders of Qing Ping Lu give us some lines of thought on the birth of codes as a response to communication needs. Pidgins, for example, have the same type of origin, that is, they answer the same kind of need, but they do this through language, while the system of Qing Ping Lu works through diagram and gesture. Of course, the communication is here very limited (statement of price, bargaining), but it is precisely this that makes the example interesting. The simple code corresponds to communication that is limited to a simple content; it is when the content becomes more complex that the form of the code becomes more complicated. From this point of view, there are certainly differences of degree between the pieces of cardboard of Qing Ping Lu and pidgins, but not a difference in kind.

To turn now to the languages used in business communication: the

TABLE 7.1. *Qing Ping Lu: Observation of 283 encounters*

Language used	
Cantonese	249
Putonghua	14
Cantonese/Putonghua	10
Hakka	2
Hunan	2
Sichuan	2
Gestures	2
Writing	2

TABLE 7.2. *Gao Di Jié: Observation of 132 encounters*

Language used	
Putonghua	86
Cantonese	38
Cantonese/Putonghua	4
Chacho	2
Tian su	2
Hu nai	2
Shantong	2

interactions observed by my students were noted down on special forms,[3] and the data is summed up in Tables 7.1 and 7.2.

It can be seen that Cantonese is THE language of communication in the market of Qing Ping Lu (249 interactions out of 283) and that the national language, Putonghua, is very much in the minority, but that this is reversed at Gao Di Jié: 88% of interactions in Cantonese in the first case, 65% in Putonghua in the second. This distribution of languages is good evidence

---

[3] The observation form used was set out like this:

Place: Date:
Product:

SEX	AGE	TYPE	THEME	LANGUAGE
M–M	30–40	S–B	Accosting	Cantonese

This would mean that a male seller about the age of 30 had accosted a buyer of about 40 in Cantonese.

for the functions they fulfil. As the language of the family, of the street, of conviviality, Cantonese clearly fulfils a vernacular function to which Putonghua cannot aspire, being the official language learnt in school, the language of administration, of the media, etc. As such, Cantonese is therefore quite naturally the language of the food market. On the other hand, Gao Di Jié is a market which draws many buyers from the north of the country. Canton is considered to be a fashionable town (the nearness of Hong Kong encourages this view) and people come to buy clothes whole-sale which will then be resold in Shanghai or Peking. So, many of the commercial exchanges take place between sellers from the south, who speak Cantonese, and buyers from the North, who speak Putonghua. Where clients do not speak Cantonese, the traders use Putonghua, the official language, whose lingua franca function is therefore obvious.

These few figures, taken from a larger research project, provide us, then, with a certain amount of information:

- They illustrate Canton's multilingualism, which is shown above all by the bilingualism of Cantonese and Putonghua.
- They illustrate the different status of each language, Cantonese being more of a vernacular language and Putonghua more of a lingua franca.
- They illustrate a power relationship since, where a choice has to be made between the two principal competing languages, it is Putonghua that is chosen. But, for the moment, we do not know if it is being adopted as lingua franca because it is the client's language or because it is the official language. In other words, does the seller submit to the customer being always right or to Northern centralism? What is certain is that Cantonese merchants are bilingual and that buyers from the North are monolingual, and this is already the beginning of a reply to the question.
- Lastly, there is the role of the market as a yardstick, which enables us to perceive major changes of language moving through society. But this last point is not specific to Canton's markets, and we shall see below that it is the same with all multilingual markets.

The Markets of Brazzaville (Congo)[4]

The language situation in the capital of the Congo is largely determined by the major trend of migration from the countryside to the town. The

[4] I here use data already published in more detail, in particular in L.-J. Calvet, *Les Langues de marché*. (Paris: Université René Descartes, 1985).

Congo is a country where the population is extremely urbanized, with 34% of its inhabitants found in two principal towns, Brazzaville and Pointe-Noire.

As far as Brazzaville is concerned, in 1917 its population was 10% of the total population of the country, with 10,000 inhabitants; in 1981 it was 25%, with more than 300,000 inhabitants, a steady rise which appears clearly in the following figures:

1917:	10,000 inhabitants
1955:	92,520 inhabitants
1961:	127,964 inhabitants
1974:	298,967 inhabitants[5]

and this has resulted in the linguistic intermingling that characterizes the town today.

Situated on the right bank of the River Congo, Brazzaville has therefore been for a long time the meeting point of migrations which began by following the route of the river. The first migrations came from the region of Stanley Pool. According to P. Duboz, 60% of the people who came to the capital over twenty years ago originated from Pool, that is, the region around Brazzaville, while only 21% of those arriving in the last five years (1975–9) come from Pool. This 'local' migration came in two major waves. One came from the North and brought with it the lingua franca of the North, Lingala; the other came from the South with Monokutuba as lingua franca, neither of these two languages being the first language of the speakers in question. These migrants established themselves in parts of the town according to their region of origin: the north of the town (the Poto-Poto and Mougali areas) for speakers of Lingala, the south (the area of Bakongo) for speakers of Monokutuba. So Brazzaville functions rather as a microcosm of the country, the two major universal languages being represented there, as well as another language, Lari, whose status is more difficult to grasp.

Lari is an urban dialect in the Kango group, an important variety, a language of the town, of the capital. People originating from the Pool region very often say, when someone asks them their mother tongue, that they 'are Lari'. This response is most frequent among people who have not been living long in Brazzaville.[6]

---

[5] P. Duboz, *Étude démographique de la ville de Brazzaville, 1974–1977* (Bangui: ORSTOM, 1979).

[6] A. Le Palec, 'Brazzaville, note sur la situation linguistique de deux quartiers', communication to the fifth Conference of AUPELF, Yauondé, 1981.

In other respects, all the ethnic groups of the country are represented in the capital, which of course reinforces its role as a 'microcosm':

Kongo group   65.5% of inhabitants
Teke group   17%
Mbosi group   11.3%
other groups   2.6%
non-Congolese   3.6%.[7]

The situation presents a sociolinguist with a question of obvious interest: what will emerge from this linguistic confrontation? Which languages are asserting themselves in social communication, and which remain confined to family use, to vernacular use? In December 1980 I carried out some research into these questions with the help of students who were taking my courses at the Marien Ngouabi University of Brazzaville and with the help of Annie le Palec, then working at the same university and preparing a thesis on the city's sociolinguistic situation. In their neighbourhoods the students handed out a questionnaire in which the central questions were: Where do you go shopping? and, In which languages? The criteria used to establish their sample were very simple: similar numbers of women and men, similar numbers of under- and over-thirties. This survey enabled us to identify an important development: three lingua francas were clearly emerging and establishing themselves, but the statistical presence of these languages varied considerably according to area. Lingala, the lingua franca of the north, was spoken in the markets in the north of the city, Lari and Monokutuba in the markets in the south. As for French, it was most used on Fifteen Years Plateau, so-called because Africans enrolled in the colonial army retired there after fifteen years of service, their income having allowed them to build houses of a higher quality than the norm. These retired soldiers were not necessarily originally from the Congo, and so did not always speak these languages and more readily used French as their lingua franca.

Here then are the percentages for the replies to the question, In which languages do you do your shopping? for four markets in the town.

POTO POTO MARKET

Lingala   65.56%
Lingala and Monokutuba   17.24%
French   10%

---

[7] Duboz, *Étude démographique.*

Lingala, French, and Monokutuba	3.5%
Lari	3.5%

MOUNGALI MARKET

Lingala	30.36%
Monokutuba	25%
Lingala and Monokutuba	16%
Lingala, French and Monokutuba	8.9%
Lingala and French	5.3%
Lingala and Lari	5.3%
Lari	3.5%
Lari, Lingala, and Monokutuba	1.7%
Lari and Monokutuba	1.7%
French	1.7%

MARKET ON FIFTEEN YEARS PLATEAU

Monokutuba and French	26.3%
French	15.7%
Lingala	15.7%
Monokutuba	15.7%
Lari and Monokutuba	10.5%
Lari	10.5%
Lingala, French and Monokutuba	5.5%

BAKONGO MARKET

Lari	57.8%
Monokutuba	20.3%
Lari and Monokutuba	12.5%
French	3.1%
French, Lari and Monokutuba	1.5%
Lari and French	1.5%
Lingala and Monokutuba	1.5%

These figures are based only on a preliminary enquiry of about 300 questionnaires, but they do show a number of clear tendencies.

First, the trade brought about by the constant migration to the city, combined with Congolese multilingualism, has posed a communication problem which has been solved by the emergence or confirmation of lingua francas. One of these, Lingala, is strongly implanted in the population that has come from the North; the other, Monokutuba, seems to be gaining ground among those who have come from the South as against the prestige language of the same group, Lari. In other words, the vernacular language has some influence in the choice of lingua franca; the 'second' language used is linked in some way to the region of origin.

Secondly, first languages are absent from the markets. No doubt, they are spoken in the home, in their vernacular function, but they are not used for trade.

Finally, it is the same with French, the official language, except for the market on Fifteen Years Plateau. But here social origin takes precedence over geographic origin and the speakers often do not have an African language in common. In this case French to an extent acts as a lingua franca, in the same way as Lingala or Monokutuba.

The Little Market of Niamey (Niger)

In November and December 1983, I was invited to teach at Niamey University and I carried out with my students research of the same kind as before. But in this case I brought together two kinds of approach. As in Canton, we observed the interactions in the market, and, as in Brazzaville, we used questionnaires.

Like Brazzaville and many other African cities, Niamey has grown rapidly in recent years, as can be seen from the figures in Table 7.3.

As far as its ethnic composition is concerned, the town has developed greatly since it was founded in the nineteenth century. If, as Sidikou writes, 'the present town grew out of five original districts based on ethnic group and clan, namely Maouri, Gandatié-Koiratégui, Gamkalle including Kalley-Zarma and Kalley-Peul (Foulankoira), Gaouey and Zongo',[8] these populations are today mixed together, and there is no longer any correspondence between district, ethnic group, and language (as the name Foulankoira might lead one to suppose: this district was originally Fulani and it is today inhabited by people from Zarma and Hausa ethnic groups). This is because immigration has had an important role in populating the town. Sidikou explains that 54.6% of people constituting his sample were not born in Niamey;[9] research by J. Yanco shows that 31% of Zarma speakers living in Niamey were born there, with 6% of Hausa speakers,[10] and 82.5% of the people in our own sample were born outside Niamey.

[8] A. Sidikou, (Niamey: Étude de géographie socio-urbaine', doctoral thesis, 2 vols. (Rouen, 1980), i. or ii. 233.
[9] Ibid. 361.
[10] J. Yanco, 'Niamey une communauté bilingue', not published, Niamey, 1983.

TABLE 7.3.

Year	Population	Source
1908	2,887	Sidikou[a]
1931	2,168	Bernus[b]
1941	4,895	Bernus
1950	12,000	Sidikou
1953	12,000	Bernus
1960	34,500	Bernus
1967	57,000	Sidikou
1975	195,874	Sidikou
1977	225,314	Census

[a] A. Sidikou, '*Niamey: Étude de géographie socio-urbaine*', doctoral thesis, 2 vols. (Rouen, 1980).
[b] S. Bernus, *Particularismes ethniques en milieu urbain: L'Exemple de Niamey* (Paris: Institute d'ethnologie, 1969).

TABLE 7.4. *Languages spoken in the markets: Replies to questionnaires*

Language	Little market	Wadata	Left bank	Yantala	New market	TOTAL	% (approx.)
Zarma	9	7	3	—	3	22	14.5
Hausa and Zarma	36	19	2	6	3	66	42.5
Hausa	11	9	—	—	1	21	14.5
French and Zarma	4	3	1	—	—	8	5.8
French	—	—	—	—	1	1	—
Zarma and Bambara	1	1	—	—	—	2	—
Songhai	6	3	2	—	1	12	8
Zarma, Hausa, and French	9	6	—	—	2	17	11.2
Zarma, Hausa, and Bambara	1	1	—	—	—	2	—

The town is a major ethnic and linguistic melting-pot (we found about fifteen different languages in our sample) and the aim of our research was to see what languages were used for communication in the markets. We therefore decided to carry out the research partly by questionnaire and partly by observation of a market in the town centre, the one known as the 'Little Market' (by contrast to the 'Big Market' which had burnt down some years before), and the two approaches gave the following results.

We can see that the majority of first languages (Fulani, Kanuri, Kotocoli, Wobe, Gourmantche) have disappeared, making way for two largely dominant languages, Hausa and Zarma (to which might be added Songhai, a dialect variety). The results of our observations in an individual market, the 'Little Market' are shown in Table 7.5.

Table 7.5 presents our observations as a whole. On the horizontal lines it shows the number of interactions in a given language, divided into three kinds (addressing the clients, business transaction, or non-business discussion) and into three types (between sellers: S–S; between seller and buyer: S–B; between buyers: B–B).

If we consider the results of these two approaches, we can see that Hausa and Zarma are clearly dominant as languages in the market, and that some first languages appear in a vernacular function between traders (Wolof) or between buyers (Gourmantche, Yoruba, Fang).

On the other hand, there is no exact correspondence between the results of these researches concerning the two principal languages (see Table 7.6).

These differences result, first, from the fact that the entry 'Hausa and

TABLE 7.5. *The Little Market: Observation of 213 encounters*

Language	Contact	Transaction	Discussion	TOTAL	%	S–S	S–B	B–B
Zarma	11	45	32	88	41.3	12	68	8
Hausa	16	31	16	63	29.5	11	47	5
French	6	12	5	23	10.7	—	22	1
Hausa/Zarma	2	12	8	22	10.3	3	16	3
French/Hausa	3	5	1	9	4.2	1	8	—
French/Zarma	—	1	—	1	0.4	—	1	—
Fulani	—	2	—	2	0.8	—	2	—
Ewe	—	1	—	1	—	—	1	—
Wolof	—	—	1	1	—	1	—	—
Gourmantche	—	—	1	1	—	—	—	1
Yoruba	—	—	1	1	—	—	—	1
Fang	—	—	1	1	—	—	—	1
Fulani/Hausa	—	1	—	—	—	—	1	—
TOTAL	38	109	66					

TABLE 7.6.

Language	Research by questionnaire		Research by observation
	Overall	Little market	(Little market)
Hausa	14.5%	14.2%	29.5%
Zarma	14.5%	11.6%	41.3%
Hausa and Zarma	42.5%	46.7%	10.3%

Zarma' did not have the same sense in the two investigations. In the replies to the questionnaire, those who said they spoke both languages in the market meant that they used one or other depending on the trader, while in the investigation by observation we were of course noting a bilingual interaction (for which the technical term is 'code-switching'). This is why the drop from 46.7% to 10.3% is logically compensated for by the rises in the two preceding columns.

But it remains the case that observing the interactions shows that Zarma has more importance than Hausa, while the research by questionnaire made the two languages equal. There is therefore a quite clear difference between what people say they do and what they really do. Everyone knows that research by questionnaire does not measure how people act but the image they have of their actions. When we can, as here, compare the two it is clear that we have the material for an interesting analysis of language attitudes.

Zarma is, at Niamey, a local language and therefore a vernacular language, which also acts as a linga franca, while Hausa is a language that has come from elsewhere, is widely spoken in Nigeria, and is expanding rapidly in Niger where it is spread by rich traders and enjoys a certain prestige. It is not surprising that some of those questioned sought to inflate their competence in this language and in their replies, to increase the number of occasions when they used it. When faced by this kind of questionnaire, there is no better way of boosting one's self-esteem than to claim to speak a language that is itself esteemed. This explanation introduces a psychological factor into the language struggle being played out in the market. On the one hand there is a dynamic of languages, for which the figures provide evidence, and on the other hand a relationship (emotional, psychological, etc.) between speakers and these languages, which can be observed in the differences between the figures from the two methods of research.

Markets and Multilingualism

We could multiply examples and describe other research, carried out at Bamako (Mali) or at Ziguinchor (Senegal),[11] but these would not provide us with new information. In Canton, Brazzaville, or in Niamey, beyond the differences, there are important points in common. First of all, there is multilingualism, which creates a problem of communication. Each time that two or more languages coexist in a community, the members of this community have to deal with the language difference in their relationships. Another point in common in our enquiries is that they looked at markets. In multilingual situations, commercial activity gives us a good picture of the solutions adopted in practice. In the face of linguistic obstacles to communication, markets show us how, despite everything, people communicate. But there remains another question: why do they use one language rather than another to deal with their multilingualism? For the division in Brazzaville into two 'linguistic zones', the absolute dominance of Bambara in Bamako, the bilingualism of Niamey and Canton are signs of power relations between human groups speaking different languages. In a market (as elsewhere in social life—markets have simply served as a convenient test) multilingualism has to be managed but this management is also evidence for a war of languages. If, for example, at the Poto Poto market in Brazzaville a seller of smoked fish was addressed in Lari, it would not be unusual for her to pretend not to understand or for her to demand an exorbitant price. This refusal to sell demonstrates a rejection of the other's language. And from this point of view the market functions as a developing agent, in the photographic sense of the term; it precipitates the power relations between language groups.

Travellers know that across the world some currencies are valued more than others. Businessmen often prefer to be paid in dollars, francs, or marks, rather than the local currency. It is the same with languages, and speakers prefer or reject this or that language, whether it is a vernacular language or a lingua franca, for reasons of prestige or hatred. There is something like a 'stock-market of languages'. But the multilingual market shows something else. In the African example which I described at the beginning of this chapter, we had trade without money and without

---

[11] See in particular *Les Langues de marché* already quoted (n. 4), also L.-J. Calvet, 'Mehrsprachige Märkte und Vehikularsprachen: Geld und Sprache', in *OBST*, no. 31 (Bremen, 1985), and L.-J. Calvet, 'Trade Function and Lingua Francas', *The Fergusonian Impact*, ii (Mouton, 1986).

language, and many historical examples demonstrate that barter is often a mute activity. Here is, for example, a description of barter in Peru, in the Andes, which is characteristic of the phenomenon.

A woman is seated in the marketplace before a pile of goods (fruit or something similar), another woman approaches her, crouches down and brings out some grains of maize, to make her own pile, thus indicating that she wants to exchange this small pile of maize with the first woman. This woman remains impassive, forcing the buyer to increase her pile of maize until she accepts its equivalence and shows her satisfaction by taking the maize. Not one word was said during the transaction.[12]

But the appearance of money calls for the use of language. People have to speak to ask the price and to discuss it; this is the basic system we saw in the market at Canton and is very limited in its possibilities of communication. This in no way implies that those involved in the barter did not speak, but simply that they did not need to speak to barter: in the market, money activated language. Where the market was multilingual, commercial activity was confronted by different group forms and the need for a lingua franca. This phenomenon, the need for a lingua franca. a common form of language, to which the next chapter will be devoted, is therefore a kind of response to the challenge of Babel. If markets do not produce, strictly speaking, common forms of language, we have seen that they are a catalyst for their emergence.

[12] E. Mayer quoted by Ibico Rojas, *Expansion del Quechua* (Lima, 1980), 65–6.

8

Lingua Francas

I have already referred to the widespread illusion that views the world as divided, in isomorphic fashion, into countries and languages, with linguistic frontiers corresponding to state and national frontiers. It is an illusion, for there is practically not one monolingual country and, conversely, languages are rarely confined to one country. We have seen (Chapter 3) that human beings were confronted by a multilingual world and the research into markets described in the preceding chapter has shown how people dealt with this multilingualism in their social practice. Through examples as different as Canton and Brazzaville, we found two general factors: the emergence of a lingua franca as a solution to the problems of communication; and, a fairly close parallel between markets and the wider sociological changes of society.

It is this emergence of a lingua franca and its relation to society that we shall now study, beginning with the example of a language whose history we shall attempt to establish, in order to bring out the factors that have influenced its growth.

The Example of Quechua

Quechua is a language spoken by a dozen million Indians in six countries of Latin America: widely in Peru, Bolivia, Ecuador, less so in Colombia, Chile, and Argentina. Its speakers are primarily spread along the Cordillera of the Andes, with some pockets in equatorial Amazonia, whose presence poses a historical problem.[1] This route, along which the language spread, coupled with its dominant position in the capital of the Incas, Cuzco, in the sixteenth century, when the Spanish arrived, has for a long time led people to believe that it originated in this region and that it spread from there to the rest of the Andes.

The Peruvian linguist Alfredo Torero has shown that this hypothesis is

---

[1] See Peter Muysken, *Pidginization in the Quechua of the Lowlands of Eastern Ecuador* (Instituto Inter-Andino de Desarollo, University of Amsterdam, 1975).

incorrect. Making simultaneous use of linguistics (the glottochronology established by Maurice Swadesh), history (the use of written archives), and archaeology (in particular, carbon dating) he has proposed a reconstruction of the language's history, according to which it originated on the coast, in the region of modern Lima, where, towards the end of the tenth century, it was confronted by Aru (a linguistic group including the present-day languages Aymara, Jaqaru, and Kawki) and by Puquina. Economic relations between the coast and the mountains were then the motive force for the spread of these languages towards the Andes, and the Inca empire, between the twelfth and sixteenth centuries, used Quechua as a language of general communication in the regions it controlled.[2] At all events, this was the situation that the first Spaniards found, and there is no shortage of written evidence for this period, which is where we shall begin our description of the spread of Quechua.

In 1575, then, the viceroy Toledo appointed by decree a certain Gonzalo Holguin as his interpreter of 'Quechua, Puquina and Aymara, which are the languages generally spoken by the Indians in the kingdoms and provinces of Peru'. In 1586, a text written in La Paz, now capital of Bolivia, noted that 'all the Indians of this province and this town speak the general language which is called Aymara, but many of them also speak and understand the Quechua language, which is the general Inca language, and there is also another regional language, spoken in some villages, which is called Puquina'. Then, in 1589, the Bishop of Cuzco asked the Jesuits to interview candidates for the priesthood in Quechua, Aymara, and Puquina 'because these three languages are spoken in many regions of the diocese'.[3]

This multilingual situation is confirmed by many travellers. In particular, Pedro de Cieza de Leon (1518–1560), who travelled from 1541 to 1550 between present-day Colombia and present-day Peru, described the peoples of the Andes speaking their own languages and the 'general' language of the region of Cuzco, Quechua, in his two works, *La Cronica del Peru* (1553) and *El senorio de los Incas* (published in 1880). The Spanish colonizers, then, found an Inca empire in which the Indians spoke different local languages, their own languages and, depending on region, one or two 'general' languages (to use the terminology of the period). These were Quechua and Aymara, Quechua being in particular the administrative language: 'Having been given the enormous task of travelling over such a

[2] A. Torero, 'Linguistica e historia de los Andes del Peru y Bolivia', in *El Reto del multilinguismo en el Peru* (Lima, 1972).
[3] Ibid. 52–8.

large country where, in every place and at every crossing, there was a new language . . . they chose the most effective solution and ordered that all natives of the Empire should know and understand the language of Cuzco'.[4]

The linguistic history of the Andes was thereafter a colonial history determined by the decisions made by the Spanish with regard to administration, education, and religion. The future of Quechua as a 'general' language or lingua franca was precarious. As the Inca empire's administrative language, in use around 1530 from the centre of Chile and the North-East of Argentina to Ecuador and Colombia, it could have disappeared with the empire, cut off from its principal function, and giving way to a diglossia of Castilian and local languages which, according to location, could have been Puquina, Aymara, or some other Indian tongue. But there were not enough Spanish troops for them to be able to impose Castilian on the indigenous peoples, and in Quechua as a lingua franca they found a ready-made instrument for the conquest and pacification of the Inca empire.[5] Of course, communication depended indirectly on interpreters trained in Castilian, and this adoption of the Inca empire's practice must have, at first, reinforced the use of the general language. But faced with this practice, the Spanish authorities, in the distant Iberian peninsula, saw things differently and in 1550 Charles I of Spain (better known to history as Charles V, Holy Roman Emperor) took a decision: 'Having examined if, even in the most perfect of Indian languages, it was possible to explain correctly the mysteries of the Holy Catholic Faith, we have come to the conclusion that this is impossible.' A. Torero comments: 'Undoubtedly, the true intention of the Emperor was to extend Castillian to the American colonies, just as the Romans had made general use of Latin in the greater part of its European possessions'.[6]

As a matter of fact, the Spanish settlers, who came to join the first conquistadors from the end of the sixteenth century, were never interested in the Indian languages. They were learnt only by priests, in particular Jesuits, and the Spanish administration used interpreters in their relations with the Indians, whom they now settled in new villages in order to control them better and make them submit to taxation. Colonial power decided to efface the traces of the previous culture. They destroyed the *huacas*, the Indian tombs, and the mummies they contained, they burned

---

[4] Pedro de Cieza de Leon, *El senorio de los Incas* (Lima, 1967), 84 (a re-publication of the 16th-century manuscript).

[5] A. Torero, *El quechua y la historia social andina* (Lima, 1974), 181.

[6] Ibid. 184–5.

the *quipus*, banned the traditional dances, etc. And, at the same time, they printed catechism books in Quechua and Aymara.

In this period, at the end of the sixteenth century, three languages were still used by the administration for control of the Indian peoples: Quechua, Aymara, and Puquina. The last of these quickly disappeared as a lingua franca 'perhaps because of its extreme tendency to split up into dialects or because of a rapid reduction in speakers'.[7] Aymara also lost ground; in particular, it only survived in the Cuzco region as a form of substratum, marking the phonology and vocabulary of local Quechua. Gradually, the traces of the Inca empire and its organization, which some have considered as 'pre-socialist' disappeared, and it is paradoxical that Quechua should have been the instrument of the destruction of the Andes society that existed before the arrival of the Spanish. In one century the Indian people were divided up into small communities that could be easily controlled, while Quechua benefited from Spanish policy.

Torero comments bitterly:

the Crown and the Clergy could be satisfied; there was no longer any need for a new evangelizing campaign. In contrast to this foreign nation, rich and powerful, there now arose a single 'Indian nation': ruralized, impoverished, socially and culturally asphyxiated. They had brought about the final reduction: the 'Indian nation' and the slave class were reduced to a single mass. Colonial domination, national oppression and social exploitation merged into one another.[8]

After that, Quechua no longer interested the Spanish authorities and we pass, at the end of the seventeenth century, to a phase when Castilian was imposed, with uneven results. It quickly took over the coastal plain, while Quechua and Aymara continued to dominate the interior. The gaining of independence by the countries of the Andes has not changed the situation much, and at the present time two languages confront each other, Castilian, the language of power, of the Creole bourgeoisie, and Quechua (and in some regions Aymara), the language of the Indians. So we have a language that came from the coast, functioning as a lingua franca for administration (in the Inca empire), which was revived in this role for a while by the Spanish crown, which then rejected it. It was a language that, in the course of several centuries became a single language under which other local languages disappeared, and spread over a vast extent of territory, all along the Andes, and that also became the sole symbol of 'Indian authenticity' in the face of colonial culture. In carrying out research in an Indian community of Ecuador on the 'language

[7] Ibid. 189.   [8] Ibid. 198.

attitude' of the Indians, I noted, for example, that speakers said that they prized their language, Quechua, because it was the language of Atahualpa (the last Inca, assassinated by Pizzarro in 1533). This reveals a sentimental and ideological attachment to the (linguistic) trace of a moment of resistance to the invader which happens to be, by an irony of history, a language that itself came from elsewhere.

What is the future for Quechua? A Bolivian linguist, Xavier Albo, gave a somewhat pessimistic conclusion to a study he made of the town of Cochabamba: 'it can be easily predicted that Quechua will slowly give ground to Castilian. But it is very difficult to calculate how many years, decades or perhaps centuries it will take before Quechua ceases to be the language of a large section of the population'.[9] What is certain, is that today, when a Quechua-speaking peasant meets a Spanish-speaking client in a market, the transaction is most frequently carried out in Spanish:[10] the lingua franca has changed sides.

Factors in the Spread of Lingua Francas

The example used here has been Quechua. It could have been replaced by a good dozen or more other lingua francas from across the world, and other case studies can be found in a small book I have devoted to this problem.[11] Such as it is, however, the example of Quechua enables us to draw up a list of factors that play a role in the emergence and spread of lingua francas, and we shall only refer to other cases to clarify certain points.

The geographical factor

We have seen that Quechua spread as a second language, then as a first language, by following a north–south route along the Andes corridor, bounded on the west by the fertile coastal plains occupied by settlers and on the east by the summits of the Cordillera which from Aconcagua (7,021 m) in Argentina to Chimborazo (6,310 m) or Cotopaxi (5,896 m) in Ecuador constitute a barrier that can be crossed only with difficulty. There is, it is true, a small Quechua-speaking group in Amazonia, in the province of Napo, but this is an exception, for the great majority of speakers of the language are to be found in a band about a hundred kilometres wide and more than two thousand kilometres long.

---

[9]   Xavier Albo, *Los mil rostros del Quechua* (Lima, 1974), 228.

[10]   At least this is what I noticed during preliminary research (unpublished) in Ecuador in the markets of Sakisili and Otavalo in the Andes, and of Puyo in Amazonia.

[11]   L.-J. Calvet, *Les Langues véhiculaires* (Paris, 1981).

All lingua francas have spread under similar conditions. It was along the River Congo that Lingala spread as a lingua franca, along the River Oubangui that Sango became the lingua franca of Central Africa, from port to port that Malay became the lingua franca of Indonesia, and the original lingua franca, a mixture of Italian and Occitan, covered the whole of the Mediterranean in the Middle Ages. Or again, it was by travelling from port to port, then along tracks that Swahili became first a sailors' language (hence its name: in Arabic 'coasts'), then crossed Africa from east to west, and so on.

Geographic factors determine how these languages spread. When they gain ground, they do so along natural routes, avoiding obstacles, obviously enough. But geographic conditions can also lie at the origin of a lingua franca's spread, and can instigate it as a lingua franca, when a natural division (in the case of an archipelago, for example) of territories and ethnic groups makes a common instrument of communication necessary. In this respect the case of Melanesia is exemplary. Its group of islands (New Guinea, Solomon Islands, Bismarck Archipelago, Trobriand Islands, etc.) has a thousand languages and possesses four lingua francas (Hiri Motu, Neo-Melanesian, Solomon Isles Pidgin, and Bislama) which are all, strictly speaking, a response to a communication problem created by geographic conditions.

The urban factor

Natural routes most often link towns, ports, and markets, and towns become like pumps in accelerating the pace of languages that are spreading. With Quechua we saw that Cuzco, the capital of the Inca empire, where Aymara was probably spoken, became the starting-point for the spread of the 'general' administrative language. Things are even clearer in Senegal, in regions where Wolof is not the local language. It can be seen, in fact, from the following table, that four to five times more people speak the lingua franca that has come from the capital to each region's principal town than in the corresponding region as a whole (see Table 8.1). There are different explanations for the role played by towns in the spread of language. First of all, towns are places with concentrations of administration and administrators, required by their work to move about across the country, to learn lingua francas more easily than peasants who do not leave their villages. Towns are also economic centres, and we saw in Chapter 7 the importance of markets in the emergence of lingua francas. This leads us quite naturally to the following factor.

TABLE 8.1. *Percentage of Wolof speakers*

In the town		In the department	
town of Ziguinchor	80.04	department of Ziguinchor	17.33
town of Podor	80	department of Podor	12.75
town of Sedhiou	40.72	department of Sedhiou	9.33
town of Bignona	37.15	department of Bignona	6.75
town of Kolda	27.81	department of Kolda	5

Note: Cf. M. Calvet and F. Wioland, 'L'Expansion du wolof au Sénégal', *Bulletin de l'IFAN*, no. 3–4 (Dakar, 1967).

The economic factor

The natural routes we have referred to with regard to the geographic factor are most often routes for trade. Roads, rivers, and ports see the passage of merchants who, besides their merchandise, transport languages used in their transactions. In this way, Quechua, originally spoken in the coastal plain of Peru, first came to the Andes through the influence of economic exchanges between the coast and the mountains; and Swahili, which originated in the island of Zanzibar, gained in importance as commerce flourished in the island.

Between 1832 and 1834 for example, forty-one ships entered the port of Zanzibar, but for the single year of 1856 the port received eighty-nine, the majority of which were American. Commerce developed strongly with the import of cotton clothes from Massachusetts and the export of cloves and ivory. The ivory had to be sought in the interior of the continent, at ever greater distances, and the spread of Swahili faithfully followed the caravan routes. In the same way, the spread of Mandingo as a lingua franca in West Africa was first linked to trading in salt and gold and, more generally, to the travels of Jula traders.[12] In all these cases, commercial relations had implications for linguistic communication; when there was no common language, a lingua franca was needed.

The religious factor

One of the problems the Spanish colonizers faced, in the sixteenth century, was to find the language most suitable for spreading Christianity; the

[12] See e.g. L.-J. Calvet, 'La Route sel/or et l'expansion du manding', in *Traces*, no. 4 (Rabat, 1980), and L.-J. Calvet, 'The Spread of Mandingo: Military, Commercial and Colonial Influence on a Linguistic Datum', in *Language Spread* (Bloomington: Indiana University Press, 1982).

use of Quechua did no harm to the language's fortunes, despite instructions from Spain. Here the relationship between Catholicism and Quechua was a matter of chance, but some religions are more directly linked to a language, in particular when there exists a fundamental text for the religion, a holy book. The advance of the religion then leads to the advance of the language. This was for a long time the case with Latin and the Catholic religion, and is still the case with Sanskrit and Hinduism, and again with Arabic and Islam. Alongside the spread of these languages and religions, a spread of writing can sometimes be observed: the Arabic alphabet is used in Muslim countries that are non-Arab speaking, the Orthodox religion has spread the Cyrillic alphabet, and so on.

Of course, these are most often scholarly languages, but Latin functioned for a long time in Europe as the lingua franca of cultivated people, and more recently, a sacred language, Hebrew, became the national language of the state of Israel, serving as a lingua franca for immigrants from every corner of the globe.

The military factor

The title of this book, language wars, naturally prepares us for an analysis of the relationship between the spread of lingua francas and military expansion, and the conquest of Latin America by the Spaniards provides a good example of the links between military success and the future of Castilian. But the army, in that it is a form of administration, also plays a not insignificant role in the history of lingua francas. For example, Bambara, the lingua franca of West Africa, was the command language of French colonial troops in Africa, and there even existed an official army handbook in the language.[13] Lingala is today the language of the Zairean army, Swahili was used by British colonial troops, and there are several other examples.

The political factor

The hesitations of the Spanish in dealing with the problem of languages, which I mentioned with regard to the religious factor, come under what one would call today 'language policy'. And policy choices are very often linked to the future of lingua francas. It was for example the language policy of German and then British colonialism which reinforced the spread of Swahili in East Africa. Similarly, it was the choice of the

---

[13] *Grammaire et méthode bambara*, by Captain Delaforge, published by the military publishing house Charles-Lavauzelle.

Indonesian Nationalist Party in 1928 which confirmed the status of Malay in Indonesia, and so on. But these choices, these problems of language planning and policy, are the subject of the third part of the book and we shall return to them at greater length.

And Yet They Do Communicate

'Eppur' si muove', this is how, it is said, Galileo affirmed that he really believed in the movement of the Earth in an undertone, when forced by the court of the Inquisition to abjure his Copernican ideas: 'and yet it does move'. We could paraphrase this famous formula and say 'and yet they do communicate', when confronted by the multiplicity of the world's languages and the difficulties that result. For what the phenomenon of lingua francas demonstrates is that wherever there is a communication problem, social practice provides a solution. Communication is established despite multiplicity. These lingua francas are therefore a way of taking up, *in vivo*, the challenge of Babel.

But any spread of language is always to the detriment of other languages, and the emergence of a lingua franca is a case of language competition. The different factors of expansion we have just described, which combine together, according to circumstances, to make the history of a lingua franca, at the same time favour one language over others and combine to establish a hierarchy of functions. On this count it is interesting to note that the lingua francas of the world are rarely spoken in the territory of just one country: they cross frontiers, extend over large territories, unlike vernacular languages, which are most often confined to a region, even a village. This fact has perhaps some explanatory value: a language will assert itself as a lingua franca as against more locally-based languages all the more easily if it is spread over a wide territory.

So there is a problem of taxonomy: what is the justification for the often-used distinction between lingua francas and international languages? For Quechua is spoken, as we have seen, in six countries of Latin America; Hausa is spoken in Nigeria and Niger, Swahili in Tanzania, Kenya, Burundi, Zaire, etc. They are all, in the true sense of the word, international languages. According to the *Dictionnaire Robert* for example, a lingua franca is 'a language serving as communication between people with a different mother tongue', which is an excellent definition, and the adjective international means 'that pertaining to the relations between nations'. It seems clear, then, that lingua francas are international languages.

However, in a short book devoted to international languages, Pierre Burney draws up a list of 'national languages that are candidates for international languages'. Besides French and English, he gives Spanish, Russian, Chinese, German, and Arabic.[14] Ralph Fasold, in *The Sociolinguistics of Society*, writes that international languages make for 'a short list of languages, mostly European: English, French, Spanish, Russian, German, perhaps Mandarin Chinese, and maybe one or two others'.[15] One language apart, the two authors are in agreement. Readers will have noted that they do not mention Quechua, Swahili, Mandingo, Malay, Lingala, etc. I could continue this list, but we have already easily exceeded Fasold's 'one or two others'. It can be seen that this distinction between lingua francas and international languages, besides the fact that it is largely Eurocentrist, brings us back to the notion of language competition that I mentioned above.

At first glance we can see in this distinction yet another trace of linguistic racism: European countries communicate among themselves with international languages, countries of the Third World with lingua francas. Or in other terms, ordinary people speak lingua francas, 'jet-set' societies speak international languages.

But most important here is the distinction between the *de facto* and the *de jure*. The languages which are used *in vivo* by people as a lingua franca to resolve their communication problems will only be elevated to the dignity of international languages, *in vitro*, when this has been legally decided (by the UN, UNESCO, etc.). On the one hand, there is the battlefield which I am describing in this second part; on the other, there is the general staff, back at headquarters, which we shall treat in the third part. Lingua francas are out in the field; to become international they have to be approved by the bureaucrats.

[14] Pierre Burney, *Les Langues internationales* (Paris, 1966), 60.
[15] Ralph Fasold, *The Sociolinguistics of Society* (Oxford, 1984), 76.

9

The Death of Languages

The idea that languages can 'die' will come as no surprise, since it is quite common to speak of a 'dead language', defined by a technical dictionary as 'a language which is no longer spoken, but which sometimes still has status in the sociocultural community and a role in teaching, in ceremonial rituals, etc., as with Latin'.[1] The Littré dictionary gives two examples, Latin and Hebrew, having defined them as 'languages which exist only in books'. More recently, the *Dictionnaire Robert* gives 'dead languages: languages which are no longer spoken', without offering any examples, but it does, on the other hand, quote Greek and Latin under the entry for Classical languages.

We might already, at this stage, wonder why Latin appears in one place as a classical language and in another as a dead language, but this would not take us very far, for there is really no contradiction between these two classifications. In fact, the only dead languages that are given as examples in the dictionaries are at the same time treated as classical languages, and Littré's definition ('languages which exist only in books') is the one most characteristic of this view since it says two things at once: a dead language is a written language, that is, it was written down while 'it was alive', remaining written down ever after, and it is no longer spoken. In other words, among the multitude of languages which have been spoken in the course of history and are no longer, there are dead languages and languages that have disappeared, hierarchically related. Latin, Greek, classical Arabic, or Sanskrit have more prestige as languages than those spoken by our ancestors who were colonized by the Romans, and which left no literature, or were not linked to a religion. At least this, briefly summarized, is what seems to be the common view of the problem.

We Speak Dead Languages . . .

Paradoxically, the languages officially considered to be dead are still spoken and written today, but in forms that would probably astonish their

[1] J. Dubois et al., *Dictionnaire de linguistique* (Paris, 1973), 326.

first speakers. When I give a course in linguistics at the Sorbonne or buy a packet of tobacco in a bar at the corner of the road, I speak Latin, in the same way that a customer ordering a plate of 'tapas' in a bar of the Barrio Chino in Barcelona speaks Latin, or a fisherman selling cod on a beach in Portugal, or a prostitute soliciting clients on the streets of Naples. Of course, some would say that in these different situations four different languages are being used: French, Catalan, Portuguese, and Neapolitan. They would not be wrong, considering the agreed difference between these four forms at least, but this takes nothing away from the fact that French and Spanish are *Latin*, but Latin deformed by fifteen centuries of popular usage, pronounced by throats used to other sounds and adapted to other syntactical habits, a bastard Latin, split into dialects, riddled with borrowings from other languages, rendered unrecognizable, but still Latin. The languages described by the dictionary as dead are still alive, we speak them every day: the Arabics spoken in the streets of Fez or Tunis are the direct continuation of classical Arabic, and Greek at its most demotic keeps ancient Greek alive.

It remains the case that if I spoke Latin to my neighbour, or classical Arabic to a Tunisian peasant, communication would be difficult, and the idea that a Welshman, an Afghan, a Frenchman, or a Czech today speak 'Indo-European' is entirely a matter of theory. We must in fact imagine 'an evolutionary process which will continue from our day until the night of time', to adopt André Martinet's formula,[2] a process in the course of which peoples were dispersed over a vast extent, initially along an east–west route, speaking local forms of the same language to begin with; these forms were then transformed from generation to generation as they became progressively more distant from the point of departure and encountered other languages. If, in a score of centuries and with a relatively limited territorial expansion, Latin was able to develop, through the effects of distance and languages encountered, to the point of taking forms as different as French, Romanian, or Portuguese, it is possible to imagine what dimensions this process might have attained in forty centuries and over a territory ten times more vast.

Latin, then, is *dead* in the sense that it is no longer spoken in the form used by Julius Caesar; it is *alive* in the sense that it continues in the Romance languages whose speakers must have thought for many years that they still spoke Latin, until the day when they realized that what they spoke no longer had much in common with Caesar's writings nor

---

[2] A. Martinet, *Des steppes aux océans* (Paris, 1986), 13.

with the speech of other regions supposed to speak Latin too. Here is a good example, the 'Strasbourg oaths' already discussed in Chapter 5. In the column on the left is the first half of the text translated into classical Latin by F. Brunot,[3] in the centre the original text with abbreviations and wrong word-divisions removed, and on the right the text in modern French.

Per Dei amorem et per	Pro deo amur et pro	Pour l'amour de Dieu et
christiani populi et	christian poblo et	pour le salut commun
nostram communem	nostro commun	du peuple chrétien et
salutem, ab hac die,	saluament, d'isti di	le nôtre, à partir de
quantum Deus scire et	en avant in quant Deus	ce jour, autant que
posse mihi dat,	savir et podir me	Dieu m'en donne le
servabo hunc meum	dunat, si salvarai eo	savoir et le pouvoir,
fratrem Carolum, et	cist meon fradre	je soutiendrai mon
ope mea et un	Karlo, et in aiudha et	frère Charles de mon
quaecumque re, ut	in cadhuna cosa, si	aide et en toute
quilibet fratrem suum	cum om per dreit son	chose, comme on doit
servare jure debet,	fradre salver deit, en	justement soutenir son
dummodo mihi idem	ço que il mi altresi	frère, à condition
faciat, et cum	fazet, et ab Ludher	qu'il m'en fasse
Clotario nullam unquam	nul plait onques ne	autant, et je
pactionem faciam, quae	prendrai, qui mien	prendrai jamais aucun
mea voluntate huic meo	vueil cest mien frere	arrangement avec
fratri Carlo damno sit	Charlon en dam seit	Lothaire, qui à ma
		volonté soit au
		détriment de mondit
		frère Charles

(For the love of God and for the common salvation of the Christian people and our own, from this day forth, insofar as God gives me the knowledge and the power, I shall support my brother Charles with my help in everything, as one should by right support one's brother, on condition that he does the same for me, and I shall enter into no arrangement with Lothair, which in my opinion would harm my brother Charles).

Any non-specialist modern reader of French would probably have difficulty in understanding the central column without the help of the column on the right, and Julius Caesar would probably not have been able to understand the central column, had it been possible to put it in front of him. It remains the case that there is some continuity between these three

---

[3] F. Brunot, *Histoire de la langue française des origines à 1900* (Paris, 1905), i. 144.

texts, or at least between the three spoken languages for which they are evidence. Latin is not dead, we still speak it.

The Disappearance of Languages

But what shall we say of the languages dethroned by Latin, languages for which we no longer have a clear picture, which were spoken in the Iberian peninsula, in Gaul or in present-day Romania before the Roman conquest? These are very clearly *dead* if we mean by this that they are no longer spoken, but this kind of death is not to be compared to the death of Latin. In the first case the languages that have disappeared have left hardly any trace other than substrata, which moreover provide the characteristics of the different Romance languages; in the second case, the dead language, Latin, has simply changed.

There are three ways in which a language can 'disappear':

– Disappearance by *transformation*. This occurs each time that, as in the case of Romance languages, a linguistic form evolves, differentiates itself geographically in the course of the expansion of the people who speak it, to give birth to a family of languages. The example of Latin, as we have said, is in this way qualitatively comparable to Indo-European, which disappeared through transformation in the same way, over a much longer period of time. But it is also comparable to the case of classical Arabic, which over a shorter period of time has been transformed into different modern 'dialects'.

– Disappearance by *extinction*. This is when, in some cases, the last speakers of a language die without leaving any descendants. For example at the beginning of the 1980s in equatorial Amazonia, in the province of Napo, there was an old couple who spoke Tete, which inevitably died with them. This disappearance of a language, the result of the disappearance of a group of speakers, does not benefit any other language, by transformation or by replacement.

– Disappearance by *replacement*. This occurs each time that a subordinate language disappears under a dominant language. This is clearly the exact opposite of the first. The transformation of Latin into one or another Romance language implies the disappearance of the languages spoken beforehand.

It can be seen, then, that languages, peoples, and races should not be confused. The people who today speak an Indo-European language are not necessarily of the Indo-European 'race', insofar as this notion makes sense, any more than all speakers of French are 'Latins'. In the same way, a large majority of the population of North Africa today is of Berber origin but Arab-speaking. In the case of disappearance by replacement, linguistic movement does not correlate with population movement, as in the example of the Tete couple mentioned above. When we examined, in Chapter 6, the bilingual families in which the children did not have the language of their parents as their first language, but the dominant language of the society in which they lived (which was for example the case with Wolof in Senegal), we had no decrease in the Fulani or Serer populations, but in speakers of Fulani and Serer. This distinction might seem ambiguous, but the whole problem here is whether language is the criterion (or one of the criteria) for the definition of a people or a nation. This discussion only concerns us indirectly, but it is necessary to stress that if there is, for example, a Chinese nation, this does not necessarily correspond to the use of this or that language, that a person can have an American passport without having English as a first language and that if an individual is a citizen of Senegal, this tells us nothing about the language or languages that he speaks.

This replacement of one language by another can be *alternating*, when in one generation there is a change of language (the son of a Fulani or Serer who speaks Wolof), but it can also be *continuous* when in the course of a long process a subordinate language slowly blends into a dominant language, and then we should describe it as *absorption*. We have hardly any historical evidence for the stages of this kind of process. Historic linguistics can show clearly how Latin was transformed into French or Catalan, through phonetic laws, through the erosion of word endings, which implied the disappearance of case-endings, grammatical modifications, and so on. But it is much less of a guide as to how the languages spoken by populations dominated by the Romans were modified under Latin until they merged with it. It is not easy to have direct access to the death of a language.

This is why the following example is interesting. It gives us some information about this process of continuous replacement of one language by another through absorption.

The Quechua of Cochabamba

In the previous chapter I quoted the Bolivian linguist, Xavier Albo, on the future of the Quechua of Cochabamba: how many years, decades, or centuries will it take before it gives way to Spanish? This was a completely theoretical question and, besides, it is not certain that Quechua cannot resist this fate. But some other academic research gives us interesting information on the situation: Elisabeth Michenot has analysed the results of contact between the Quechua of Cochabamba and the official language.[4]

First, she describes two forms of Quechua, not fixed and differentiated forms, but tendencies between which the language fluctuates. She calls one of these Quechua 1 (Q1), spoken in the countryside by peasants who are for the most part monolingual, and the other Quechua 2 (Q2), the language of the towns, spoken in particular by shopkeepers and tradesmen, but also the language of administration and the radio. The first form of the language could be characterized as a 'purer' Quechua, the second as having borrowed a lot from Spanish, but besides this 'linguistic' judgement, the second form is also considered socially prestigious, because it is spoken by people who enjoy a certain standing. What are the relations between these two forms? We shall describe them through two simple problems, the vowel system and the phrase-structure.

Quechua normally has three vowel phonemes, i, u, and a, that is, a triangle of vowel sounds which is usually described as follows:

$$i \qquad u$$
$$a$$

As always in these cases, the phonemes show a certain amount of allophonic dispersion, that is, they can be produced phonetically in different ways. So, the phoneme /i/ can be phonetically produced [e] and the phoneme /u/ can be phonetically produced [o]. The word /urqu/, 'hill' can be produced [orqo], the word /qulqi/, 'money' can be produced [qolqe], etc.

In the form Q1, spoken by the peasants, these forms e and o, which are not phonemes, but phonetic variants, come into conflict with the phonemes /e/ and /o/ of Spanish in borrowed words, creating a certain fluctuation: the Spanish word /uniko/ is pronounced [oneko], the Spanish term /peso/ is pronounced [piso], [pesu], or [pisu], etc.

On the other hand, in the form Q2, spoken in the towns and much more influenced by Spanish, the triangle of vowels has five sounds:

$$i \qquad u$$
$$e \quad o$$
$$a$$

[4] Elisabeth Michenot, 'Parler-Pouvoir: Études des caractéristiques du quechua et des conséquences de la situation de contact avec la langue officielle. Cochabamba, Bolivie', doctoral thesis under the supervision of D. François (Paris, Université René Descartes, 1983).

the e and the o appearing both in loan words from Spanish and in authentically Quechua words. So there is /mesa/ for the Spanish word *mesa*, 'table', and /perqa/ for the Quechua 'wall' otherwise produced /pirqa/. Here the vowel system of Quechua has been infiltrated and reorganized by the vowel system of Spanish.

From the syntactical point of view, statistically the most frequent expression in Q1 (which E. Michenot christens 'preferred expression') is characterized by relatively short sentences in which the verb is found at the end, while in Q2 the tendency is to longer utterances, with subordinate and relative clauses, etc.:

Q1	80% of verbs in final position	3 to 4 terms per utterance
Q2	25–30% of verbs in final position	7 to 10 terms per utterance

So the same content will be expressed by a single utterance in Q2 and by four utterances in Q1. In Q2 we would say, approximately: 'If you want to give your cow the fodder that you have treated in order to cure this illness, you'll have to wait three weeks'; in Q1, one would say: 'You've treated the fodder against this illness; you want to feed your cow; don't give it this fodder; you'll have to wait three weeks for that'.[5]

We have, therefore, in Q2 a kind of infiltration of Quechua by Spanish, one system being slowly taken over by the other, not only on the lexical front (loan words) but also on the phonological and syntactical fronts. But it must immediately be added that Spanish also shows the same dual tendency: on the one hand a popular Spanish, marked by the influence of Quechua, on the other a developed Spanish, closer to the Iberian model. The first, called 'Andes Spanish' is generally considered to be the one spoken by people whose first language is Quechua, but the author stresses it is increasingly gaining ground among underprivileged classes of society as a first language and suggests a parallel relationship between the two languages, for which she gives this schema:

Quechua 1 = popular Spanish
Quechua 2 = 'developed Spanish'[6]

---

[5] Elisabeth Michenot, 'Parler-Pouvoir: Études des caractéristiques du quechua et des conséquences de la situation de contact avec la langue officielle. Cochabamba, Bolivie', doctoral thesis under the supervision of D. François (Paris, Université René Descartes, 1983), 253–5.

[6] Ibid. 313.

E. Michenot stops there and concludes simply with the hope that Quechua will resist Spanish. I would prefer to stress that if in these two cases we have a socially dominant form, considered to be 'legitimized' because it is spoken by the elites (Quechua 2 and 'developed' Spanish) the two pairs nevertheless show an important difference since Spanish is the purer form, the least marked by contacts with the version of Quechua that is considered to be legitimate, while for Quechua it is on the contrary the form marked by contact with Spanish. We can then imagine that the differences between Quechua 2 and Andes Spanish will gradually lessen and that if Quechua is in the end threatened with disappearance, the absorption will take place at the point where Quechua 2 and Andes Spanish come into contact, the day when the people who think they speak Quechua are no longer understood by the speakers of Q1 but are understood by speakers of Andes Spanish.

The Death of Languages

What, then, in this kind of case, is the death of a language? It is difficult to give a reply to this question without preliminary agreement as to what we mean by a 'language'. Let us first take two examples. The sentence 'Der Militär-Attaché kokettierte mit der Dame auf der Terrasse',[7] (the military attaché flirted with the woman on the terrace), which comprises only words borrowed from French, is clearly German, in the same way that the sentence, 'Le fourgue s'est fait cornancher par une michetonneuse', (the fence was laid into by a tart), which comprises only slang words, is clearly French. In both cases, syntax, word-terminations, conjugation, and grammatical words indicate the language. For a language is made up of three components: syntax, phonology, and lexis. Now the lexis has always undergone more change than the other two components, due to semantic variation and, above all, borrowings. Who remembers now that the words 'admiral' and 'magazine' are Arabic words, that 'tomato' and 'chocolate' are Aztec, that 'puma' is a Quechua word or that 'maize' is an Arawak word? All these words are both French and English, naturalized perhaps, but still French and English. Languages have always been enriched by these borrowings, these travelling words, and this has never brought their individuality, their uniqueness into question.

On the other hand, when a language sees its sound-system merge into the sound-system of another language, when its sentences copy the

---

[7] Example quoted by P. Burney, *Les Langues internationales* (Paris, 1966), 16.

sentences of another language, it is then in danger of being absorbed. The phonology and syntax are the basic structure of a language, the lexis is only the surface decoration. What puts Quechua 2, in the example above, in danger of absorption, is not the fact that it borrows words from Spanish; nearly half of the vocabulary of English is of French origin, and English is not thereby threatened with disappearance. It is because, for one thing, Quechua 2 adapts its words less and less to its own phonology and, for another, it tends to align its syntactical structures with those of the dominant language. It is clear that I am not able to say, in the present state of affairs, whether the Quechua of Bolivia will be finally absorbed by Castilian (and anyway this process will take a very long time), but this example gives us some idea of the way in which languages can die on the battlefield and shows us what there is on the other side of the fence, when, as in the case of Latin, a language dies through transformation, through absorbing a subordinate language.

The idea that languages can die leads us naturally to the obvious metaphor of 'dying languages'. Is it possible to detect the signs which reveal that a language is in danger of disappearing? It is certainly easy to measure the statistical symptoms of the approaching death of a language (although human action can always reverse the course of affairs). In the same way that a rate or index of commonality can be measured, that is, the relationship between the number of speakers of a language and the number of speakers who have this language as a first language,[8] so the index of regression of a language can also be measured, that is, the proportion of speakers who no longer speak the language of their community of origin.[9] For example, if we take 1,000 people originating in a cultural group whose language is L, and 400 of them do not speak this language, the relation 400/1,000 or 0.4 can be considered as the index of regression for L. This approach consists in following the disappearance of a language from a statistical point of view, and it can of course be refined by taking into account age and sex, opposition between town and country, etc., in order to determine the different factors of regression. But it is equally possible to read the 'danger-signs' in the very form of a language, to sketch in some way a symptomatology of the disappearance of languages. The research work done on this question is too extensive to be summarized

[8] See e.g. L.-J. Calvet et al., *Rapport de mission à Ziguinchor* (Paris: CERPL, 1985).

[9] Cf. M. Dieu and P. Renaud, 'A propos d'une étude statistique du multilingualisme au Cameroun: Quelques problèmes methodologiques', in P. Wald and G. Manessy, *Plurilingualisme* (Paris, 1979), 69 et seq.

here[10] and I will content myself simply with recalling the problem of 'fluctuation', of which Quechua was a quick example. This is the fact that certain phonological contrasts in a language tend to disappear, to be replaced by a haphazard alternation (or 'fluctuation') a fact which is evidence for the destruction from within of the whole system.

It is therefore possible, first, to measure in statistical terms the tendency of a language to disappear, that is, to evaluate the regression in the number of speakers, and, secondly, to read the signs of probable or imminent disappearance in the form of the language itself, the symptoms of the slightest differences in relation to the language absorbing it. For the death of a language always has non-linguistic causes (power-relations, and so on) whose evolution and effects can be followed from both the sociolinguistic and the linguistic point of view.

Linguistics and Sociolinguistics

Here, then, we have a good example of what sociolinguistics is, that is, the study of the effects of social issues on language. The disappearance of a language is not only a statistical fact, which appears in a decrease in the number of speakers, it is also a fact of pure linguistics, and can be discerned in precursory signs. This problematic, briefly mentioned, leads us to a more theoretical consideration. There is a tendency within linguistics to think that only the descriptive and formalist 'hard kernel' counts as science, while the other approaches (psycholinguistic, sociolinguistic, etc.) are rejected as peripheral, as what some German linguists have christened, not without humour, as 'soft linguistics' or 'hyphenated' linguistics (since, in German, hyphens separate linguistics from psycho-, socio-, etc.). An example of this tendency in France is Jean-Claude Milner who criticized this 'antilinguistics, aimed particularly at helping linguists put up with themselves: sociolinguistics, semantics whether generative or non-generative, ideological inquiries, the names matter little',[11] and even if Milner's problem is to put up with the coexistence of Lacan and Chomsky within his own thinking (it is for example amusing that

[10] See e.g. N. Dorian, *Language Death: The Life Cycle of a Scottish Gaelic Dialect* (Philadelphia, 1981); W. Dressler, 'On the Phonology of Language Death', in *Papers from the 8th Regional Meeting*, Chicago Linguistic Society (Chicago, 1972); B. Schlieben-Lange, 'The Language Situation in Southern France', *Linguistics*, 191 (1977); A. Fernandez-Garay, *La Mort des langues, bibliographie critique* (DEA report, Université René Descartes, 1986).

[11] J.-C. Milner, *L'Amour de la langue* (Paris, 1978), 126. Translated by Ann Banfield, *For the Love of Language* (Macmillan, 1990).

psycholinguistics does not appear on his list, between sociolinguistics and semantics), this kind of rejection is worth pausing over for a moment. In fact, the linguistic currents of this second half of the twentieth century are faced by a fundamental choice. Either they remain, in the Saussurian tradition, with the analysis and description of *langue* (this is the choice made by schools otherwise as different as Martinet's functionalism and Chomsky's generativism) or they regard the *parole* in which this language is manifested as the only source for determining the social aspect of communication. So *langue* and *parole* mark out two approaches, one regarded as formal linguistics and the other, by the adherents of the first, as 'informal' and peripheral.

There is clearly no reason for regarding the approach through speech as naturally less scientific than the approach through language. The problem is rather that in reducing language to a code, to a structure, or to rules for the production of sentences, the adherents of the first approach make their task considerably easier, while the second approach is only in its infancy and still has teething troubles. I myself at one time had a tendency to treat this debate in categorical terms, to set sociolinguistics in opposition to linguistics, to such an extent that it might have seemed an attempt to replace the linguistics of language with a linguistics of speech. In fact, there is no question that the formal description of languages is necessary; the only point to be discussed is its imperial pretension to constitute the whole of linguistics. This is why the brief description of the Quechua of Cochabamba and the discussion of a possible symptomatology of the death of languages seem to me to be important. They of course provide us with information about the process of absorption of one language by another, but they also show us how descriptive linguistics (and it does not matter which descriptive theory is chosen) overlaps with sociolinguistics, how social facts are present at every level. This means, in general, that there is only one linguistics, and this can be emphasized by naming it social linguistics or, if it is preferred, it means that sociolinguistics is the whole of linguistics. More particularly, as far as this book is concerned, it means that language wars does not occur only in the conflicts between different languages, but that they can appear within language itself. This comes back, in another guise, to what I wrote at the beginning of Chapter 5: no matter how monolingual we are, we are all multilingual.

PART III

Among the Administrators

10

Language Policy and Planning: First Approach

The five preceding chapters all, from different angles, touched on the same subject, that is, how speakers experience and manage multilingualism. We treated different topics (the family, markets, lingua francas) and we used different approaches (research by questionnaire or observation, description of languages, reconstruction of the history of languages through the study of documents). But, whatever the topic or approach, in every case the lesson of our analysis and research was the same: social relationships lie behind language relationships, and the linguistic phenomena we have described are the evidence for this. We are now going to leave the battlefield, the *in vivo* management of multilingualism and the relationships between languages to turn to the *in vitro* management of these problems, that is, the direct and deliberate intervention by those with political power into the domain of language. To begin, we shall in this short chapter clarify some key terms and propose definitions which will serve as reference points.

Language policy and language planning have been much discussed for many years, ever since the American linguist E. Haugen launched the phrase 'language planning' in a 1959 article devoted to the language situation in Norway.[1] The date shows that, from what we might call an 'etymological' point of view, language planning is a recent phenomenon, if we suppose there is a correspondence between the appearance of a thing and the appearance of a name for it. Is it to be concluded from this that for the last forty years we have been witnessing the emergence of a new social concern at the same time as a new branch of applied linguistics or of sociolinguistics? Matters are not so simple, for if we consider that the management of multilingualism is a branch of language policy, then it is as old as multilingualism and the myth of Babel itself. History teems with examples of human intervention into language, well before anyone described these interventions as language 'policy' or 'planning'. The case of

---

[1] E. Haugen, 'Planning for a Standard Language in Modern Norway', *Anthropological Linguistics*, 1: 3 (1959).

Charles I of Spain deciding in 1550 to impose Castilian on the Indians of South America enables us to observe a sequence of stages that are characteristic of this kind of intervention:

- The stage of reflection on the language problem, of analysis of the situation (here limited to a single question: can the catechism be taught in Aymara or in Quechua?).
- The decision-making stage (here, the decision to use Spanish in order to evangelize the Indians).
- Finally, the stage of application or implementation of the decision (which in this case would imply teaching Spanish first and religion after).

This sequence will enable us to give a better definition of policy and planning, terms which we have used somewhat vaguely until now and which are sometimes used as alternatives for each other, as if they were synonyms. We shall treat language policy as the conscious choices made in the domain of relationships between language and social life as a whole, and more particularly between language and national life; and language planning as the research and implementation of the means necessary for the application of a language policy. So, to return to the example given above, Charles I's decision was a choice of language policy, and the eventual implementation of this choice in the field in South America was language planning.

Language policy, as I have just defined it, appears therefore as linked to the state. This is in no way a theoretical assertion on my part, but rather the recording of a fact, and we cannot exclude the possibility that language policies may either transcend frontiers or, on the other hand, apply to a restricted group, a community smaller than the state in which it coexists with other communities. In the first category, we might mention the community of deaf-mutes, who can hold world congresses and take decisions, pass motions on the subject of teaching (should the deaf be taught sign language or should there be an attempt to teach them speech?), or again the community of Esperantists, to whom we shall return in another chapter. In these two examples, we have a diaspora which by definition is not limited within frontiers. In the second category, we might mention linguistic minorities, Bretons in France, Tibetans in China, for example, who can have a platform or demands comparable to a language policy. On the other hand, the passage to action that constitutes language planning most often requires state intervention. The Bretons have not, technically, the means of applying their language demands on their own.

If the notion of language planning implies, therefore, the notion of language policy, the converse is not true and one could give a long list of policy choices relating to language which have never been carried out. But language policies that are not applied (or are inapplicable, for lack of political power) are not for all that to be ignored, for not all of them have the same function. It is necessary to distinguish between practical function and symbolic function. When a newly independent state decides to take a local language as its national language, this decision will be considered a practical one insofar as it is followed by planning that introduces the language into schools, into administration, and the like, until it replaces the colonial language in all areas of national life. But the same decision will be considered symbolic, if it is never applied, or if at first it cannot be applied. This was the case with the Indonesian Nationalist Party which decided in 1928 to promote Malay to the status of national language, for this was still in the colonial period and they had no means of making their decision effective. But, by asserting the existence of a national language, the party made a symbolic assertion of the existence of an Indonesian nation as against the Dutch occupation. It needed twenty years and the independence of Indonesia for this decision to become a practical one and to be applied.

There is also a third distinction which will help us to describe and analyse different language policies, that is, the contrast between action on one language and action on a number of languages. In fact, language policy (and, also, planning) can aim at action on the form of the language, that is, standardizing the national language. An intervention of this kind can take place at three different levels:

- On the level of writing, when it is a case of providing the language with an orthography or of modifying an existing orthography, or even of changing the alphabet.
- On the level of lexis, when it is a case of creating new words (by borrowing or neologisms) to enable a language to carry content previously carried in another language (political and scientific vocabulary, etc.).
- Lastly, on the level of dialect, when a language recently promoted to the rank of national language exists in several regional forms and it is necessary either to choose one of these forms or to create a new form that borrows from the different varieties.

But language policy can also intervene in the relations between languages, in multilingual situations, when it is necessary to choose a national

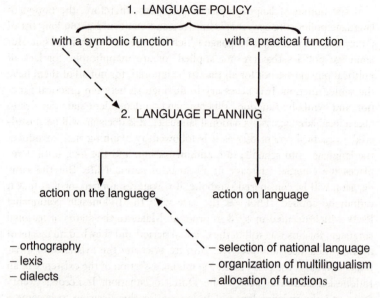

FIG. 10.1 In this schema the arrows with straight lines indicate the logical link between a language policy with a practical function and the language planning that implements it, and the arrows with dotted lines indicate the possibility of a link between apparently alternative solutions.

language among several competing languages, or organize regional multi-lingualism, or decide on languages for teaching, for media communication, and so on. This case is the most common, as will be shown in the examples we shall develop in the following chapters. But these two kinds of action can overlap; an intervention into languages can lead to the promotion of a national language over which policy will then have a standardizing effect.

These different definitions and the relations between these terms can be summarized in Figure 10.1.

At the beginning of this chapter I mentioned that the expression 'language planning' was launched by E. Haugen in 1959. It was J. Fishman, in a short book published in 1970,[2] who added the phrase 'language policy', and this pairing, policy/planning, became more and more frequent, although, as I have said, the terms were not always defined precisely. For

___

[2] J. Fishman, *Sociolinguistics: A Brief Introduction* (Rowley, Mass., 1970), 108.

Haugen, planning came under applied linguistics,[3] while Fishman discussed it in a chapter with the title 'Sociolinguistics'. And more recently, C. Ferguson and J. Das Gupta wrote in the preface to a collection of essays on language planning:

Language planning is a latecomer to the family of national development planning. Although deliberate attempts to change or preserve languages and their use may be as old as economic policy making efforts in human societies, and thus long antedate the modern concept of planning, it is only very recently that these activities in the language area have been recognized as an aspect of national planning.[4]

The term 'planning' became current in the field of economics in the sense of 'organization according to a plan'. There is a reference here to the role of the state, to which I have already referred, since the state is responsible for the plan. But the fact that language planning appears in this text in the context of 'national planning', that it is compared to economic planning, poses another problem. For the very use of this term 'planning' puts language in the class of things that can be planned, like schools, birthrate, development, construction, etc., in the class of phenomena on which those with power can act, which they can control and direct. But the central problem is never raised, a problem that I would formulate in this way: to what degree is it possible to apply planning to language?

The idea of language planning implies three things: two properties of language and the capacity for human action:

– It implies first of all that language changes, a fact which is not open to question. This is amply demonstrated by the history of language.
– It implies also that the relationships between languages can change, and here again we have ample evidence that this hypothesis is correct.
– But, above all, language planning also implies that it is possible to intervene on these two points, that it is possible to make *in vitro* changes to language and the relationships between languages.

Now the discourse of linguistics has always more or less assumed the opposite. By contrasting norm and description, modern linguistics presents itself as a science whose telos is not to give rules, or to establish correct usage, but to describe rules and usage. Language development,

[3] E. Haugen, *Language Conflict and Language Planning: The Case of Modern Norwegian* (Cambridge, Mass.: Harvard University Press, 1966), 24 and 26.
[4] J. Das Gupta and C. Ferguson, 'Problems of Language Planning', in *Language Planning Processes* (The Hague: Mouton, 1977), 4.

whether it is of one language or of the relationships between languages, is a matter of social fact and not of planned intervention. The linguist explains this development but he does not instigate it. This is why the very notion of language planning is a kind of challenge to linguistics.

When the British writer George Orwell wrote his novel *1984* in 1948, no one took his thoughts on language seriously, in particular, his idea of a totalitarian power intervening daily, through the agency of 'grammarians' governing vocabulary, in order to fashion 'Newspeak', a new language. It is necessary, in fact, to distinguish two things that the author runs together in the novel. First, there is totalitarian intervention that seeks to rule over people's minds through language (if the sentence 'Down with the chief' was decreed to be ungrammatical, would the population cease to think 'down with the chief'?) and secondly, there is the technical possibility of changing language by decree. So, to go into more detail, it is necessary to distinguish between, on one hand, the attempt to modify the perception of social experience by modifying the language ('joycamp' means forced labour, 'minipax' is an abbreviation for Minister of Peace, i.e. Minister of War), with the idea that speakers analyse their experience through words, and that any semantic modification will modify their experience of the world. Then, on the other hand, there is the desire to create a logical language, without any irregularities, in which for example a root can function as noun, verb, or adjective by the simple addition of a word-ending ('speed' as noun or verb, with 'speedful' in place of 'rapid' and 'speedwise' in place of 'quickly' . . .), or again adjectives are organized by opposition with the use of prefixes (instead of 'dark', one might have for example 'unlight').

In the first article devoted to linguistics that I ever published, I criticized this overall conception point by point.[5] Today, the great increase in operations of language planning and of works devoted to describing and analysing them makes one think that, paradoxically, Orwell was perhaps right and the linguists wrong.

---

[5] L.-J. Calvet, 'Sur une conception fantaisiste de la langue: La 'Newspeak' de George Orwell', *La Linguistique*, 1 (1969), 101–4.

11

Case Studies: The Management of Multilingualism

In this chapter and those that follow, we shall describe a number of actual language policies, which will then provide us with a basis for discussion. We shall begin with language policies that had to deal with a substantial amount of multilingualism but which had no intention of reducing it to monolingualism.

The Case of China

In the People's Republic of China there are said to be about fifty different languages that can, for ease of exposition, be divided into two groups: Han languages and minority languages.

The term 'Han' describes the Chinese ethnic group (in Chinese a difference is drawn between *han zi ren*, 'people of the Han race', people of the Han ethnic group, or Chinese, and *zhong guo ren*, 'people of the middle country', Chinese citizens). The Han group includes the different Chinese tongues spoken in China, though the official view is that in fact there is one language with a number of dialects. These languages number eight:

1. the language of the North, spoken by 70% of the population, and often called 'Mandarin' in the West
2. Wu
3. Hsian
4. Kan
5. Northern Min
6. Southern Min
7. Yüeh
8. Hakka, or Keija[1]

Maurice Coyaud has divided these dialects into two zones (see Table 11.1). Here is his description of his classification:

[1] A. Rygaloff, *Grammaire élémentaire du chinois* (Paris, 1973). See in particular the maps, pp. 250–1.

Table 11.1.

Zone 1 (south-east of China)	Zone 2 (mandarin dialects)
1. Canton	7. Peking, Manchuria, bassin du Huang
2. Kan Hakka	8. Hankou, Nanking
3. Amoy swatou	9. south-east, Sechuan, Yunnan,
4. Fujian	Guizhou, Guanxi, Hubei
5. Wu	
6. Xiang	

There is no intelligibility between languages of the first zone and those of the second zone (as between French and Spanish); there is no or very little intelligibility between languages of the first zone. We can say then that these 'dialects' are in fact different languages. On the other hand, Mandarin is a single language with three dialects as indicated.[2]

So on one side we have speakers of a language from the Han group, who represent 95% of the total population (70% for Mandarin, 25% for the other languages, about 250 million speakers), and on the other there remain 5% speaking so-called 'minority' languages (but 5% of more than a billion inhabitants makes these minorities far from insignificant in size; they number as many people as the population of France), belonging to four different families: the Altaic group (Mongolian, Uighur, Kazakh, etc), the Tibeto-Burman group (Tibetan, Yi, etc.), the Tai group (Zhuang, Buyi, etc.) and Miao-Yao which constitute an isolated group.

Since the thirteenth century, the language spoken in the North has become, under the name of *guan hua*, 'x, , 'language of civil servants', a sort of administrative and intellectual lingua franca (it is what will be called 'mandarin' in the sixteenth century, based on a Portuguese word, *mandar*, to order). At the same time two written languages co-existed: *wen yan*,/¤¥ , 'character language', the written language of those in power, of administration, of the educated, that is, the socially dominant written language, and *bai yan*, ¥ ¤¥, 'white or easy language', very close to the written language of the North, in which all well-known novels and plays were written. In 1919, at the time of the movement of 4 May, an anti-*wen yan* movement was born (*wen yan* being perceived as an instrument of domination), along with a movement in favour of a *guo yu*, Œ»y 'national

[2] M. Coyaud, *Questions de grammaire chinoise* (Paris, 1969).

language', with the idea of marking the existence of a single China linguistically. It was this idea that was taken up after the Revolution of 1949, under the name of *pu tong hua*, ·¶‡q, , 'common language', the expression 'guo-yu' continuing to be used in Formosa. We shall now describe Chinese language policy since the Revolution as far as it concerns the Han languages and the minority languages, leaving for another chapter the problems involved in reform of the alphabet.

At the time of its foundation (1921), the Chinese Communist party adopted the principle of the right of minorities to autonomy and (this is what concerns us) their right to education in their own languages. After 1949 the preamble to the Constitution in fact stated that 'China is a unified multinational state', that 'each nation is free to enrich its language', while article 39 stipulated that the administration of autonomous regions should be carried out in the one or several languages of the region, and article 40 that it was necessary to aid national minorities in developing their culture. So much for the principles.

In reality, the language policy of the Chinese government varied considerably, as it followed the fluctuations of politics, and these variations can be considered under the headings of four major periods: 1949–1956, 1956–1965, the Cultural Revolution, and since 1976.

1949–1956: Linguistic Diversity

We have just seen that the Chinese Constitution guaranteed the rights, in particular the linguistic rights, of minorities. In this period there were two planning efforts. One, under the aegis of a Committee for the Reform of Minority Languages, established in 1951, worked on a census of the languages, their alphabet, and so on. The other, under the aegis of an Association for the Reform of Language (created ten days after the Revolution, it became in 1952 the Committee for Research into the Reform of Language, and in 1954 the Committee for the Reform of Language) worked on Chinese and resulted in October 1955 in two conferences, devoted respectively to the 'reform of the written language' and the 'standardization of modern Chinese'. It was from the second conference that the definition of a 'common language', Putonghua, emerged.

Throughout this period a number of minorities were aided in the development of teaching in their language, an alphabet (in general derived from the Latin alphabet) was given to languages without writing, reading and writing were taught, and the Institute of Minority Languages established groups of trained people from the autonomous regions, while in the regions of Han ethnic groups, teaching was given in local languages:

Cantonese in Canton, Shanghaiese in Shanghai, etc. It was on this second point that the conference of October 1955 changed things.

1956–1965: The Putonghua Programme

The common language, defined as consisting of the pronunciation of the Peking dialect, the syntax of the Northern dialects, and the vocabulary of modern literature in *Bai Hua* ('plain talk'), was henceforth to be the single language for teaching in the Han regions, and its promotion was to be considered a priority. On 6 February 1956 the 'Directives of the State Council regarding the promotion of the common language' were published. They referred to the action to be taken with regard to adults—the Minister of Education having himself published on 17 November 1955 a similar text concerning the action to be taken with regard to school-children.[3]

It was decided to teach language and literature in Putonghua from the beginning of the school year of 1956. Other subjects would also have to be taught in Putonghua, but this was delayed for two years, and this course of action was supported by the opening of an education centre for teachers in Peking, by the broadcasting of information on language in the press and on radio to help the teaching body. This programme, which mobilized resources and was accompanied by a reform of the alphabet which we shall discuss later (Chapter 15), did not however involve the minority groups, who during this period followed the policy begun in the preceding period, which was generally a policy of bilingual teaching.

Dayle Barnes[4] observes that speakers of Han languages other than Mandarin had more or less accepted the idea of bilingualism and that, in 1957, when this 'great movement of adjustment' was launched in the spirit of the 'hundred flowers', the Putonghua programme was not controversial. Even if those directing it thought that a common language ought to lead to the disappearance of dialects, people did not feel the promotion of Putongua necessarily led to the disappearance of their local languages. In the writing of Alexis Rygaloff, in 1973, we find an attempt at evaluating what the programme might bring about:

The history of this language is clearly not long enough to have produced noticeable effects. So we should take care not to suppose that dialects in Canton, Shanghai, Fuzhou are already giving way before the new national model. But even though there is a lack of authoritative information that would enable us to make a judgement on progress and determine how far the extreme diversity that existed

[3] Dayle Barnes, 'The Implementation of Language Planning in China', in J. Cobarrubias and J. Fishman (eds.), *Progress in Language Planning* (Berlin, 1983), 295.

[4] Ibid. 297.

before these attempts at unification has been undermined, it can be said that a very great majority of the Chinese population is well on the way to becoming bilingual. In principle, only the population of Peking are excepted from this.[5]

This hypothetical description corresponds quite well with the situation as it could be observed on the spot twelve years later. While carrying out research in Autumn 1985 into 224 students of the Bai Yun Shan campus, at the Institute of Foreign Languages in Canton, I observed that the majority did not have Putonghua as a first language, as is shown in Table 11.2 by replies to the question, 'at what age did you learn Putonghua?'

TABLE 11.2. *At what age did you learn Putonghua?*

At primary school	144
Putonghua the first language	49
At secondary school	12
At university	10
At nursery	9

1966–1976: The Cultural Revolution

During this period, for which it would be pointless to provide a general outline, as it is well known, the Putonghua programme continued (although schools and universities ran into a number of 'difficulties'), but, more importantly, the policy aimed at minority groups changed considerably. In the struggle against 'revisionism', the very idea of the autonomy of minority groups was considered by some as contrary to the unity of the party, their languages and customs were compared to bourgeois practices and the trained groups from the minority groups were largely purged.

In 1974, a delegation of American linguists was invited to China for a month's visit and, on their return, its members published an account of their meetings.[6] Some passages of this account illustrate the sudden change of direction in an interesting way. At the Central Institute for Nationalities, whose theoretical (and, before the Cultural Revolution, practical) aim was to work on national minorities, Professor Fei Xiao-tong explained to the delegation that 'the immediate goal of Chinese linguistics is the popularization of Putonghua'.[7] In a chapter devoted to the theory of

---

[5] Rygaloff, *Grammaire élémentaire du chinois*, 5–6.

[6] W. Lehmann (ed.), *Language and Linguistics in the People's Republic of China* (University of Texas, 1975).

[7] Ibid. 21.

language in China there is a reference to Stalin's old idea that the world victory of Socialism should lead to the emergence of a single international language.[8] Documentary evidence for this period is lacking, and it is not possible to see whether in this period it was thought that at first, before world victory, Putonghua would become China's only language. But it is easy to imagine that anything that came under minority particularism or nationalism had to be fought against with the same vigour as the traces of the Chinese past, such as the Confucian philosophy or religion. The same American linguists wrote that the department of languages of the Central Institute for Nationalities was training interpreters and translators for the minority languages. We learn in passing that, since the Cultural Revolution, courses on linguistics had been removed from the syllabus as too theoretical and, more importantly, that the interpreters being trained were in fact speakers of minority languages who were learning Putonghua. The single exception to this profile was made up of several Han speakers who, according to the authors, were studying Tibetan,[9] which confirms the general impression: on the pretext of training interpreters, Putonghua was in fact being taught to students who did not speak it, that is, the official language was being spread more than speakers of local languages were being trained. The exception in the case of Tibetan is to be explained by the very special attention that central government was paying to Tibet.

Since 1976

The death of Mao Zedong, then the arrest of the 'gang of four' and the return to power of Deng Xiao Ping, brought about the same disorder in the domain of languages as elsewhere. The Putonghua programme continued, and was even expanded by the use of television, but the national minorities rediscovered the prerogatives they had lost, more and more books and dictionaries were published, research increased, and so on.

We can imagine, then, that the model of society at the end of this process is one of a general bilingualism (except for the people of the North whose first language corresponds more or less to the national language), which can come in two types:

First, there is a 'Sino-Chinese' or Han bilingualism, between Putonghua and a Han 'dialect'. This is the case in Canton and Shanghai, for example, and we can wonder how long these languages, which are no longer taught in school, will be able to resist Putonghua, even if they do not appear to be threatened for the moment. This bilingualism covers

[8] W. Lehmann (ed.), *Language and Linguistics in the People's Republic of China* (University of Texas, 1975), 133.   [9] Ibid. 110.

about 25% of the population (1,008,200,000 inhabitants according to the 1982 census).

Secondly, there is a 'Sino-minority' bilingualism, where the first language is a minority language, Kazak, Korean, Tibetan, etc. In these cases, it seems that the future of the languages is more assured, not only because they are taught and used for administration, in conjunction with Putonghua, but especially because all these national minorities, who occupy 50% of Chinese territory and are situated on the margins of the empire, are in a sensitive geographical position, on the frontiers of the former USSR and because those in power do not particularly want to upset them. This bilingualism covers 5 to 6% of the population.

So it does not look as if China, confronted by its own multilingualism, has sought to change this into monolingualism, if an exception is made of the interlude of the Cultural Revolution. The national minorities have a bilingual development and it is the Chinese 'dialects' which are most threatened by the Putonghua programme. We shall see this more clearly when we treat the problems of writing.

The Case of India

According to the census of 1951, 782 different languages and dialects were spoken in India, a number which mounted to 1,652 in the census of 1961. The difference between these two totals does not really mean that the number of languages doubled in ten years (!), but provides a good example of the difficulties to be overcome in drawing up an inventory of the languages spoken in a given territory. On the one hand, the 1961 census took into account 103 languages which were not included in 1951; on the other hand, the simple fact of asking people what their language is sometimes poses a problem, and finally the number of languages listed, whatever that number is, does not mean much: many of these languages might have very few speakers. This is the case with India, as Mahadev Apte emphasizes:

For several hundred of these mother tongues there are very few speakers. For example, there are altogether 64,432 speakers for 527 languages. As many as 210 of these have no more than one or two speakers each. Another category of 400 languages has a total of 426,076 speakers. Quite often a single mother tongue gets enumerated under several slightly different names. People often give the names of their castes, localities, or occupations when asked about their mother tongues.[10]

[10] Mahadev Apte, 'Multilingualism and its Socio-Political Implications: An Overview', in W. O'Barr and J. O'Barr (eds.), *Language and Politics* (The Hague, 1976), 141–2.

Be that as it may, and whatever the real number of languages in India, the country presents us with an astonishing multilingualism, in both multiplicity of languages and of kinds of language. There are Indo-European languages like Hindi, Gujerati, Kashmiri (73% of the population), Dravidian languages like Telegu or Tamil (24%), Austro-Asiatic languages (1.5%), and Sino-Tibetan languages (0.7%), with Hindi being on its own the first language of about 30% of the population. This multilingualism is complicated by the fact that, despite the multiplicity of competing languages, Indians are, individually, rarely multilingual. In 1961 for example, 7% of the population, that is, 30 million people, declared a knowledge of a second language (English for 11 million, Hindi for 9 million) which simply means that India had no lingua franca capable of unifying the country linguistically.

To understand the present situation, we have to go back to the history of the nineteenth century. The centre and north of the country experienced a violent religious conflict between Muslims and Hindus, which was paralleled by linguistic and political conflict. The Hindus, who mostly spoke Hindi, were more modernist in their politics; they were not opposed to the anglicization of the country's elites and attempted to get the British authorities to recognize their language in the same way as Urdu, the Muslim language, which was already used in the courts.

Paradoxically, these two languages were mutually comprehensible and their differences were much more to do with human action than with their nature. Urdu, written in the Arabic alphabet, had borrowed extensively from Arabic and Persian, while Hindi was written in Devanagari, the alphabet of Sanskrit, a language from which it had borrowed extensively. As the Muslims had adopted a hostile position since the beginning of the British presence, it was the Hindus who made some gains, as for example, the replacement of Urdu by Hindi as state language in Bihar in 1861. In fact their objective was to have their language adopted in all the central and north-eastern provinces, and a petition which circulated through the 1880s gives an idea of the tone of the campaign: 'No gentleman would ever condescend to educate . . . females in Urdu or Persian, because books written in these languages are generally obscene and tend to have a demoralising effect on the character'.[11]

In fact, only the highly Sanskrit form of Hindi and the highly Persian form of Urdu are poles between which communication does not take

---

[11] Quoted by J. Das Gupta, *Language Conflict and National Development* (Berkeley, 1970), 103.

place, due to major lexical differences, but there was a popular form, covering variants of Urdu and Hindi, Hindustani, which could have served as a unifying language for the north of the country. Gandhi attempted to play this card. He had Hindustani adopted as the official language of his party, the Indian National Congress, in 1925, and he was followed in this by Nehru, who declared in 1937 that the language 'would bring Hindi and Urdu closer together and will also help in developing an all-India linguistic unity'.[12] But this solution met opposition both from extremist Hindus and Muslims and from all the people of the South, speakers of Dravidian languages, for whom Hindi, Urdu, and Hindustani were all equally foreign languages. So the debate (linguistic and political) was centred around the opposition between two political tendencies, the Hindu tendency represented by the National Congress and the Muslim tendency represented by the Muslim League. This conflict found a half-solution at the time of independence, in Partition (the creation of Pakistan, an Islamic republic, where Urdu is the national language).

But the existence of Pakistan did not resolve India's language problems. The first sittings of the Constituent Assembly, which met in 1946, took place in English and Hindustani, while a huge campaign in favour of Hindi was organized, with the Hindus arguing that Hindustani was a concession to Urdu, that is, to the Muslims. In 1949 a parliamentary vote revealed the precariousness of the situation, since 78 deputies voted for Hindi and 77 for Hindustani. But this Hindu/Hindustani problem, a continuation of the Hindi/Urdu problem, hid from view another problem, mentioned above, the problem of the whole south of the country where the leading languages were Kannada, Tamil, and Telugu. The Constitution adopted delaying tactics: English would remain the official language of the Union for fifteen years and would then be replaced (in 1963) by Hindi, while the different states could choose their official language.

This set the Union on the way to redrawing the boundaries of the states on linguistic grounds. It was in 1952 that a Communist deputy from Bengal put down a motion aiming to adjust state frontiers according to the language situation, a motion which was rejected by 261 votes to 77. But the political situation in the south was difficult. A certain Potti Shri Ramulu, who undertook a hunger-strike in order to obtain the creation of a Telugu state, died at the end of 1952. The violent disturbances that followed forced the government to vote through, in August 1953, the

---

[12] Ibid. 112.

creation of the state of Andra Pradesh, whose official language is Telugu.[13]
Thereafter, different states of the Union adopted different official languages and today there are, for 28 states and territories, twelve different official languages: English, Assam, Bengali, French, Gujerati, Hindi, Marathi, Oriya, Panjabi, Tamil, Telugu, and Urdu.

The situation is therefore extremely complex, for these official state languages are not necessarily spoken by the whole of the population, as Table 11.3 shows.[14]

So we have a local situation on different levels, where it is possible to find, paradoxically, states where few speak the official language (Urdu in Jammu and Kashmir, Hindi in Rajasthan) and where, between State and Union, there can be three official languages, to which may be added the several other languages spoken.

There was still the problem of the Union's language and the 1963 decision that the Constitution had imposed upon itself. In fact, the situation in the southern States made the adoption of Hindi as single official language impossible and an Official Language Act was voted through in 1963, stipulating that English would remain alongside Hindi as official language, a law which was reinforced by a 1967 amendment: English would keep its place for an unlimited period.

The Case of Guinea

In 1958, when General de Gaulle offered French territories a referendum on whether to join a new federal community, Guinea was the only country in Africa to vote 'no' and prefer independence. Guinea is also unique in having chosen a language policy of 'decolonization'; unlike all the other African countries previously colonized by France (I am not speaking here of the countries of North Africa), it very quickly promoted African languages to the rank of national languages, to be used for the training of adults and in education. For this reason and for others more directly political, Guinea has played an important role in Africa for twenty years, and for many Africans opposed to the policy of their own countries, Sekou Touré, the chief of state, was the symbol of the struggle against neo-colonialism. This is why the analysis of this language policy has especial interest.

[13] Mahadev Apte, 'Language Controversies in the Indian Parliament: 1952–1960', in *Language and Politics*, 216–17.
[14] According to the 'Eleventh Report of the Commissioner for Linguistic Minorities', quoted by Apte, 161, 163, 190.

TABLE 11.3.

Name	Official language	Principal local language (%)	Principal minority languages (%)
States			
1. Andhra Pradesh	Telegu	Telegu (85.9)	Urdu (7.1) Lambadi (1.62) Tamil (1.55)
2. Assam	Assamese	Assamese (57.14)	Bengali (17.6) Hindi (4.4) Bodo (2.9)
3. Bihar	Hindi	Hindi (44.3)	Bihari (35.39) Urdu (8.93) Santali (3.57)
4. Gujarat	Gujarati and Hindi	Gujarati (90.5)	Urdu (2.8) Sindhi (2.42) Bhili (1.34)
5. Haryana	Hindi	Hindi (88.6)	Punjabi (8.1) Urdu (2.77)
6. Himachal Pradesh	Hindi	None	Pahadi (38.4) Hindi (10.6) Mardeali (16.7)
7. Jammu and Kashmir	Urdu	Kashmiri (54.4)	Dogri (24.4) Pahar (6.84)
8. Kerala	English	Malayalam (95.04)	Tamil (3.12)
9. Madhya Pradesh	Hindi	Hindi (78.07)	Rajasthani (4.9) Marathi (3.8) Gondi (3.2)
10. Maharashtra	Marathi	Marathi (76.5)	Urdu (6.8) Hindi (3.1) Gujarati (2.7)
11. Mizoram	English	Kannada (65.1)	Telegu (8.6) Urdu (8.6) Marathi (4.5)
12. Nagaland	English	None	Konyak Ao (15.4) Sema (12.8) Angamai (11.4)
13. Orissa	Oriya and English	Oriya (82.3)	Kui (2.9) Telegu (2.2) Santhali (2.1)
14. Punjab	Punjabi	Punjabi (67.2)	Hindi (35.2)

TABLE 11.3. *Continued*

Name	Official language	Principal local language (%)	Principal minority languages (%)
15. Rajasthan	Hindi	Rajasthani (56.49)	Hindi (33.32) Bhili (4.13) Urdu (2.5)
16. Tamil Nadu	Tamil	Tamil (83.1)	Telegu (9.9) Kannada (2.8) Urdu (1.8)
17. Uttar Pradesh	Hindi	Hindi (85.3)	Urdu (10.7) Kumauni (1.3) Garhwali (1)
18. West Bengal	Bengali	Bengali (84.28)	Hindi (5.4) Santhali (3.27) Urdu (2.3)
Territories			
1. Andaman and Nicobar Islands	English and Hindi	None	Nicobar (21.9) Begali (21.8) Malayalam (10.5)
2. Chandigarh	English	No figures	
3. Dadra and Nagar Haveli	English	Varli (51.47)	Gujarati (19.5) Konkani (12.9) Dhodia (6.9)
4. Delhi	Hindi and English	Hindi (77.3)	Punjabi (11.9) Urdu (5.7) Bengali (1.3)
5. Goa, Daman, and Diu	English	Konkani (88.8)	Gujarati (5.5) Marathi (1.8) Urdu (1.5)
6. Lakshadweep	English	Malayalam (83)	Mahl (16.7)
7. Manipur	English	Manipuri (64.46)	Tangkhul (5.6) Thado (3.6) Mao (3.6)
8. Pondicherry	English and French	Tamil (88.2)	Malayalam (5.6) Telegu (4.4)
9. Tripura	Bengali	Bengali (65.2)	Tripuri (24.8) Manipuri (2.4)

TABLE 11.4. *Main languages spoken in Guinea with number of speakers*

Fulani (Peul)	1,200,000
Malinka	750,000
Susu	650,000
Loma (Toma)	350,000
Kpelle	300,000
Kisie	250,000
Basari	75,000
Koniagi	60,000
Baga	40,000
Nalou	25,000
Toubakay	20,000
Landouma	15,000
Lele	15,000
Dialonka	10,000
Yola	4,500
Mikifore	4,000
Kono	3,000
Konianke	2,500
Mandenyi	2,000
Tomamian	2,000

According to the census carried out in 1982 under the auspices of the World Bank, there are in Guinea about twenty African languages (see Table 11.4).

The figures above relate to first languages, and it should also be noted that three of the languages in this table, Fulani, Malinka, Susu, have a role as regional lingua francas. It was the eight languages most widely spoken that the Guinea Democratic Party chose as national languages for their launch, from 1962 onwards, of a language-planning operation in two areas, adult education and schools.

Adult Education

Four successive literacy campaigns were pushed forward in the eight national languages. The first two, in 1962 and 1964, were entirely control-led by the Guinean state, the third, in 1970, was launched with the help of UNESCO. This was the period when, after its congress in Tehran, the international organization decided to change its policy towards literacy. In order to avoid the return to illiteracy that had been discovered when a number of campaigns had been evaluated, it was decided to promote *functional literacy*. The principles are quite simple: to teach literacy in the mother tongue or in a regional language that the adult already speaks (which was not always the case beforehand: people were taught to read and write in English or French, though Guinea was an exception) and to link this teaching to economic development. So, for example, growers of millet would learn reading, writing, and new agricultural techniques at the same time, and they would continue to use their new knowledge after the campaign, since they would continue to receive brochures, technical manuals on the cultivation of millet, manure, the plough, etc., at the same time as, in some cases, newspapers, radio programmes, and the like.

But the country's policies in foreign affairs came into conflict with the necessities of the literacy campaign. In 1971 Guinea broke off diplomatic relations with UNESCO, and the campaign launched the previous year had scarcely any effect. It was taken up again in 1973, but it seems without great success (there has been no reliable evaluation of any of the four campaigns).

Schools

Educational reform was begun in 1968: education was given entirely in the regional language, that is, one of the eight chosen languages, in the first year of primary school. The plan consisted of advancing each year by one year, so as to cover the whole of the primary-school years by 1974. At the same time, French was introduced as a taught subject at the rate of four hours per week, from the third year. Then secondary education was given in French, with the national languages remaining as taught subjects and no longer as teaching languages.

In fact, this programme soon encountered several difficulties. First of all the training of teachers caused a problem. Existing teachers had been educated in French and it was necessary to teach them to read and write a national language, and then to teach them grammar and arithmetic in this language, while young teachers had to be trained within a very short time. Specialized colleges of education were opened, with responsibility for providing the teachers needed, but another problem got in the way, a lack of teaching materials. The only printer in Conakry, the capital, was overwhelmed and the manuscripts prepared by researchers in education often remained as manuscripts, in desk drawers. By 1978, the programme for the introduction of national languages into schools was four years behind. It was decided to reduce the number of teaching languages from eight to six, by the suppression of Basari and Koniagi for which there was a lack of qualified teachers. In 1983, these six languages were introduced into the second year of secondary education, although according to the original plan, this should have taken place in 1976: the plan was running eight years late. Along the way, yet another difficulty was encountered, the dialectical diversity of the languages. So an Academy of Languages was created in 1972, with particular responsibility for working on the problem of the unification of dialectical forms.

It was in this general context of relative failure that in 1984 the sudden death of Sekou Touré occurred. In the reaction against abuses of power which followed, the new rulers decided to return to education entirely in French. The Academy of Languages was now instructed simply to work on the hypothesis of a single national language for the unification of the country, which would be adopted after an interval for consideration lasting six years, that is, in 1990.

We shall not discuss here these new decisions by the government of Guinea, but we shall try to survey the reasons for the failure, for it is quite obvious that if Sekou Touré's language policy had succeeded, his successors would have left it alone.

First of all, there were technical reasons: the absence of written materials for adults, and the scarcity of school books meant that the planning advanced in a void, without solid foundations; it was the same for the teachers and instructors of literacy, who had received insufficient training; finally, linguistic reform was perhaps begun too quickly, without carrying out preliminary language studies (description and transcription of languages, dealing with dialectical variants, etc.).

But there are perhaps more important political reasons for the failure, since if really necessary it is possible to teach without books, without blackboards, without exercise books, but it is difficult to go against the views of parents and teachers. The country was emerging from a long period in which French had always been the language that enabled a rise in social status; even if it was a rise for individuals and not groups as a whole, it was still visible, tangible success. The pupils' parents in particular all knew that their children could not obtain qualifications and 'succeed' in life without being able to handle French correctly. The introduction of national languages into schools therefore required a campaign of explanation which did not take place and neither the pupils' parents, nor the teachers, nor the elites were convinced of the merits of the reform. If it is added to this that the division of the country into eight (then six) language zones posed technical problems for those, like civil servants for example, who had to move around the country for professional reasons and whose children might have to change teaching language, it can be seen that the government was the victim of excessive haste and a bureaucratic notion of language planning. In this respect, there is much to learn from the experience of Guinea, even if it did not in the end advance the cause of African languages, since the gulf between the hopes that some placed in it and the results obtained was so large.

Discussion

The language policies of China, India, and Guinea, which we have just described, have a number of points in common.

In all three cases, the state was confronted by a multilingual territory, and in all three cases we can discern a tendency to the creation of monolingualism. Guinea, having tried to organize a state with eight, then six national languages, is moving towards the choice of a single language; for a long time India has dreamt of establishing Hindi as the sole national language; and China, while respecting minority languages, is trying to institute a Putonghua monolingualism in the Han majority. In other words, underlying these language policies is the idea that the state is embodied in one nation and this nation in turn is embodied in one language.

Also, in all three cases, there is the confirmation of a distinction between the state and the nations it includes, which is in contradiction with the tendency to monolingualism that I have just emphasized. This is clear in Guinea where a distinction is made between the official language and the national languages (the eight then six African languages retained); it is also clear in China where a co-existence between the state language, Putonghua, and the languages of the national minorities, is being slowly established, and in India where there is a distinction between the two official languages of the Union (English and Hindi) and the languages of the different states and territories. This contradiction is the result of two forces which do not necessarily work in the same direction, the *in vivo* management of multilingualism, which we discussed in the previous chapters, and the *in vitro* management of this multilingualism, management by planners. In other words, language policies reveal a double conflict: on the one hand, a conflict between social practice and state power, on the other, a conflict between language frontiers and state frontiers. We have here a kind of language war which we shall call 'internal', a war which sets languages against each other within the framework of a single state. And, behind this language war, we can see a struggle for power, with the language of the capital, or of the dominant ethnic group, attempting to impose itself as the only language, excluding others, and with speakers attempting to impose their culture upon others.

In the cases of Guinea and India, that is, in situations of decolonization, there can also be found the search for a linguistic individuality that is free of any trace of linguistic colonialism. Whatever the differences between the two situations, the project is in effect the same, to demonstrate that it is possible to establish a modern state without French or English, to found it, as far as the structures of communication are concerned, on one or more local languages. In this respect, however, these countries are hardly being innovative since they are attempting to reproduce a model imported by the colonial powers they wish to free themselves from, a model of the monolingual state. Here again we find a distinction we introduced earlier between practice and symbol: in India English remains the official language for practical reasons, while for symbolic reasons there has been an attempt to replace it with Hindi.

Another interesting point, in comparing our three examples, is the moment at which the problem of language planning began to arise: at the time of the revolutionary movements of 1919 in China, then after the revolution of 1949; at the time of the British occupation in India, then at the time of independence; at the time of independence in Guinea.

That is to say, the language problem does not arise in a void, but emerges either in the context of the establishing of the state, or in the context of resistance to a foreign power. Once again, the war of languages is nothing but the linguistic aspect of a wider war. And if we take the key date of the official appearance of the state (through independence or revolution) as our reference point, we shall see that Guinea is different

TABLE 11.5. *Emergence of the language question*

	Before the birth of the state	After the birth of the state
Practical problems	How to address the people, make propaganda, campaign for independence	Managing political life, education, general emancipation, reduction of minorities, secure state power
Symbolic problems	How to assert national identity, oppose colonialism	Reinforce national unity, mark one's frontiers

from the other two countries in that the linguistic problem was posed after the establishment of the state, while in China and India it was posed beforehand. All this can be easily summarized in a small table.

So, as far as China is concerned, the claim made for a 'guo yu' in 1919 was a case of symbolism, but the Putonghua programme after 1949 was practical, even if, linguistically speaking, these two notions are synonymous, and relate to the same language. In India, the opposition between Hindi and Urdu, or the pro-Hindustani positions of Gandhi and Nehru were symbolic before independence, but the debates of the Constituent Assembly on the language of the Union were eminently practical. This link between the language question and the state question, illustrated here by examples where in the end some provision had to be made for multilingualism, shows us how important an issue language is. Despite the tendency displayed by all three countries to respect local languages and diversity, there emerges a stronger inclination, the impulse of those in power towards monolingualism: to impose one's own language on those under one's administration.

12

Case Studies: Language Planning and Nationalism

We shall now discuss the cases of Norway and Turkey, where the problem is not so much how to deal with multilingualism (even if these countries are not really monolingual, with Kurdish in Turkey, and Lapp in Norway), but how to deal with the language itself. In both cases we encounter the same political desire to shape the national language in order to shape the country. We shall see how an idea of the nation is constructed through action upon the language.

The Case of Norway

As in the previous examples, the origin of the Norwegian language problem is a political event. After three centuries (from 1523 to 1814) of domination over Norway, Denmark, which had been involved in the Napoleonic Wars on the side of Great Britain, was obliged by Bernadotte to abandon this domination and give way to Sweden (the Treaty of Kiel, 1814). Denmark had, however, tried a last-minute manoeuvre to avoid this loss of sovereignty, and granted Norway an extremely liberal constitution, called the 'Eidsvold constitution' and a parliament, the *storting*. These provisions, which Sweden accepted, led to the debates we shall now discuss.

E. Haugen, whose work on the Norwegian situation is authoritative, distinguishes five varieties of language at this period:

1. *Pure Danish*, used by some immigrants and above all in the theatre, which had been dominated by Danish actors.
2. *Literary standard*, that is, Danish pronounced with a Norwegian accent, primarily used by teachers in schools and in church by pastors.
3. *Colloquial standard*, the daily speech of the educated classes, a compromise between the preceding and the following types.
4. *Urban sub-standard*, spoken by the people, varying from city to city.

5. *Rural dialect*, spoken by peasants and fishermen, varying from one parish to another.[1]

Speakers of the language types at either extreme of this classification did not understand each other, that is, a peasant speaking his rural dialect and a teacher speaking the standard literary language were unable to communicate. On the other hand, there was mutual communication between each level and the following or preceding type.

So the linguistic trace of the long Danish domination co-existed with the diversity of the people's Norwegian dialects. The nationalist elites wished to bring about a unification of the country by language, in order to mark the difference between what was Danish and what was Norwegian. Two approaches to the problem quickly came into conflict. On the one hand, Knud Knudsen (1812–1895) proposed that the foundation should be the spoken language of city people, *byfolkets talesprog* and that the pronunciation of Danish should be Norwegianized in order to move towards a 'nationwide Norwegian pronunciation', *den landsgyldige norske uttale*. On the other hand, Ivar Aasen (1813–1896) proposed that the foundation should be the rural dialects which he considered to be the heirs of old Norwegian, and he devoted several works to the grammar and lexis of this language, to which he gave different names: the language of our common people ('vort almuesprog'), the true language of the Norwegian people ('det rette norske folksprog'), the national language ('national sprog'), Norwegian national language ('norskje landsmaal') and, finally, Norwegian ('norsk'). It was in fact the term 'landsmaal' (country language) which came to designate what was then only an idea of a language, an approach perfectly defined by the ambiguity in Norwegian of the word 'land' which, like 'country' in English can refer to the countryside as well as the nation. It was around this notion that those 'of the left' in Norway mobilized; it meant for them fighting for the linguistic unification of the Norwegian nation and against the linguistic superiority of the dominant classes.

In contrast, the partisans of Knud Knudsen mobilized around the idea of 'rigsmaal', national language (a word created on the model of the German 'reichssprache'), that is, the standard literary language which its adversaries mockingly christened 'dansk' or 'dansk–norsk' (Danish or Danish–Norwegian). So, at the end of the nineteenth and beginning of the twentieth centuries, the country was troubled by a conflict between the alternatives *landsmaal/rigsmaal*.

---

[1] E. Haugen, *Language Conflict and Language Planning: The Case of Modern Norwegian* (Cambridge, Mass.: Harvard University Press, 1966).

The debate very quickly concentrated on problems of the alphabet: how to distance the orthography of *rigsmaal* from the orthography of Danish and bring it closer to *landsmaal*. So, from 1905 onwards, the date when Norway finally achieved independence through dissolution of its union with Sweden, language commissions succeeded each other and reforms of orthography voted through by parliament came at a steady rate (1907, 1913, 1916, 1923, 1934, 1936, etc.). Haugen, for example, comments on the 1923 situation thus: 'Two bold orthographic reforms within a decade had given Norwegian *rigsmaal* a completely new face, which could not easily mistaken for Danish'.[2]

But differentiating *rigsmaal* clearly from Danish was only part of the aim; the other scheme, that of unifying Norway linguistically, remained. For the linguistic translation of the social division still persisted: on one side the dominant classes using a standard language quite close to the written language (*rigsmaal*), and on the other, the lower classes using a form closer to local speech (*landsmaal*). Although somewhat schematic, this description is not far from reality. In any case, it was adopted by the Norwegian Communist Party who, in the 1930s, played an important role and continued to repeat that the struggle for a language of the people was part of the class struggle.

For, throughout the history of Norway, the language debate is inseparable from political debate. Since the first writings of Knudsen and Aasen, the two linguistic poles of which we have spoken have often changed their names: *dansk/norsk*, *rigsmaal/landsmaal*, *bogssprog/landsmaal*, *bokmaal/landsmaal*, and finally, today, *bokmal/nynorsk*, but this pairing has always represented the same political opposition between two approaches, which can be crudely described as a right-wing and a left-wing approach to nationalism. So the reform of the alphabet, voted through in 1938, when the Communists were well represented in parliament, was abolished in 1941 under the German occupation, accused of 'introducing the dictatorship of the proletariat into the domain of language', then re-established in 1945, after liberation.

The following anecdote gives a good illustration of the climate. In 1959, André Bjerke translated into Norwegian the musical comedy by Alan Jay Lerner, *My Fair Lady*, adapted from Shaw's *Pygmalion*. To show the contrast between the cultivated English of Professor Higgins and the 'vulgar' cockney of Eliza Doolittle, he used on the one hand Bokmal (the book language) and on the other, Nynorsk (the folk speech of Oslo). The

[2] Ibid. 103.

linguistic situation in Norway was perfectly suited to such a transposition. But, in the programme for the play, the translator wrote an introduction which relaunched the controversy: 'In Norway we have the paradoxical situation that Professor Higgins is being instructed by Eliza Doolittle on how he is supposed to write and speak his mother tongue correctly. In this country, Eliza Doolittle is not in the gutter, selling wild blossoms; she is in the Language Commission, circulating language blemishes.' It can be seen that Bjerke is in favour of Bokmal, and he specifies, in a very provocative manner, that his principal written source for Eliza's language had been a work on standards published in 1957. An example will demonstrate the extent of the controversy. Where the English text has Higgins saying: 'This is what the British population | Calls an elementary education' he translated: 'Her i Landet Kalles denne talen | For den nye laereboknormalen' (In our country this speech is called the new textbook norm).[3]

To repeat, the whole debate that I have just summarized is a debate between elites: in 1946, a Gallup poll aimed at capturing the opinion of Norwegians on the language problem found that 80% of the population were in favour of amalgamation of the two languages, and that 75% thought this amalgamation should take Bokmal as its basis. In other words, discussion of the language problem, however democratic, did not really reflect the 'spontaneous' beliefs of the population, who were more interested in standards and less anti-Danish than the planners.

The Case of Turkey

The Turkish 'language revolution' (*dil devrimi*) was also the by-product of political events.[4] In 1923 Mustafa Kemal was elected President of the Republic, supported by a nationalist, secular, and anti-Ottoman movement, and he launched into a series of measures aimed at modernizing the country. We shall consider here only the measures that concerned language and made up the 'language revolution'. At the time Turkish was written in Arabic characters and the official form, the one used by the elites, was full of borrowings from Arabic and Persian, which made it practically incomprehensible to a large majority of the population. Mustafa Kemal then launched the country into a great reform of the language, and his course of action was underlined by a number of decisions, of which an incomplete list is given below.

---

[3] E. Haugen, 265 et seq.

[4] I am here using primarily L. Bazin, 'La Réforme linguistique en Turquie', in *La Réforme des langues, histoire et avenir*, i (Hamburg: Buske Verlag, 1966).

- The founding, in the summer of 1928, of a language commission with responsibility for perfecting a new alphabet. The reason given was that Arabic characters transcribed the sounds of Turkish quite inadequately. For example, the eight short vowels and the three long vowels of the language could not be rendered by the three vowels of Arabic and the same character, the Arabic waw, served for o, ö, u, ü and v.[5] The Commission therefore established an alphabet called Turkish, using Latin letters and transcribing phonetically and with great precision the phonemes of the spoken language.
- This alphabet was established by the National Assembly in December 1928 and immediately used in education, then spread by the civil service which progressively replaced the old alphabet on its printed forms with the new one. The operation was completed by June 1930.
- The suppression in 1929 of the teaching of Arabic and Persian in schools.
- The requirement, from 1931, that the Koran be read in Turkish and no longer in Arabic. This was a logical consequence of the preceding measure, but for an orthodox Muslim it represented a real heresy, since the text of the holy book had been dictated by God in the chosen language.
- The founding in 1932 of a 'Society for the Study of the Turkish Language' (Türk Dil Kurumu), with responsibility for beginning a 'purification' of the language, that is, to replace words based on borrowed words with others based on Turkish etymons. The Society looked for old words that had gone out of use, words from living dialects, even words borrowed from languages in the same linguistic family, such as Azerbaijani. This research relied extensively on the goodwill of people ('scholars, professors, teachers, civil servants, officers', writes Bazin) who sent thousands of index-cards to the Society for the Study of the Turkish Language that were then carefully sorted and published. In 1934, a volume of 1,300 pages based on the analysis of 125,000 index-cards was published (*Tamara Dergisi*) which was followed from 1939 by a *Söz Derleme Dergisi*.
- The promulgation in June 1934 of a law requiring citizens to take a name of Turkish origin. It was on this occasion that Mustafa Kemal, leading by example, took the patronym of Ataturk, 'father of Turkey'.
- The publication of dictionaries of ancient and modern Turkish or of other languages in the same group (Kirghiz, Yakut), of grammars and

[5] Ibid. 162–3.

textbooks recording the reforms, of popularizing works for the public, etc.

It can be seen how radical and provocative this reform was in an Islamic country. Ataturk's aim was not only linguistic, and this 'revolution' was of course the linguistic translation of a secular, modernist, and anti-Ottoman struggle. It remains a fact that it transformed the language, and L. Bazin notes that 'even when transcribed from the former Arabo-Turkish system into the new Turkish–Latin alphabet, Ottoman texts of the last period are, in the great majority, incomprehensible to a Turk of less than sixty who has not followed specialized courses (at university level)'.[6] From this point of view, the experience of the Turkish 'language revolution' is unique in the history of language planning.

Discussion

Norway and Turkey have this in common, then, that a campaign has been fought over language, but a campaign that goes well beyond language, to reveal national policy.

If Norwegian language policy aimed, unsuccessfully, at establishing a single national language, this is because the language was considered to have two functions, to unify and to differentiate. Before being Norwegian, that is, before unifying the country, the language which has been confusedly sought since Knudsen or Aasen had, first of all, to be not Danish. It had to mark the country's difference. This desire to assert oneself through differentiation, which was first of all applied to the writing system, with the idea of imposing Norwegian pronunciation on the transcription of the language, shows that a political campaign can take the *form* of the language itself as its terrain. The Turkish 'language revolution' is a perfect example of this. We have already said that the Turks' action on language, which transformed it in a very short time, should be interpreted as the linguistic side of a modernization policy based both on opposition to the remains of the Ottoman empire and on a desire for secularity. So in this reform a really heavy blow was struck against Islamic tradition: the change of alphabet, the suppression of courses in Arabic and Persian in schools, the reading of the Koran in Turkish— all of this could not but be perceived by religious people as deliberate aggression.

[6] I am here using primarily L. Bazin, 'La Réforme linguistique en Turquie', in *La Réforme des langues, histoire et avenir*, i (Hamburg: Buske Verlag, 1966), 155.

But what we can learn from the two preceding case studies is much wider in scope and much more general, as we shall see below.

The first point concerns the relationship between nationalism and language policy. In both cases, a particular notion of the country appears behind the reform of language; in both cases, there was a desire to reinforce the country's foundations by strengthening the language's foundations. Norway wished to assert its existence as separate from Denmark, Turkey wanted to break with its Ottoman past. If the goal was the same, the means, however, were very different. The high number of successive reforms adopted by the Norwegian parliament shows that the country managed its planning democratically: public discussion, parliamentary debates, votes. In contrast to these debates and hesitations, these turnings back of the clock, the Turkish 'language revolution' seemed to go on its way without being halted by any obstacle, and it is a fact that the language situation in Turkey developed more quickly in fifteen years than in Norway over 150 years. Such efficiency has a price, however, and this is exactly the difference from Norway. In Turkey we have extremely rigorous management of language planning. Whatever Mustafa Kemal's modernism, however great an appeal was made to the population, in particular for the collection of new words, his methods of government were extremely authoritarian. Only a strong power can make such a deep impression on the language and in such a short time.

In the preceding chapter, in particular with regard to India and Guinea, we saw that language policies which aimed at influencing multilingualism were in the end influenced by the facts and led into confirming the difference, which was otherwise often denied, between state and nation, into establishing a difference between the official language and national languages. Here it is evident that with both Norway and Turkey, we have the opposite situation: the idea that there is a correspondence between state and nation, a double equation, state = nation = language, and also the idea that it is possible to act upon the nation-state by acting upon the language. At the same time, these language policies shed a strong light upon what lies behind nationalism, except that hatred, racism, and the rejection of others are manifested here not in relation to the colour of a person's skin but in relation to lexical borrowings, rules of writing, pronunciation, alphabets, etc.: a war of languages.

Another point of similarity between the two policies is the notion of linguistic 'purity'. In both cases, we find the same search for linguistic authenticity, for a line of descent from the ancestors. When Mustafa Kemal decides to clear the language of its Arabo-Persian vocabulary, to seek out authentically Turkish words to replace these borrowings, we have a sort of return to the source which, as L. Bazin underlines, is not without ambiguity.

By 'Turkish' the workers of the 'language revolution' meant any language, ancient or modern, belonging to the Turkish family: from the language of the Orkhon inscriptions to the living speech of Turkestan, the Caucasus, the Volga, Siberia, etc., via Uighur and Chaghatay, without forgetting, of course, Anatolian and Balkan dialects.[7]

Aasen's researches on rural dialects and old Norwegian adopted the same approach, as was the desire to found a new orthography upon an authentically Norwegian pronunciation, that is, as we saw, a non-Danish pronunciation. This search for lexical 'purification' depends upon two principles, both of which are open to dispute. The first, which I shall call the Antiquarian principle, consists in believing that purity is a function of age: 'the older, the better'. The second consists in believing that purity is a function of indigenousness: 'the more it originates from here, the better'. But even before we question these two principles, the very notion of purity itself is open to dispute, and we shall return to it in a later chapter devoted more particularly to the influence of language policies upon vocabulary.

But, above all, the two examples we have just described give a complete panorama of the different domains in which language planning will intervene when it attempts to act upon language:

– Writing: whether it is a question of modifying the orthography or of changing the alphabet, as in the Turkish or Norwegian case, or of providing languages previously not written down with an alphabet, as in many countries (in particular in Africa) the problem of writing is at the centre of many language policies, and a chapter will be devoted to it later (The war of writing).

– Lexis: the problem approached in Turkey was, as we saw, primarily one of 'purification', of a return to the source, but language policies are more often confronted with the problem of modernizing the vocabulary, of adapting the language to areas of communication (science, teaching, etc.) for which it has not previously been used, that is, the problem of neologisms and word-borrowings to which a chapter will also be devoted (the war of words).

---

[7] I am here using primarily L. Bazin, 'La Réforme linguistique en Turquie', in *La Réforme des langues, histoire et avenir*, i (Hamburg: Buske Verlag, 1966), 167.

- Dialects: when a previously subordinate language acquires the status of official or national language, the problem of dialect variants often arises, and the example of Landsmaal is good evidence for the difficulties that may be encountered when an attempt is made to unify divergent forms, to standardize the unifying language. In the Norwegian example, this search took place in an ideological atmosphere influenced by German Romanticism, by the idea that the people are the carriers of linguistic authenticity. Elsewhere there is a tendency to impose the dialect of the capital, or of the social or ethnic group in power, but in all cases, whatever the principle of standardization, whatever the criterion chosen to decide what the official form of the language will be, we find an attempt (which is after all quite understandable if we take the point of view of *raison d'état*) to reduce difference to similarity, by a sort of centralizing attack.

- Linguistic environment: on 9 December 1938, 300 street-name signs in Oslo were changed in order to conform to the new, recently adopted orthography, which was the municipality's way of symbolically asserting its adherence to the reform of writing; and, throughout the successive reforms which we have mentioned, it is possible to get an idea of the political views of Norwegian newspapers simply by looking at the orthography they used. In fact this anecdote has a broader value for, generally speaking, any language planning that affects the form of the language needs to make use of the environment, to keep putting the results of the reforms before the eyes and ears of the language's speakers. Whether it is street-name signs having their orthography or language changed (as in Algiers in 1967, in the middle of the Arabization campaign, when, one fine day, signs in Roman letters were swept away) or car registration plates, road-signs, shop-signs, the text of the Koran, etc., the language environment is an important semiological issue which supports language planning, at the same time as being a yardstick for non-linguistic power relations. Convincing evidence for this can be found by glancing at the shop signs of a town like Paris, by comparing what can be seen in a rich, tourist shopping area like the Avenue de l'Opera (signs in Japanese and English) with a neighbourhood of immigrant workers like Belleville (signs in Arabic, Chinese, Hebrew). The nationalism which leads some to refuse to use foreign signs is matched by the economic relationships that lead others to advertise the name of their company in the language of potential clients. The struggle is not the same, but in both cases it is embodied in the domain of language.

13

Case Study: The Language Struggle of the Jivaro of Ecuador

Let us begin with some precise terminology: the 'Jivaro' never call themselves 'Jivaro' but 'Shuar'. In fact, the term 'jibaro' means 'peasant' in Spanish, with a pejorative connotation, and was applied to the people living in Peruvian and Ecuadorian Amazonia by the first arrivals from the Iberian peninsula, in the sixteenth century. I have kept it for the title of this chapter, for reasons of clarity, since the Shuar are practically unknown in Europe, as is their culture, especially if their famous practice of head-shrinking, the 'tsantsas', is excluded. But from now on I shall describe this people by using the name that they use: Shuar. There are, in Amazonia, around 150,000 Shuar, divided into two groups of citizens by the Protocol of Rio de Janeiro: 120,000 are considered to be Peruvians and 30,000 to be Ecuadorians. What I shall describe here is the language policy in the schools of Ecuador, making use primarily of notes taken during a stay in Sucua, the 'capital' of the Ecuadorian Shuar in July 1980. At the time I was able to have meetings with people responsible for the 'Federation of Shuar Centres', to visit schools and examine the many documents published by the Federation.[1]

To the east of the Andes, between the River Pastaza to the north, the Morona to the east and the Maranon to the south, the Shuar are very dispersed in the Amazonian forest, and live in small, isolated villages. The absence of communication routes makes relations between these groups

[1] I have published a description of this policy, which I here partly repeat in 'Les Jivaros et les mégahertz', *Les Nouvelles Littéraires*, 4 Sept. 1980, and in 'Écoles radiophoniques chez les Shuars', *Le Monde Diplomatique*, no. 336 (Mar. 1982). I also make use of Alain Dubly, *Evaluacion de las escuelas radiofonicas de Sucua, 'Radio-Federacion'* (Quito: INEDES, 1973), which is relevant only to the first year of the experiment. Rafael Mashinkiash, *La educacion entre los shuar* (Sucua, 1976), a study that stops at 1972, before the introduction of radio into schools; Miguel Alioni, *La vida del pueblo shuar* (Sucua, 1978), the work of a missionary who stayed with the Shuars from 1908 to 1912 and gives, in particular, information of the traditional number system, and *Solucion original a un problema actual, Federacion de centros Shuar* (Sucua, 1976). All works published in Sucua are published by the Federation of Shuar Centres.

difficult, and the organization of traditional schools even more so. It was for this reason that the Salesian missionaries who had come to spread the gospel organized, from 1934 onwards, education in boarding-schools. This type of schooling, by cutting off the children from their family environment, made it possible both to convert them to Christianity and to teach them Spanish culture and language. Two factors gradually came together to modify this educational policy. First, the fact that the Salesians became increasingly concerned about Shuar culture and sought ways of ensuring its survival in face of the dominant Castilian model. Secondly, the fact that the Shuar themselves took control of their own destiny. In 1964 the Federation of Shuar Centres was founded: local representatives were elected in the two hundred or so existing centres (each centre consisting on average of about fifteen families), who in their turn elected those responsible for the twenty-four regional associations who sent their delegates to the Federation. This Federation acts as a Shuar state within the state of Ecuador. It looks after production co-operatives, the registration of births, marriages, and deaths, land registry, real estate, the development of animal husbandry, education, health, the sale of crafts and folk art, and so on.

In 1966 the idea of a Shuar radio station emerged. With financial help from the Salesian missionaries, two young Shuar attended training courses at the radio school of Riobamba, in the Andes, with the idea that they could, once trained, run a radio station which would broadcast from Riobamba into Amazonian territory. But the mountains are a natural barrier that radio waves cannot cross, and so it was decided to install a broadcasting station in Sucua in 1968: *Radio-Federacion*. To do this, international aid was sought and the radio station was financed by humanitarian associations in Germany, Italy, Holland, and by UNESCO, for the Shuar wished to keep control of the money, by multiplying the sources of finance. Matters then proceeded fairly quickly:

- In 1968, five hours broadcasting a day, in two languages (Castilian and Shuar), from Monday to Saturday, two hours in the morning, one at midday, two in the evening.
- In 1969, this rose to seven hours a day, plus two hours on Sunday.
- In 1970, eleven hours broadcasting a day, still in the two languages, and two hours on Sunday. But these broadcasts, aimed at the Shuar people, did not change the fact that at school their children continued to learn Spanish language and culture.
- It was in 1972 that the important step was taken. To support the

recently established bilingual schools, teaching by radio was begun, with broadcasts now from five in the morning to ten in the evening every day. At the same time, the first one-kilowatt transmitter was replaced by three transmitters, two of 5 kw and one of 10 kw.

The idea of bilingual schools was based on a few simple principles:

– To be taught in Castilian is a psychological shock for Shuar children, a sharp break in relation to their environment and culture, and it is preferable to begin schooling in the language spoken in the family.
– All languages can cope with modernity, given a minimum of planning.
– Shuar culture and heritage should be promoted.
– The national language, Castilian, should also be studied.

On this basis, the Shuar put into action a system of schooling which respected the national curriculum, that is, it prepared pupils in Castilian for Ecuadorian exams and also combined it with a specific curriculum:

(1) The radio programmes were inspired primarily by the Shuar environment and culture: readings taken down from the oral tradition, the study of myths, of customs, of language, but also of local botany and zoology, as well as traditional crafts (weaving, construction of musical instruments, of canoes, of kitchen utensils).
(2) Subjects for school essays drew directly on local daily life. For example I noted, while going through the pupils' exercise-books, the following topics: the myth of the black panther, the life of the President of the Federation, descriptions of a Shuar assembly, a traditional feast, etc.
(3) There were translation exercises between the two languages, and the teaching of grammar for both was extremely traditional, that is, formal grammar.

So the teaching model was in no way modern. In the Spanish part of the teaching, national curricula were scrupulously respected (this was the subject of an agreement with the Minister of National Education), and in the Shuar part, the same curricula were adapted to local realities and language. So the only original thing in the experience was at the beginning, in its bilingualism and biculturalism. No other Indian group in Ecuador has achieved a system like this (although the Quechua are, for example, much more numerous than the Shuar), and everywhere the teaching is in Spanish.

The introduction of radio, from 1972 onwards, was the second piece of originality in the school curriculum.

In the course of the school year 1972–3 thirty-one centres used broadcasts for the first year of primary school. In 1975–6, broadcast radio programmes reached the fourth year, and in 1980, during my stay in Sucua, Radio Federacion's airwaves were devoted to school broadcasting from 8 o'clock in the morning to 1.30 in the afternoon. The broadcast programmes covered the whole of the primary years and were picked up in 153 centres. In each of these, the teacher had the aid of a 'tele-helper' recruited by the Federation, who guided the radio listening while the teacher was occupied with pupils at another level: each lesson lasted forty minutes, with twenty minutes listening and twenty minutes working on the material.

Since 1972, these radiophonic schools have steadily developed, while illiteracy has declined, along with the number of pupils in religious and state schools, where the teaching is only in Spanish. The figures relating to this, as provided by the Federation, are in Table 13.1.

In the bicultural schools, the relationship between the two teaching languages develops gradually throughout the years of schooling: 90% Shuar and 10% Spanish for the first two years, 70% Shuar and 30% Spanish for the next two years and, from the fifth year of primary school, the two languages share the timetable equally.

There is nothing new in any of this. Radio was used for many years in Senegal, for example, when the method of the Centre de Linguistique Appliquée de Dakar was applied to the primary years, and the use of two languages, a local language and a national language, is not a novelty either, as we saw with the example of Guinea. The originality of the Shuar example comes from something quite different, in that we have here a language policy that is atypical and exemplary on several points.

First of all, it is unusual in that it is not linked to the State. It is the

TABLE 13.1.

	Number of pupils	
	1972	1979
Bicultural radiophonic schools	506	3,419
Monolingual church schools	1,660	500
Monolingual state schools	1,790	906
Illiterates of school age	1,148	500

policy of a minority, decided by and put into action by that minority; as such this educational reform contrasts strongly with the cases we have so far described (without, for all that, being unique: we might for example mention the schools organized by militants in the Basque region).

Secondly, it is also unusual in that this case of human intervention into languages is not a form of social domination but, on the contrary, a liberation. Accepting the status of national language conferred on Castilian, the Shuar have quite simply organized a bilingualism between a vernacular, their own, and a lingua franca, the state language. That is, within their group they have accepted the reality of national conditions. When the Indians of Ecuador meet for a congress, all of them, Colorado, Quechua, Shuar, etc, speak Spanish to each other; their problem is to maintain their languages in their respective nations, which is what the Shuar are attempting to do.

Lastly, the Shuar case is exemplary because it shows what it is possible to achieve, it pushes back the limits of the impossible. Of course, the geographic situation of these people, far from the capital, difficult of access, in part explains their relative autonomy. But this takes nothing away from the fact that the Shuar have negotiated with the government practically as equals, that they found their sources of finance on their own and, finally, that they give an astonishing example to all the peoples of the world.

There is another point on which their practice is interesting, their intervention into language itself. For every time that an attempt has been made to introduce a language that has only recently been written down into a traditional system of teaching, that is, a language supported by an oral tradition but not yet possessing a metalanguage to carry grammatical and mathematical discourse, then there arises the problem of neologisms, of creating a vocabulary. Now, here too, the Shuar have themselves solved the problem. I shall give only one example, the number system.

The traditional Shuar number system works on base 5: to count they use the hand (*uwej*), then the foot (*nawe*), showing the fingers and naming them: *chikichik* (one), *jimiar* ('pair of fingers', i.e.two), *menaink* (three), *aintiuk* ('two pairs', four), *uwej* ('hand', five), *nawe* ('foot', ten). There is a special name for six (*wigni*), then for seven, eight, and nine the form *hiraku* is added to the names of the first series: *jimiar hiraku* (seven), *menaink hiraku* (eight), and *aintiuk hiraku* (nine). The meaning of *hiraku* is not very clear (perhaps 'of the other hand').

It can be seen that this system makes counting beyond ten difficult, which does not denote a deficiency at all, but provides the interesting anthropological information that the Shuar world had little need of counting. The missionaries' introduction of writing, of decimal numbers and figures, followed by the establishing of bicultural education, have forced this system, in which counting depended on the body (the finger, the hand, the foot), to disappear before another, more or less copied from the Spanish system. The uniqueness of the solution thought up by the Shuar lies in the respect it shows for tradition through designating the missing numbers by reference to their graphic form. In this way six has been christened *ujuk* (that is, 'monkey tail', which recalls the form of six), seven is *tsenken* (the name of an agricultural implement in the form of a seven), eight is *yarusk* (the Shuar word for the ant) and nine is *nsumtai* (word for the index finger, used for painting decorative motifs on the face in the form of a nine). Hundred is termed *washin* (the name of a pot used in fishing) and thousand by *nupanti* ('many'). The decimal numbers work like this:

1. *chikichik*
2. *jimiar*
3. *menaink*
4. *aintiuk*
5. *uwej*

so far these are the traditional terms, then:

6. *ujuk*
7. *tsenken*
8. *yarusk*
9. *nsumtai*
10. *nawe*
11. *nawe chikichik*
12. *nawe jimiar*, etc.
20. *jimiara nawe*
21. *jimiara nawe chikichik*, etc.

For 30, 40, etc, they say 'three feet' (*menainka nawe*), 'four feet', for 110 *washin nawe*, 111 *washin nawe chikichik*, etc.

Here, therefore, we find a double transformation: on the one hand a move from the gestural to the pictorial (they used to count by showing the fingers, now they write), and, on the other hand, from a number system using base 5 to one using base 10, that is, the decimal system. In the beginning the body was the measure of everything, as in a great number of other cultures. In the Torres Strait, between Australia and New Guinea, there is even a system that makes it possible to count up to 33^2 by going through the joints of the body, giving them a succession of names. But the number system using base 10, introduced by Spanish colonization, was perceived from a pictorial point of view as foreign and so it was necessary to adapt it to daily experience. The solution was not sought in the internal logic of the language (by, for example, adopting the traditional form '*hiraku*') but in an external logic, by playing on the written form of the digits: 7 resembles an agricultural implement, 8 resembles an ant, etc.

One can see the political value of the Shuar case, which should be appreciated in the light of the fate reserved for other Indian cultures in South America and, more widely, for minority cultures around the world. In most cases, the war of languages is revealed in the division of classes by age. The children learn the national language, often inherited from a colonial period, at school while the adults eventually learn to write a local language. This situation, if it does not lead to the introduction of local languages in school, means that first languages are gradually limited to uniquely group functions, confined to family use, and are at the risk of eventually disappearing. In particular, the fact that the children do not learn to write the same language as their parents opens a gap between them which could, in one or two generations, be fatal for the first language.

For their part the Shuar have adopted a radical solution (and not only in the field of language, but also in the management of their economy, their land, etc.) and provided themselves with the technical means for carrying it out. On these grounds, this microcosm of language policy and planning is exemplary. It shows us that the language empires that are slowly being established across the world, whether they speak French, English, Russian, or Spanish are not an inevitable misfortune and that it is possible to fight for a space for difference in a universe tending towards uniformity.

[2] System described by Wyatt Gill, quoted by Lucien Lévy-Bruhl, *Les Fonctions mentales dans les sociétés inférieures* (Paris, 1951), 209–10. For a wider discussion of number systems, see Geneviève Guitel, *Histoire comparée des numerations écrites* (Paris, 1975).

14
The War of Writing

Writing is the graphic representation of language, a means of preserving speech, and thus an instrument of second-degree communication. Surely, then, establishing an orthography is simply a technical matter? Given a language that is not transcribed, linguists can study its phonology and devise an alphabet which is as consistent as possible and best adapted to the language's sounds. They then propose this alphabet to those who decide who, as they should, decide; next, manuals of literacy and pamphlets are printed. In short, we have the classic scenario of language planning as it might be imagined in theory. From this we might conclude that establishing an alphabet is something that is both technical and neutral. But this is not really the case and we shall see that the form taken by the graphic notation of a language can be an ideological and political issue.

The Mandingo Alphabets

Despite the widespread belief that all African languages come from an oral tradition and only encountered writing through being colonized, we know today that a number of them had already been transcribed before the colonial era. In the last century, S. Koelle described a writing system for the Vai language.[1] In addition D. Westermann has pointed to writing for the Bassa, Nsibidi, and Noum[2] languages, and more recently D. Dalby has studied notations for languages in West Africa.[3] But these alphabets, often inspired by the Arabic alphabet (that is, transcribing consonants by characters and vowels by diacritics), did not spread widely and were, in fact, mostly used for magical purposes.

As far as Mandingo is concerned (spoken in different dialectical varieties, Bambara, Malinke, Jula, etc, in Mali, Burkina Faso, Senegal, Guinea,

[1] S. Koelle, *Grammar of the Vaï Language* (London, 1854).
[2] D. Westermann, *Les Peuples et les civilisations d'Afrique* (Paris, 1970).
[3] D. Dalby, 'The Indigenous Script of West Africa', *African Language Studies*, no. 8 (1967), no. 9 (1968), no. 10 (1969).

Gambia, the Ivory Coast, Guinea Bissau, Sierra Leone, and Liberia), Gérard Galtier has noted a consonantal alphabet, 'Masaba', recently invented and used in some Bambara villages in Mali,[4] and there is also 'Nko' (in Bambara, 'I say') invented in Guinea, in the region of Kankan, by Souleymane Kanté, and used for some handbooks printed in Conakry. Parallel to these endogenous attempts at transcribing the language, Catholic and Protestant missions have used Roman letters to work out their own alphabets, which differed on points of detail,[5] but it was only in the context of literacy campaigns launched by UNESCO that there developed any official concern with the problem of unifying these methods of writing.

In 1966 a meeting of experts was held in Bamako (28 February–5 March), with responsibility for proposing alphabets for six languages (Mandingo, Fulani, Tamasheq, Songhay-Zarma, Hausa, and Kanuri). The discussion very quickly turned to a choice between a uniquely Roman alphabet, which would facilitate language learning for people already literate and the use of current typewriters, or an 'Africa' alphabet, developed by the International African Institute (IAI) and already in use in Anglophone countries. The commission responsible for Mandingo finally proposed a Roman alphabet, transcribing, for example, nasal vowels with an 'n' and not with a tilde and not using the phonetic signs of the IAI, but this proposal was not taken up in full by any of the countries; each adapted it on points of detail. So, for the same prenasalized stop, the transcription 'mb' is now in use in Guinea, Senegal, the Ivory Coast, and Gambia, and 'nb' in Mali and Burkina Faso. Open vowels are transcribed in three different ways, and, to give another example, the word meaning 'eight' is written *segin* in Mali, *seyin* in Guinea, and *séegin* in Burkina Faso. This is clearly a ridiculous situation, since a book printed on one side or other of the frontier does not use the same transcription for dialects of the same language, which are mutually comprehensible when spoken, and since people who have just learnt to read the official language of their country have to learn another alphabet if they wish to have any understanding of texts published in their language but in a neighbouring country.

Without going further into the details (in particular, the 1966 alphabet seems more coherent than those which were adopted), we should consider the reasons for this rejection of a unified alphabet. Naturally the different

[4] G. Galtier, 'Problèmes dialectologiques et phonographématiques des parlers mandingues', thesis under the supervision of Lionel Guerre and Serge Sauvageot (University of Paris VII, 1980), 244 et seq.
[5] Ibid. 255–9.

countries put forward technical reasons: either the desire to be as close as possible to local pronunciation, or the desire to have the same alphabet for all the languages of the country (this is for example the case with Mali, where the 'Africa' alphabet has been adopted for languages other than Bambara). But if we step back a little, we can soon see that there was a desire to show a distinctive identity in the choices made. The experts who came together at Bamako in 1966 were Western (French, American, Russian) and African, but it is possible that some people saw the influence of the West in the alphabet proposed as an interference in local cultures, hence their desire to alter it. That those who decide these matters should want to adapt what the experts propose is quite normal, but the goal of the meeting was to unify the transcription of the languages in different countries, yet the result was quite different. Here we find again what we encountered in the example of Norway, a desire to mark national specificity by the very form of the transcription adopted. So Bambara in Bamako and Malinke in Kita, Mali are transcribed using the same alphabet, while the Malinke of Kankan, Guinea, although very close to the Malinke of Mali, uses another alphabet. Malinke is first thought of as Malian or Guinean, and as Malinke only second. Suppose that, on the pretext of real dialectical differences, a different alphabet was used to write French in Belgium, Quebec, and France, but the same alphabet was used for the French of Paris and Marseilles: we would have a comparable situation, with an emphasis placed on the national aspect (France and Belgium) while in fact the Parisian accent can be considered to be closer to the Brussels accent than that of Marseilles.

But, however ridiculous these parochial language policies may appear, in using the transcription of languages to mark national differences, writing is not what is at issue in power relationships, as it is in the examples now to be described.

The Soviet Example

Before the Revolution, Russian was the official language of the Empire (apart from the Baltic states, Poland and Finland), and there was little tolerance for minorities: 'one Tsar, one religion, one language'. Soviet policy, for its part, was based on a long-term vision, the idea of a process leading to a society without frontiers of class, religion, or nation, in the heart of which a unique culture would be born, generated by all the cultures involved, a process that would go through three stages: 'rastvet', the flowering of the different cultures, 'sblizheniye', their coming together, and finally 'sliyaniye', the emergence of a harmonious unity. As far as languages are concerned, a parallel process would lead to a world language:

(1) Development of national languages after the victory of Socialism.
(2) Selection by the people of one language, from among all the national languages with equal rights.
(3) Progressive transformation of this interlanguage into the principal means of communication.
(4) Transformation of one of the regional interlanguages into a common world language.[6]

This is the context within which it was decided to fight illiteracy, extremely widespread at the time, through the use of mother tongues. Those which were not yet transcribed were given a Roman alphabet, and those which were already written in Arabic characters were, despite Muslim opposition, given a new system of transcription so that they too would be written in Roman characters. At the beginning of the 1930s, the Roman alphabet was the clear victor, and then, between 1935 and 1940, the policy was changed and all languages (except those which had a very ancient alphabet like Armenian and Georgian) were changed to the Cyrillic alphabet, the one used for Russian. So some languages, like Tadzik, had three alphabets in twenty years: Arabic, Latin, Cyrillic. In the course of this period, literacy made enormous strides, as Table 14.1 shows.

But this remarkable progress does not remove the question I wish to pose: why these changes of the alphabet? Why suppress the Arabic alpha-

TABLE 14.1.

	Literacy rates		
	1897	1926	1939
USSR	28.4%	56.6%	87.4%
Ukraine	27.9%	63.6%	88.2%
Georgia	23.6%	53%	89.2%
Armenia	9.2%	38.7%	83.9%
Turkmenia	7.8%	14%	77.7%

[6] Rory Allardice, 'Language Equilibrium in the Soviet Union', dissertation submitted in partial fulfilment of the degree of Master of Arts (University of York, 1984), 7–9.

bet, why use the Roman alphabet in order to end up with the Cyrillic alphabet? The linguist Jan Knappert gives us a first clue:

In Southern Siberia, the Turkic dialects, of which the most prominent were Türkmen, Özbek, Kara-Kalpak and Kirghiz, were not used in literature; one literary language was in use for most of Türkestan: Jaghatay (Djagadai), written in Arabic characters. Soon after the Russian revolution, different orthographies were devised for each of these dialects, based on the Roman script. About ten years afterwards, in the middle 30s, those Roman alphabets were abolished, and replaced by newly designed orthographies based on the Cyrillic script. This and the many Russian loanwords give the impression that the purpose of these languages is only to be stepping stones for students whose higher degrees will be all in Russian. In this way the speakers of the Turkic dialects will be tied to Russian as the central language of the country, and will be less conscious of their relations with their neighbours. They are not able to understand them as soon as the conversation turns to a more educated subject: then Russian has to be used.[7]

G. Lewis, for his part, underlines the fact that in the process of the modernization of languages, 70 to 80% of words borrowed came from Russian.[8] Alongside this change of alphabet, the teaching of Russian was made obligatory in all schools in 1938, on the theory of 'two currents' (dva potoka), which amounted to a division of functions: the vernacular function for local languages, official, scientific, and lingua franca functions etc., for Russian. More recently, during a conference held at Tashkent in 1975, it was suggested that Russian should be taught from kindergarten, then in 1979, at another conference in Tashkent, under the title of 'The Russian language, language of friendship and co-operation of the peoples of the Soviet Union', it was suggested that students should be required to write their dissertations in Russian. Demonstrations followed in Tbilisi (Georgia) and Tallin (Estonia), and there was trouble in other Baltic republics, petitions from Georgian intellectuals, etc., as some speakers realized that their language was slowly merging into Russian.

So here we have a phenomenon of assimilation of the USSR's languages by Russian, which owes nothing to dialectical materialism and everything to power relationships and language policy. The relations between Russian and the other languages can be easily approached through the help of two statistics: 3.1% of Russians are bilingual, that is, speak another language from within the USSR; 42.6% of non-Russians are bilingual, that is, speak Russian.[9] In this process of assimilation,

---

[7] Jan Knappert, 'Language in a political situation', *Linguistics*, 39 (1968), 59–67.

[8] Glynn Lewis, *Multilingualism in the Soviet Union* (The Hague, 1972).

[9] B. Comrie, *The Languages of the Soviet Union* (Cambridge, 1981).

changes in alphabet have played a not insignificant role. For those in power, the Roman alphabet, chosen at the beginning, had the advantage of appearing to be ideologically neutral: they did not wish to see the Bolsheviks compared to Russian imperialism. As for the suppression of the Arabic alphabet, its aim was of course to try to cut religious roots in the regions where Islam was powerful. After this, once Soviet power was assured, the change to Cyrillic, added to the words borrowed *en masse* from Russian, would reduce the differences between the languages, to the benefit of Russian. This form of linguistic imperialism naturally took different routes, working at once on school and university policy, language planning, the media, but the apparently minor problem of the alphabet played, as we have seen, an interesting role. The semiological difference between two alphabets protects languages by separating them, and Kirghiz or Tadzik for example are less susceptible to influence from Russian if they are written in Arabic characters than if they are written in Cyrillic characters.

But in China the very opposite situation is found: the unity of writing protects the diversity of languages.

The Chinese Example

We have already discussed, in Chapter 11, Chinese language planning; here we shall treat only the problem of writing, which needs to be separated into two issues: the simplification of characters and Pinyin.

Character Reform

It is well known that Chinese writing has the special characteristic of not really being linked, from the phonetic point of view, to a particular language: a person speaking only the Peking dialect cannot communicate orally with a person speaking only the Canton dialect, but they can both read the same newspaper and communicate in writing. The characters refer to ideas before referring to sounds, and a person can read them without knowing how to pronounce a single Chinese word, in the same way that a comic strip can be read without words. How many of these characters are there? According to Zhou Yougang, there are:

- a basic set of 6,763 characters, of which 3,755 are frequently used and 3,008 less used.
- 16,000 other characters which, with the previous ones, are enough to

print all ancient and modern books (which raises the number to close to 23,000).
– 34,000 other characters of little actual use.[10]

In sum, to read current publications it is necessary to know about 4,000 characters; a well-read person would know more than 30,000. This means that learning written Chinese requires an exceptional effort of memory, and simplifying the characters has always been a problem. Without going back as far as the Qin period, we might mention the movement of 4 May 1919, which gave the idea of simplification an anti-feudal significance. Then there was the government of Nanking which in 1935 attempted an abortive simplification of 324 characters; in this regard it was a precursor of the Socialist government which, in October 1955, published a list of 515 simplified forms and 54 simplified particles. It should be understood that a Chinese character is composed of a certain number of elements or strokes which should be followed in a given order, and that the reform of 1955 reduced the average of 16 strokes per character to an average of 8, which can be considered progress. To take a current example, the classical character for the horse ¤, is made up of ten strokes, while the simplified character, ¤, has only three. Of course, this reform has some disadvantages, in particular, it removes a certain intelligibility in the characters where the sense can sometimes be read off from the composition. Thus the word pronounced *ji* in Mandarin and meaning 'calculate, plan' was written ›p, a composite character in which can be seen, on the left, the root for the spoken word and on the right the number ten: to know one's numbers up to ten. The simplified character, ›p, masks this etymology, in the same way that the character, ¤fi, 'cart, vehicle' shows a cart seen from above, with its axle, its wheels, its body, a message which disappears in the simplified form, ¤fi.

This first wave of simplification went fairly well, even if it posed and still poses a certain number of problems in communication with Taiwan, Hong Kong, and overseas Chinese who still use the classical characters. It is true that every means at the disposal of state propaganda were used to launch the simplified system and in 1974 there were, for example, some strange slogans which ran together the struggle against Confucius, the struggle against Lin Biao and the struggle for character simplification:

---

[10] Zhou Youguang, 'Modernization of the Chinese Language', *International Journal of Sociology of Language*, no. 59 (1986), 13–14.

shenru pi lin pi kong tuidong hanzi gaige
'going in depth with criticism of Lin Biao and Confucius, pushing ahead Chinese character reform'
kong laoer shi fandui hanzi biange de zushiye
'Confucius was the grand master of those who opposed Chinese character reform'.[11]

So, for a young Chinese of today, cloud, *yun*, is written ¶‡ and he would probably not recognize the same sign in the classical character ¶‡. In this way he loses a whole graphic etymology which can be found embedded in this classical character. First, in the composite character there is the presence of *yu*, rain, «В then there is the history of the character itself, three thousand years old, which can be read on bones, seals, and bronzes, etc. Here we have a good example of the difference between the historic evolution of a form of writing and conscious intervention into this form of writing; on the one hand, thirty centuries of history, and on the other, twenty years of reform. In this way, everyone can read, in the character *dong*, "F, 'is' the etymological composition, with the sun /Ø rising behind a tree / , but this composition is clearly absent from the simplified form "F.

This first campaign for simplification was generally accepted into daily life, primarily through the influence of school. On the other hand, a second list of simplified characters, launched in 1977, was soon withdrawn, in face of numerous protests (in particular, the writer Pa Kin published an article opposing the new reform). The arguments of the opposition were primarily cultural: we will end up by no longer being able to write true Chinese, calligraphy is our national art and it uses the classical characters, etc. It seems to me that today the situation has stabilized on this point. The teaching of classical Chinese in school has begun again, and one can even see, here and there, classical characters reappear in public inscriptions or in the press, without causing a problem. So the writing paper of the Institute of Foreign Languages in Canton, where I have taught, has for a heading the classical character for the first syllable of the name of the town. Although it has to be said that the text was written by Mao.

If we examine this intervention into the writing system too swiftly, its policy implications can seem to be different to those we found in the Soviet example of alphabet change. It is, however, necessary to stress that

---

[11] Chin-Chuan Cheng, 'Contradictions in Chinese Language Reform', *International Journal of Sociology of Language*, no. 59 (1986), 88.

one aspect of this standardization brings us back to the same problem. Recalling that a Chinese character associates a written sign and a semantico-syntactical function, Yang Jian stresses that the desire of the Chinese government to standardize writing involves

> proceeding to a selection of the characters most useful for modern Chinese, simplifying how they are written as much as possible, and defining their sense (and their pronunciation). In consequence a number of characters created for the use of dialectical expressions are excluded, and also expressions whose characters are considered to be incorrect phonetic signs.[12]

It can be seen that this raises a number of problems. To mention just two:

– What is a useful character? Who decides its utility?
– What is modern Chinese? Who defines the notion of modernity?

At the same time, then, certain difficulties in the transcription of dialects emerge (if, as Yang Jian writes, specific characters are 'excluded'). But the problems posed by this simplification have, from this point of view, nothing in common with those posed by Pinyin.

The Reform of Pinyin

The idea of Romanizing Chinese writing is nothing new. The missionary Mateo Ricci had already used Roman letters to transcribe the language and, in the modern period, in parallel with the Romanizing systems put forward by sinologists (the best known is the Wade notation), numerous attempts at alphabets have emerged. We might mention the 55 semi-Chinese, semi-Western characters proposed in 1892 by Lu Kan-chang;[13] *Zhuyin Zimu*, an alphabet based on the characters (1918); *Guoyu romazi*, 'National language romanization' (1928); *Beifangu latinhua xinwenzi*, 'Latinized New Writing of the Northern dialect' (1933), and finally Pinyin, adopted in 1958, that is, three years after the decision taken by the government to make teaching of the common language Putonghua general. We shall see that there is a link between these two decisions.

Many reasons have been officially put forward to justify the use of Pinyin:

– to aid the teaching of characters,
– to aid foreigners in learning Chinese,

---

[12] Yang Jian, 'Problèmes de chinois contemporain', *La Crise des langues* (Paris, 1985), 426.
[13] John de Francis, 'Language and Script Reform in China', in *Advances in the Creation and Revision of Writing Systems* (The Hague, 1977).

TABLE 14.2.

	Boys	Girls	TOTAL
Can you write Pinyin easily?			
Yes	81	77	158
No	37	5	42
Not very well	19	5	24
Do you agree that Pinyin should replace characters?			
Yes	40	33	73
No	94	53	147
Don't know	3	1	4

– to deal with the problem of place-names and personal names,
– to aid the spread of Putonghua,
– to write out telegrams, etc.

So this Romanization of the language appears as an auxiliary transcription, which would not replace the character system but, on the contrary, would make learning it easier. At least in theory, for at the beginning of the Pinyin campaign a sentence of Chairman Mao was often quoted: 'our written language must be reformed; it should take the direction of phonetization common to all the languages of the world',[14] and the recurrent intervention of one leader after another makes one think that the final aim was to impose Pinyin as the sole form of written Chinese. During my research in Canton, I posed two questions linked to this problem in a questionnaire for students: can you write Pinyin easily? and do you agree that Pinyin should replace the characters? Table 14.2 shows how the replies divided.

The arguments put forward by the minority in favour of reform were, in order of frequency, the simplicity of Pinyin, its speed of use, the possibilities of greater use of typewriters and contacts with foreigners. Those against reform referred to the beauty of the calligraphy, the fact that the characters are part of Chinese culture, contacts with overseas Chinese, and the problem of homophones. There are in fact many words that are pronounced in the same way, and so are written in Pinyin in the

[14] W. Lehmann (ed.), *Language and Linguistics in the People's Republic of China* (University of Texas Press, 1975), 51.

same way and are only distinguished by their characters. For example, Pinyin makes no distinction between *li* 'coarse, boorish', «Z, *li*, 'plum tree', §ı , *li*, 'lining of clothing', œG*li*, 'habitation', ¤‰*li*, 'carp', ˆU, etc., or again between *yuan dan* 'New Year's Day' and 'egg'. This is a strong linguistic argument against Pinyin.

But only one person out of the 224 questioned noted that the imposition of Pinyin could imply the death of languages other than Putonghua. The fundamental difference between characters and any alphabetic system is that the latter would record one given language, while it is possible, as we have remarked, for a person speaking Han to read a newspaper without knowing how to speak Putonghua. Now Pinyin is, of course, the Romanized transcription of Putonghua, which means quite simply that imposing it in place of characters would lead to 'dialects' being relegated to the class of unwritten languages. The Han languages other than Putonghua would gradually lose their literary and cultural functions, become limited to the group function and reduced to the domain of orality.

So a Romanized transcription which, at the beginning, might have appeared as a technical solution to a particular problem, i.e. the difficulty of learning the characters due to their great number, becomes in fact an instrument that serves the imposition of one language, the official language, upon the different Han groups speaking other languages.

Discussion

It is not the first time we have met the problem of writing systems in this book. We have seen that replacement of the Arabic alphabet by a Roman one was an aspect of the Turkish 'language revolution', and that the politico-religious opposition between the Muslims and Hindus of India could be symbolically reduced to the choice of a writing system: the Arabic alphabet for Urdu and Devanagari for Hindi.

The examples analysed in this chapter show us more clearly still that writing can be an area of conflict. In the case of Mandingo, as in the case of Norway described in Chapter 12, the choice of transcription was dependent on what I called a 'parochial language policy': a desire for particularism, for national originality, which in order to be 'different' from others risks putting obstacles in the way of communication, which is after all the principal function of language.

The example of Indonesia and Malaysia is, from this point of view, also interesting. At the beginning of the century there were two orthographic systems for the same language, Malay: one developed in 1901 by Ch. van Ophuysen and used in the Dutch East Indies (the present Indonesia), and the other developed in 1904 by Wilkinson and used in Malaysia, each system with characteristics borrowed from the writing of colonial languages, Dutch on the one hand, English on the other. In 1947, the newly independent Indonesia promulgated a new orthography which in particular broke with the traces of the Dutch method of writing (for example the oe for the sound /u/). Then, in 1961, an attempt was made to launch a common system for the two countries, the 'Melindo' system (for Melayu Indonesia), but political conflict between Malaysia and Indonesia meant that it was never applied and it was only later that the same orthography was used for the same language: EYD (Ejaan Yand Disempurnakan, 'perfected orthography'), made official in Malaysia in 1969, in Indonesia in 1972, and in Singapore in 1976. In this sequence we can observe the characteristic tendencies of the problems raised in this chapter, some of which have already appeared in the examples described above: the desire to break free from colonial orthography, as in the Norwegian case, the desire to formulate a national orthography, as in the different countries where Mandingo is spoken, and finally the desire to go beyond these oppositions and unify the writing system.[15]

But the example of the USSR's policy concerning minorities is much more eloquent. The change from the Arabic alphabet to the Roman alphabet and then to the Cyrillic alphabet could of course be a result of planning confusions, of chance changes, but we have seen that it was rather a desire to bring minority languages as close as possible to the Russian language in order to ensure the supremacy of the latter. As for the Chinese example, to reform the characters does not pose much of a cultural problem (there is only the risk of losing the history carried in the signs), but it would be much more serious if Pinyin were to replace the traditional writing system since, as we have seen, Romanization would no longer be the writing system for the several Han languages, but the transcription of just one of them, the official language.

Thus writing is linked to power in different ways. Symbolizing the group (as in the Hindi/Urdu case) or the country, it can be the object of an emotional attachment, of a nationalist or group reaction, or inversely, an opposition, a rejection. In this sense, it can be compared to several other semiological systems working on two levels: the level of denotation,

---

[15] Cf. Pierre Labrousse, 'Réformes et discours sur la réforme, le cas indonésien', *La Réforme des langues* (Hamburg, 1985), ii. 340–2.

on the one hand (the writing system is a writing system . . . , and this tautology could sum up its function), and the level of connotation on the other (this alphabet or that system connotes the past which is identified with or rejected). There is already, in this symbolic function of writing, cause for conflict, for 'the war of writing', as I wrote at the head of this chapter. But writing can also be where direct, aggressive intervention takes place, whether it is, as in the Soviet case, the imposition of the writing system of the dominant language on subordinate languages, with the writing system being only the first step of a wider offensive, or, as in the case of Pinyin, cutting languages off from their graphic roots. The writing system would then appear to be one means of oppression among others, a symbolic oppression certainly, but only at first, for it paves the way for the exercising of much more concrete power relationships.

15

The War of Words

I said earlier that when a language policy is applied to language and not languages, that is, to the form of languages and not to their relationships, it can be applied at three different levels, to writing, to lexis, and to dialect forms. Here we shall discuss intervention in the lexical domain.

First Approach

There are two kinds of justification for intervening in the lexical domain.

In some cases, action on lexis is a response to a threat. People think that the language is being invaded by a foreign vocabulary and it is agreed that this vocabulary should be driven out of the lexis in order to replace it with an autochthonous (indigenous) vocabulary. This defence of the lexical 'purity' of the language is a frequent occurrence, and we shall have an opportunity to analyse it in the next chapter, taking the example of French.

In other cases, action on lexis comes from a desire to enrich the language. People think that in order to adapt the language to the necessities of modernity, to allow it to carry content which it has not carried until now (teaching, politics, sciences, etc.), it should be given a new vocabulary.

This intervention in the domain of lexical creation generally develops between two opposing tendencies, on the one hand, borrowing, that is, the use of a term existing in another language, and, on the other, indigenous neologisms, that is, coining a new word from roots belonging to the language. The use of the term 'borrowing', traditional in linguistics for referring to what I shall call 'travelling words', those which move from one language to another, is of course open to dispute. The term means, etymologically, an 'advance of money' and implies that this 'loan' is followed by a 'return'. Now words that are borrowed are not returned, but the image was created to refer to plagiarism in literature, and plagiarists are bad at paying their debts. Be that as it may, these two tendencies, borrowings and neologisms, are not only characteristic of language policy, that is, bureaucratic action on language; speakers also tend towards them spontaneously. For here we must distinguish between two types of lexical creation, one that I shall call spontaneous, as practised daily by speakers of a language and which defines the way in which the language supplies its local needs, and the other which I shall call planned, as practised by linguistic policies, that is, the decision to create words. So we have spontaneous neologisms or lexical creativity, and programmed neologism or lexical creation, the intersection of the two pairs giving four possibilities:

Creation by	Spontaneous	Planned
Neologisms	1	3
Borrowings	2	4

(1) Spontaneous neologisms, invented by speakers in response to a communication need and based on the structures of word-formation and derivation of the language: this is, for example, the case with the French word for railway, 'chemin de fer', road of iron.

(2) Spontaneous borrowings, appearing in the same conditions as the preceding category. The speakers find themselves faced with a reality or practice for which their language has no name and in order to deal with it they use a word from another language. This is the case with 'camping' or 'parking' in French, with of course some phonological adaptation and, sometimes, the appearance of new sounds in the language doing the borrowing.

(3) Programmed neologisms, that is, a word coined from the structures of the language by a group of linguists, a terminology commission, in order to name what has not been named until now or was named by a word borrowed from another language. For example, 'remue-meninges' in French to replace the English 'brain-storming'.

(4) Lastly, programmed borrowings, chosen from another language by the same commission in the same situation, for example, the Arabic word 'zarrah' chosen to designate the atom in Malay.

The Example of Bambara

During the colonial period, the Bambara language spoken in Mali used two kinds of spontaneous lexical creation together, one borrowing directly from French and the other coining new words from the structures of the language. Here are some examples:

words borrowed from French: alimete (*allumette*, match), asiyeti (*assiette*, plate), balansi (balance), diwen (*vin*, wine), foto (photo), kamiyon (*camion*, lorry), sofere (chauffeur), tabali (table), were (*verre*, glass), etc.

indigenous neologisms: baganfagayoyo (place where beasts are killed = slaughterhouse), farikolonyenajekene (body-distraction-square = stadium), negeso (iron horse = bicycle), pankuru (canoe that flies = plane), etc.

It is difficult to know why, with these spontaneous creations, some words were borrowed and others created; the division between the two types does not appear to be significant. For contemporary realities, we find 'tren' (train) and 'negesira' (iron way = rail), but we also find almost synonymous pairs, 'sar' and 'misidaba' (cow hoe = plough), 'glasi' and 'jikuru' (water stone = ice), etc. It is nevertheless clear that, whichever method is used, it is for naming objects that come from another culture and were introduced by colonial power: spontaneous lexical creation, whether a borrowing or an indigenous neologism, is a response to a concrete semantic problem.

Then came independence, linguists, literacy campaigns, and language planning; an official move towards a 'Bambarization' of neologisms began. So, although the Bambara word 'peresidan' had been used for 'president' since the beginning of colonization, in an obvious borrowing from French, 'jamanakuntigi' was created, which means word for word 'master at the head of the country'; where the word 'politigi' was used for 'politics', 'nyetaasira' was created and this last example is worth pausing over for a moment. The term 'nyetaasira', coined by the linguists of the Division Nationale d'Alphabetisation Fonctionelle et de Linguistique Appliquée (National Division of Functional Literacy and Applied Linguistics), means word for word 'the road of progress'. This word-formation to convey the notion of politics is clearly taking an ideological view; obviously the neologists were thinking of their country's politics, or the politics of progressive countries, but can the politics of a Hitler or a Pinochet be considered a 'road towards progress'?

During a training course for linguists that I gave in Bamako in April 1984, I suggested, at the end of a discussion of this problem, the carrying out of a short inquiry into the reception of these neologisms: how were Bambara speakers decoding these words? We took two words from the political neo-vocabulary coined by the DNAFLA, 'nyetaasira' for politics and 'barakelawaserer' which means word for word 'band, group of workers', used for 'proletariat', and we asked different people in the street who spoke Bambara what they thought these words meant. Not one of them gave the sense proposed by the terminology commission, and the replies centred around the following notions:

nyetaasira: the route of progress, to progress, progress, future, these last two glosses being the most frequent in the replies obtained.

barakelawkasera: union, group of workers, category of workers, but several people replied that they did not understand the term, that it did not exist in Bambara.

Obviously, it can be imagined that, since usage produces meaning, these terms may end up by entering the language through sheer amount of use, if they are so used in official texts and the media. We see examples of this all the time in other languages and the French word 'logiciel', coined to replace the word 'software' borrowed from English, is a good example. But this is not really the problem. What is striking here is the coexistence of two approaches to lexical creation: a quantitative approach, which considers which forms are already used or are likely to be understood by the greatest number, and a qualitative approach, which considers which forms are the purest, the closest to the structures of the language.[1] Now in the Bambara example, it was the qualitative approach that was preferred to the quantitative approach, and this decision is evidence for both the reality of power and an ideological reality.

First, the reality of power: the language, treated here as lexical creativity, does not belong to those who speak it, but to commissions of linguists who arrogate to themselves alone the right of deciding what is linguistically 'pure' or 'impure'. Nor am I here describing a specifically Malian phenomenon, but a general one; all terminology commissions, whether they sit in Paris, Montreal or Peking, show the same characteristic, which we shall find in very different situations but all equally significant. In a thesis on the subject of teaching the deaf in Tetouan, Morocco, Hassan Ben Jelloun[2] described, for example, the establishing of a code, in this case a sign language, which was directly influenced by Moroccan teachers and American co-workers: the signs which would be used by the deaf were primarily created by people who could hear.

---

[1] This distinction, quantitative/qualitative, is borrowed from Andrée Tabouret-Keller, who used it in a discussion on the subject 'the standardization of languages' at the 13th International Colloquium of Functional Linguistics, Corfu, 24–29 Aug. 1986. At this same colloquium I presented a paper, 'L'enjeu néologique et ses rapports à l'idéologie', from which this chapter is adapted.

[2] Hassan Ben Jelloun, 'Pédagogie des jeunes sourds au Maroc, cas de Tetouan, problèmes linguistiques', thesis under the supervision of F. François (Université René Descartes, Paris, 1986).

Secondly, the ideological reality: the choice of the 'pure' form rather than a borrowing reveals here the desire to break free from colonial languages, from Western influences and, more generally, from dominant languages. But again, we can find the same phenomenon in other situations, and official efforts in France to 'deanglicize' the vocabulary come under the same nationalist tendency. More significant still, from this point of view, is action on place-names. Many countries changed their names after independence: the Belgian Congo became Zaire, Dahomey became Benin, the Upper Volta became Burkina Faso, Dutch Guinea became Surinam, and so on. Many towns had their names changed: Leopoldville and Elisabethville in Zaire becoming Kinshasa and Lumbumashi, Mazagan and Port-Lyautey in Morocco becoming El Jadida and Kenitra, etc.

In all these cases, whether it is a matter of place-names or of general vocabulary, we can see, behind the power of those who assume the right of giving names, the appearance of ideology. First there was colonial power, which christened places in its own way, showing no interest in whether these countries or towns already had a name, with the colonial ideology appearing in the names themselves. Then there was national power, rechristening places with names more or less taken from tradition, with the nationalist ideology opposing local names or words to the names and words imposed by others.

Neologisms and Ideology

In the example from Mali I have just described, there was at bottom a simple choice to be made: either to borrow a word from French, and accept a word from outside, or to create a Bambara word, with the desire to imprint the (linguistic) mark of (political) independence on the vocabulary. S. Takdir Alisjahbana has given a more complex and richer example regarding Indonesia:

In the coining of Indonesian modern terms during the Japanese occupation in Indonesia, for example, the preference in the determination of Indonesian modern terms was as follows: first to look for an existing Indonesian word; if there was no adequate Indonesian word for that concept a search should be made in the various local languages. If there was also no fitting word in the local languages either, an attempt would be made to find an Asian word. The internationally used terms came last.[3]

[3] S. Takdir Alisjahbana, *Language Planning for Modernization: The Case of Indonesian and Malaysian* (Mouton, 1976), 28.

It was in this way that, faced with the word 'autonomi' which was used by all speakers of the Indonesian language, the terminology commissions were led to propose the word 'swantantra', considered to be more 'local'; it was in this way that the Arab word 'zarrah' to designate the atom was preferred to a borrowing from Greek through the intermediary of modern European languages.

This overlapping of levels of lexical research is interesting because it shows us that the central problem here is to give the lexis of the language a nationalist imprint. By giving priority to the Indonesian lexical stock, and then to other local languages, and then to Asiatic languages, before accepting a term of European provenance for want of anything else, the notion of linguistic nationalism is rendered somewhat elastic. It appears most frequently in the choice of a language, for example the choice of Malay (renamed Bahasa Indonesia, the Indonesian language) as national language in place of the colonial language, which was Dutch. We saw earlier that it can appear in the choice of a writing system (this was for example the case with Turkey), but here it appears in the search for an indigenous vocabulary, the notion of 'indigenousness' being defined relatively, by concentric circles, passing from the most local to the regional, the national and, finally, the continental, etc.

These problems of lexical creation have brought us back to nationalism, and also to religious conflict, when for example Hindi borrows its neologisms from Sanskrit, while Urdu borrows from Arabic and Persian. They also bring us back to political loyalties, when in the countries of the East, words composed for the political vocabulary of German, Czech, etc., are copied into Russian. This lexical problem, just like the problem of writing described in the previous chapter, raises the question of the link between technical (in this case, linguistic) intervention and ideological background.

Intervention into language by programmed neologism normally implies four stages.

The first stage is a description of the language's system of lexical creativity (derivation, word-formation, etc.). For example, if the description of a language like Fulani shows that a lexeme always comes in the form R + te + WM (root + thematic element + word-class marker) words can be created by borrowing R and deriving the word according to the schema above.

This is an obvious point, but it can never be sufficiently repeated that language planning, just like sociolinguistics as a whole, is inseparable from the description of languages. Sociolinguistics encompasses linguistics, it is, to use Saussurian terms, a setting of the linguistics of *langue* within a linguistics of *parole*.

The second stage consists in making a survey of the lexical deficiencies and then of the available stock (regional words, trade and professional vocabulary, borrowings, etc.). To adopt an economic metaphor it is to describe both demand (the needs, the concepts for which a linguistic sign has to be found) and supply (the available stock). In this stock there may sometimes be signs that can be used by working on what they signify, by enlarging their semantic field. This is for example the case with Fulani, when the terminology commission proposes the word [Mɓedu], 'sieve' to mean 'circle' or the words meaning the lathes of a hut roof, [ŋorol or jurol] to mean 'meridians' and 'parallels'. In this way the vocabulary of geometry or geography is constructed by borrowings from within the language.

In the third stage, the missing words have to be coined whenever the available stock is insufficient, while respecting the rules of the languages elucidated in the first stage. When spontaneous creation has already made a choice (as in the case of 'politigi' or 'peresidan' in Bambara), solid arguments are needed to refute it and impose the planners' choice instead. It is here that the problem of choosing between indigenous neologisms and borrowings occurs.

There is, finally, the trying out of these terms in the field, by transferring them to the test bed of use by the speakers of the language. From the linguist's point of view, the goal to be attained is the greatest clarity, the greatest efficiency of vocabulary. This is not something to be decreed, but to be tested in the to-and-fro between the planner, 'the blacksmith of words', and the user. This experimenting does not in itself present major problems. But the linguist is not the only one involved and we have seen that politics and ideology interfere a lot in this domain. And the political authorities rarely consider that the people (the users of the language) have anything interesting to say.

The four stages I have just outlined constitute an ideal schema which is rarely realized: the linguist is here in a delicate position and he should act as a watchdog in attempting, in the face of political power, to see that the rights of the language and its speakers are respected.

A language has rights from two points of view. There is conformity to the rules of lexical production, of course, but also respect for what I would call 'acquired rights', as in the case of Bambara where it is difficult to see why it was necessary to replace an international term, integrated into the language and understood by all, like 'politigi' by an 'autochthonous' or 'pure' term that no one, apart from its creators, understands.

Speakers have rights insofar as the speakers of a language are the collective creator, the driving force of linguistic evolution, and it is difficult to see how any neologistic enterprise can develop against or without them.

For the speaker is, in the end, the person who is most notably absent when it comes to official intervention into language. All language planning implies a very particular idea of language: the idea that intervention can be effective, that through laws and decrees it is possible to replace a development which, as the history of languages shows, is principally the result of the action of speakers and the product of time. The development of languages and of the relationships between languages is a historical and social fact, the fruit of a long history, while language policy is, on the one hand, a considerable acceleration of this development, and, on the other, an attempt to replace history by intervention through a kind of legislation. There is, then, something of a scientific paradox for the linguist in intervening in an activity whose presuppositions go completely against all that he knows about language, in passing from the description and analysis of the relationship between language and society to direct action upon this relationship. But above all, this intervention, whether it concerns lexis, writing, the unification of dialects, or the relationship between languages, has an undeniable political background. What happens with language planning is that when those in power are confronted by language a small number of planners are set into action and they then impose their decision on a large number of the 'planned'. Sociolinguistics, which has shown how social differences, power-relations, have their linguistic counterpart, is today implicated in a set of planning practices which reinforces the power of the state over language, even when the aim of these practices is the struggle for the linguistic liberation of peoples. Desiring, for example, to replace a language inherited from colonialism by a subordinate local language, language planning risks behaving like political regimes which claim to de-Stalinize a regime with Stalinist methods.

To return to the lexical problem that is the theme of this chapter, it can be seen that the desire to enrich the vocabulary of a hitherto subordinate language, to give it the means to carry a content previously carried by the former dominant language, is an intervention with a democratic aim that runs the risk of being carried out in bureaucratic fashion: the civil servants of language are the reason that language is taken away from its speakers. At the same time it can be seen that this war of words goes against all that we know of the history of language. Cross-breeding has always been a great provider of lexis, languages live by reciprocal borrowings, so attempts at purification, the rejection of foreign words and of spontaneous lexical productivity introduce a contradiction between nationalism and science, as well as between a group's reactionary attitude and common necessity. Between the scientific paradox and political compromise, the planner finds himself faced with the eternal problem of the relationship between science and the world, between the monastic and the secular. For there is no language planning without linguists, and they have to negotiate unceasingly with those with political power, people whose objectives are rarely scientific, they even have to negotiate with themselves, between their own scientific and ideological positions. This problem, which we have discussed here with regard to lexis and the war of words, could, as we have seen, be discussed with regard to any aspect of language planning, and it leads us to an unavoidable difficulty: without some democratic control over language policy, it risks becoming the modern form of what I called not long ago 'linguistic cannibalism'.[4]

---

[4] L.-J. Calvet, *Linguistique et colonialisme, petit traité de glottophagie* (Paris, 1974).

16

Trench Warfare: The Case of French

There is not much talk of language policy and planning in France. In some of the countries that we have discussed, Turkey, Norway, China, for example, these problems are or have been discussed daily; although (we shall come back to this at the end of the book) the number of those who make the decisions remains confined to a few bureaucrats, information is or was widespread. There is nothing like this in France, where it might be supposed that similar problems do not occur and where, nevertheless, dealing with the language situation is a question that goes back a long way into the past.

The Growth of French

The history of the international growth of the French language is already a long one, and if, following tradition, we admit that French has been spoken since the ninth century (the Strasbourg Oaths being the first written trace of the language), it is also well known that three or four centuries later French had spread widely through Europe and outside it. The Crusades certainly played an important role in the spread of the language both into other Romance countries and into the East (Armenia, Greece). The victory of William the Conqueror at Hastings in 1066 and the occupation of England that followed established French across the Channel. The language also spread to the elites of countries on French frontiers, in Italy (it was in French for example that Marco Polo dictated the accounts of his travels), in Germany and the Low Countries. The University of Paris drew foreign students. In short, old French did very well alongside Latin, as F. Brunot describes:

In the minds of men of the time, French rose, if not to the level of Latin, at least as close to it as was possible for a common idiom . . . French rose to a demi-universality. In many respects, it even seemed for a while that it would not just make itself known but also establish itself at the expense of the indigenous languages, particularly in England.[1]

[1] F. Brunot, *Histoire de la langue française* (Paris, 1905), i. 359.

This growth continued for centuries, as the importance of Latin declined. In the middle of the eighteenth century, French was spoken in all European courts, studied in all middle-class families, used in diplomacy and for treaties, and the situation can be summed up in this telegraphic formula: 'general decline of Latin, static influence of Italian, and weak competition, in Europe at least, from English, German and Spanish'.[2] It is easy to understand why the Academy of Berlin chose the universality of the French language (cf. Chapter 4) as the subject of its annual competition in 1782. At this period, French was the only language that could aspire to the role of a cultural lingua franca in Europe, the only one that could aspire to replace Latin.

This undeniable advance needs to be analysed more precisely. To do this, we should distinguish first, between geographic growth and functional growth and, secondly, between European growth and overseas growth.

First of all, the fact that a language is used over a vast territory should not be confused with the fact that it is used with several functions. A language's increase in number of speakers is easy to understand, but it can happen that, without a rise in the numbers speaking it, a language can increase in the number of functions it fulfils. This is, for example, the case with a subordinate language, which had a primarily group function, when it becomes a national language, a vehicle for political discourse, a means of teaching, etc. In the course of its history French has experienced both types of growth.

Its geographic spread (and therefore the numbers speaking it) took place in two stages.

First of all, it spread over Europe (France itself, and certain parts of countries on the frontier, in Belgium, Luxembourg, Switzerland, and Italy), but this geographic spread very quickly stabilized and we can agree with Franck Schoell when he writes: 'In sum, for the last seven or eight centuries, French as a mother tongue has only just been able to maintain its position. If it has recorded significant progress, this has only been within the political frontiers of the state, to the detriment of Flemish, Alsatian, Niçois, Corsican, Catalan, Basque, Breton'.[3]

We have in this case what I shall call 'continuous French-speaking', that is, a practically uninterrupted territory where French is spoken (even if this comes under different states, but we know that linguistic and political frontiers only rarely coincide).

---

[2] F. Schoell, *La langue française dans le monde* (Paris, 1936), 17.
[3] Ibid. 14.

Then, across the world, the French language was exported when its speakers emigrated, to Louisiana or Canada for example, and also during the colonial period, when it gained a significant number of speakers as a second language, constituting what I shall call 'fragmented French-speaking', which is also functionally diversified. This leads us to the second type of expansion, functional expansion.

For if French in France and the francophone parts of Belgium or Switzerland, in the zone of 'continuous French-speaking' is used for a large number of functions, from group functions to the most official, it is a very different matter with 'fragmented French-speaking'. Its status in Martinique, where it coexists with a dominated language, Creole, should not be confused with Quebec, where it coexists with a dominant language, English, nor with 'francophone' Black Africa, where it dominates the numerous local languages but is spoken only by a minority of the population in situations that are themselves minority situations. In all these cases, the French language has experienced different increases in functions, and to these should also be added its international, diplomatic role, which we mentioned above.

The Reasons for the Growth and Subsequent Decline of French

It is not easy, even with the comfort of hindsight provided by distance in time, to explain the reasons for the success of the French language, and one can only suggest a number of factors which have all, in different degrees, played a role.

First of all, there is the demographic factor, insofar as French was, until the nineteenth century, the language most spoken in Europe as a first language. F. Schoell quotes figures that are significant from this point of view: there were in 1801 (date of the first census) $27^1/2$ million inhabitants in France as against 9 million in England and Wales, in 1835 there were 35 million Frenchmen, 26 million British, and 29 million German.[4] This numerical superiority explains a good deal, in the same way that the fact that there are today little more than 60 million speakers of French as a first language as against more than 200 million for English explains the present situation.

The national factor then played an important negative role. Until the nineteenth century Europe was divided into small kingdoms (for example Italian unity was only accomplished in the second half of the last century),

[4] Ibid. 21 and 354–5.

which were not very democratic, in which the elites spoke French and the people had hardly any right to speak in public. It was only with the relative democratization of these states and the education of the broader classes of society that national languages began to play a role and that national consciousness slowly appeared. As a matter of fact, the people who would slowly gain economic, cultural, and political power across Europe, were no longer the nobles who took a delight in speaking French and were familiar with French literature but a generally monolingual middle class with no special reason to be impressed by French culture. National languages, which had for a long time been the victims of the spread of French, would therefore compete with French as the language for conveying culture, and then replace it.

There are other factors which are often mentioned: France's economic power, the prestige of its kings and especially of its literature, but it is necessary to insist on the fact that these factors are inseparable from the two preceding ones. It is because France was a state that had been established a long time and had a large population, that it was able to profit from the relative weakness of its neighbours in all domains, including the domain of language.

These factors, which in part explain the growth of French in Europe, also explain the curbing of this growth at the end of the nineteenth century. As modern states established themselves, the function of cultural lingua francas, that had been filled by Latin and then French, disappeared. The colonial era, which took over, in part masks this profound transformation, but something fundamental changed at the end of the last century, which is accounted for by two events which were little noticed at the time. I am thinking first of all of the foundation in 1883 of the 'Alliance Française pour la Propagation de la Langue Française dans les Colonies et à l'Etranger'. During the previous centuries, the growth of French which we have just sketched received no institutional support, and the fact that a need was felt to 'propagate' French clearly shows awareness of a crisis: an expanding language does not need to be defended. The other event, which is completely different and to which we shall return at greater length in the following chapter, is the growing interest in artificial languages for international use, which manifested itself in the same period (Volapük dates from 1879, Esperanto from 1887, and Ido from 1907). The proliferation of plans for constructed languages shows that there was a place to be occupied, that a function was no longer being fulfilled: the promoters of these languages all thought they could replace French. They could not know that they were in fact living through an interregnum and that if the conditions for the growth of the French language no longer existed, a transformation was taking place in the international situation which would give birth to another growth, the growth of English.

Skirmishes in Quebec

The first fruits of this transformation appeared on the other side of the Atlantic. When France ceded Canada to the British crown in 1763, by the Treaty of Paris, common law was extended to the territory, but then, in face of the protests of the French-speaking population, the French *droit civil* was re-established in 1774. In 1791, the Constitution divided Canada into two provinces, high Canada and low Canada (the latter 90% French-speaking), and the legislative elections of 1792 are a good example of the linguistic conflict that was developing between the English and French languages. After the elections, there arose the problem of the Presidency of the Assembly. Jean-Antoine Panet, a French-speaker, put himself forward and was opposed by the candidacy of an English-speaker. The debate, as it is transcribed by the *Gazette de Québec* of 20 December 1792 is not without interest. McGill puts forward the candidacy of W. Grant against Panet in these terms: 'An essential quality for the Speaker is a perfect knowledge of the French and English languages . . . if an interpreter is necessary for communication between the Speaker and the King's representative, it would be the interpreter who would be the voice of the chamber and not the Speaker'. To this Panet replied, not without humour, 'that the King of England spoke all languages, and made treaties with all nations in their own languages as well as in English, that Jersey and Guernsey were French, and that to object to a member on the basis of language could not prevent him from being Speaker'.[5] It is an amusing debate, which may raise a smile, and it reappears in different places and on different subjects: what the language for the law should be, for example, or for the army, or for debates in the Assembly. Alexis de Tocqueville, in his *Voyage en Sicile et aux Etats-Unis*, describes a scene he observed in a civil court in Quebec, which displays a similar tone:

When we came into the hall a slander action was in progress. It was a question of fining a man who had called another *pendard* (gallows-bird) and *crasseux* (skin-flint). The lawyer argued in English. *Pendard*, he said, pronouncing the word with a thoroughly English accent, 'meant a man who had been hanged'. No, the judge

[5] *Gazette de Québec*, 20 Dec. 1792, quoted by G. Bouthillier and J. Meynaud, *Le choc des langues au Québec, 1760–1970* (Montreal, 1972), 117.

solemnly intervened, but who ought to be. At that counsel for the defence got up indignantly and argued his case in French: his adversary answered in English. The argument waxed hot on both sides in the two languages, no doubt without their understanding each other perfectly. From time to time the Englishman forced himself to put his argument in French so as to follow his adversary more closely; the other did the same sometimes. The judge, sometimes speaking French, sometimes English, endeavoured to keep order. The crier of the court called for 'silence' giving the word alternatively its English and French pronunciation. Calm re-established, witnesses were heard. Some kissed the silver Christ on the Bible and swore in French to tell the truth, the others swore the same oath in English and, as Protestants, kissed the other side of the Bible which was undecorated. The customs of Normandy were cited, reliance placed on Denisart [author of a well-known work on jurisprudence], and mention was made of the decrees of the parliament of Paris and statutes of the reign of George III. After that the judge: 'Granted that the word *crasseux* implies that the man is without morality, ill-behaved and dishonourable, I order the defendant to pay a fine of 18 louis or ten pounds sterling'.[6]

After this gently burlesque description, Tocqueville turns to the barristers' language:

The lawyers I saw there, who are said to be the best in Quebec, give no proof of talent either in the substance or in the manner of what they said. They are conspicuously lacking in distinction, speaking French with a middle-class Norman accent. Their style is vulgar and mixed with odd idioms and English phrases. They say that a man is *chargé* of ten louis, meaning that he is asked to pay ten louis. *Entrez dans la boite*, they shout to a witness, meaning that he should take his place in what the English call the witness-box. [Standard French would have *banc*, meaning 'bench'][7]

There are more reports of the same kind. In 1806 an English traveller, John Lambert, noted that: 'The French have a large majority in the House of Assembly, their number being thirty-six to fourteen British. The speeches are therefore mostly in French: for the English members all understand and speak that language, while very few of the French members have any knowledge of English.'[8] So Canada was no longer French, but it was the English who were bilingual, and this situation, characteristic of power relationships, suggests that French was then the dominant language. Nevertheless, and it is here that the change of which I have spoken showed through, English began to influence French. Tocqueville, as we

[6] Tocqueville, *Journey to America*, tr. G. Lawrence (Faber, 1959), 187.
[7] Ibid.
[8] G. Bouthillier and J. Meynaud, *Le choc des langues au Québec, 1760–1970* (Montreal, 1972), 124.

saw, observed this influence in the barristers' language; the same Lambert observed it in the street:

A curious sort of jargon is carried on in the market-place, between the French, who do not understand English, and the English who do not understand French. Each endeavours to meet the other half-way, in his own tongue; by which means they contrive to comprehend one another, by broken phrases . . . The intercourse between the French and the English has occasioned the former to ingraft many anglicisms in their language, which to a stranger arriving from England and speaking only boarding-school French, is at first rather puzzling. The Canadians have had the character of speaking the purest French, but I question whether they deserve it at the present day.[9]

In 1855, Jean-Jacques Ampère, son of the physicist and Professor of French Literature at the Collège de France, was shocked by what he heard:

I had scarcely disembarked when a quarrel that arose between two carters brought to my ear expressions which are not to be found in the dictionary of the Academy, but which are also a sort of French. Alas! Our language is in the minority on shop-signs, and when it does appear, it is often altered and corrupted by the proximity of English. I read with sadness: *manufacteur de tabac*, *syrup de toute description*, the feeling for gender is being lost because it does not appear in English, and plural signs disappear in places where it is absent in the rival language. It is a distressing sign of foreign influence over a nation that resists, defeated by grammar after being defeated by arms![10]

These different texts in fact show us two different things: on one hand, the influence of English over French, obvious in the anglicisms noticed by our authors, and on the other hand the preponderance of English in commercial life (signs, the market, etc.). On this terrain the factors which until then had favoured the promotion of French were ineffective.

Throughout the nineteenth century, French Canadians pursued the struggle for their language's rights with notable success. In 1848, the British Parliament repealed the article of the Act of Union which proscribed French, and in 1867 article 133 of the Canadian Constitution gave French the status of official language in the Parliaments of Ottawa and Quebec, and in the courts, and specified that the laws should be printed in both languages. But all of this made little difference to the real relations between the languages. I spoke, in the title of this section, of skirmishes, and this is indeed the case: small squabbles here and there, irrelevant to

[9] Ibid. 123.
[10] J.-J. Ampère, *Promenade en Amérique: États-Unis–Cuba–Mexico* (Paris, 1855).

the real problems. In 1865, the Abbé Chardonnet, delivering the sermon of St John the Baptist in the cathedral of Quebec, employed a warlike tone which on its own would justify this book's title:

> And honour to all those of you who, without taking away anything from the sacred right of our national language, have taken up a foreign weapon in the struggle, have snatched it from the hands of your adversaries, and wielded it yourselves. . . . Everywhere, in our public squares, in our streets, in our offices, in our salons, you can hear the sound of the invading pronunciation of a foreign language. . . . Very well, it is a battlefield where the struggle still goes on and where, less than on any other, can we hope to win alone. It is the field of our way of life, the vital struggle for our language and customs.

But this flight of oratory was hardly more effective that the *Marseillaise* which, as we know, has never won a war, even when sung with the utmost conviction. Confronted by English, which was spread by economic growth, French appeared above all as the language of the Catholic religion: 'the language that guards the faith', 'be good French-speaking Christians', these themes launched by the Church, which found itself in the front line of the language struggle, show that the two languages involved corresponded to very different social realities.

The 'victory' of 1867, and the other gains which have followed up to the present day (education was of course one terrain for guerilla warfare, but there was also the coinage, which was made bilingual in 1936, and, from 1953 to 1962, a long campaign was fought for the right to write cheques in French) made little change to the situation, and there is nothing to prove that law 101, which protected the use of French in public life and was the last stage of the war, has really changed it either. But the example of Quebec is interesting in that it can be taken as a lesson, as a prefiguration of what is today, in France, the 'defence of French'.

The 'Defence' of French

Between the sixteenth and the nineteenth centuries, the major preoccupation of the state, in the linguistic domain, was to ensure the supremacy of French over the other languages of the country. On 15 August 1539, the Edict of Villers-Cotterêts, often quoted, stipulated that henceforth legal instruments should be: 'delivered, recorded and issued to the parties in the French mother tongue'. But it was not just Villers-Cotterêts: 'These prescriptions were renewed by Charles IX in article 35 of the Edict of 1563, the so-called *Roussillon Ordonnance*. They were further extended to ecclesiastical justice in 1629. The use of French for public instruments was enacted in 1621 for Béarn, in 1684 for Flanders, in 1685 for Alsace and in 1700 and 1753 for Roussillon', writes Xavier Deniau,[11] and this list is far from complete. In all these examples, and up until the law of 2 Thermidor, Year II ('Law declaring that from the day of its publication, no public instrument, in any part of the republic's territory, may be written in anything but the French language', and those who contravened this were liable to six months in prison and, for civil servants, dismissal), we may observe intervention into languages (in the plural) by the state, an intervention guided by a single principle: the imposition of monolingualism on France. Today state intervention seems to have changed direction; the priority is not action on languages but also on the language (in the singular), and in the last thirty years in France we can find echoes of what we have just seen in Quebec.

Ever since the first attacks of 'Franglais', language specialists, solemnly attending at the bedside, tell us that French is in a bad way. They diagnose two recurring kinds of illness, some internal and some external.

Internally, that is, at the level of the language, the same complaint is heard on all sides: the language is going downhill, the French speak it (and write it) worse and worse, and a recent book bears a title that is significant from this point of view, *The Crisis of Languages*.[12] In it one finds, alongside essays devoted to different languages of the world (Hebrew, Chinese, Spanish, Korean, etc.), four chapters devoted to French, in Quebec, France, Belgium, and Switzerland. The diagnoses here are different: in Quebec, a crisis of orthography; in France, the relationship with standard French, etc. And this is not something new: already in 1909 G. Lançon published a work entitled *La Crise du français*. But the profound ambiguity of these examinations of 'the crisis of the language' resides in the contradiction that, although beginning with the diagnosis of an 'internal illness' they come to treat it as an 'external illness', for the sickness of French has a name, the name of another language, English. To find convincing evidence, it is enough to run through the legal texts. J.-P. Goudaillier[13] has drawn up a list of decrees concerning language published between 1973 and 1980. All concern vocabulary and all attempt to replace English words by French words in fields as varied as broadcasting, public works, oil, transport, information technology, medicine, defence,

[11] X. Deniau, *La Francophonie* (Paris, 1983), 82.
[12] *La Crise des langues*, texts collected by J. Maurais (Paris, 1985).
[13] J.-P. Goudaillier, 'Sprache und Macht: Wie ein Gesetz in Frankreich die Sprache reinigen will', *Dialect*, no. 6 (1982), 28–37.

the aerospace industry. Since then, more ministerial decrees on terminology have appeared, concerning tourism (17 March 1982), telecommunications (27 April 1982), broadcasting and advertising (18 February 1983), airborne and spaceborne remote-sensing (20 October 1984), and even the 'vocabulary of old people' (13 March 1985). Alongside these proposals for neologisms, the legislative arsenal is also equipped with punitive texts, like the law 'relating to use of the French language', known as the 'Bas law', which allows for the conviction of companies who do not use French in France (for example, British Airways was convicted because it had released airplane tickets in English), and a circular of 14 March 1977 stressed that 'the law makes the use of French obligatory in written texts and inscriptions, and prohibits the presence of foreign expressions when equivalent French terms exist, in the following fields: supply and demand of goods and services, in the news and presentation of radio and television programmes'.[14]

Between Ineffectiveness and Chauvinism

In fact, French language policy has discovered terminology, 'a new science' according to Philippe de Saint-Robert, 'Commissar-general of the French language',[15] whose powers, according to the decree of 9 February 1984, cover in particular the co-ordination of 'work carried out on the subject of terminology'. Full of confidence from this discovery, it has launched itself into a crusade against word-borrowings, especially borrowings from English. Saint-Robert, in the preface I have just quoted, poses the problem aggressively:

Should a language defend itself? Of course it should, although a number of lazy minds, who think of themselves as independent thinkers, suggest as a shiningly obvious truth that a defensive attitude is already an admission of weakness. The fact that all living organisms are born threatened is less an admission of weakness that an admission of mortality; language behaves like a living organism which, throughout its existence, sees some of its cells die, others born, and keeps renewing the spirit that animates it.

This metaphor of the language as a living organism is an old one, and here as elsewhere it has the weakness of leaving out of consideration the language's driving force: does a language develop through its speakers or

[14] J.-P. Goudaillier, 'Sprache und Macht: Wie ein Gesetz in Frankreich die Sprache reinigen will', *Dialect*, no. 6 (1982), 30.
[15] Preface to *Guide des mots nouveaux* (Paris, 1985).

through terminology commissions? For, more deeply, this approach to the problem raises two questions, a question of effectiveness and a question of ideology.

The question of effectiveness is obvious, and we have encountered it throughout the third part of this book. In the previous chapter I wrote that cross-breeding has always been a great provider of lexis and that languages live by reciprocal borrowings. This was not a theoretical position; I was simply drawing the lesson of the history of languages, of all languages. Such borrowings have never been the product of official decisions, they were 'proposed' by speakers who used them and 'accepted' or 'rejected' by other speakers whose collective linguistic practice makes language. Of course, they are evidence for power-relationships: words are not borrowed from just any language and in just any field. It is possible to read in the lexical strata of a language, in the borrowings it has made at different periods from other languages, the types of relationship the speakers of this language had with those of other languages, that is, economic or social relationships. But the borrowings are here only symptoms, they are not the illness, if there is an illness. In other words, the real invasion of the French language by English words testifies first of all to a technical supremacy in the English-speaking countries, and if one considers this to be an 'epidemic', then we should study the epidemiology that teaches us that one does not fight illness by decrees, that one does not bring it to an end by prohibiting its entry. The terminology commissions which have flourished in the last fifteen years or so and the power conferred upon them by the law are a little reminiscent of an arboriculturalist who tries to treat a wilting tree by painting its yellowed leaves green rather than by improving the soil. The question of the effectiveness of such an approach to the problem is therefore open. We saw, on the subject of neologisms, that it is completely possible to modernize the vocabulary of a language, even if this sometimes poses ideological problems, but in the case referred to the aim was to create new words to refer to notions which until then had not been referred to in the language in question. On the other hand, the desire to replace an already existing (and borrowed) vocabulary by another, an autochthonous one, implies the intervention of a highly planned state. In the case of Turkey which we studied in Chapter 12, one can of course stress the modernist and secular tendencies of Mustafa Kemal Ataturk which were the driving force of the 'language revolution', but it is impossible to pass over the profoundly authoritarian and xenophobic aspect of his policy in silence. It is here that the struggle against foreign terms borrowed by French poses a problem.

In December 1985, while the Haut Conseil International de la Francophonie was meeting in Paris, Pierre Bercis (President of the Social Rights of Man) published a strange article in *Le Monde*. Lumping together the people who would today refuse to defend the French language with those who in the past collaborated with the Nazi occupiers, he wrote:

The fate reserved for the French language has enormous significance. In the same way that the loyalty of those who have decided to react against its humiliation is philosophically or politically significant. They are, very nearly, those who chose or would have chosen Resistance: true Gaullists, convinced Socialists, Communists. . . . As for the others, people like Doriot, their claim is that nothing can be done and that it is better to 'go over to the barbarians' and to draw as much advantage from this as possible. At the same time the masses applaud Pétain, then de Gaulle, believing each of them to be right in turn.[16]

Further on, this defender of the rights of man made this call for repression: 'Despite what the government believes, persuasion is not enough. The amount of corruption caused by the search for easy profits is so great that the government will never succeed in making the fifth column see reason, except by sanctions that are as exemplary as they are severe.' Of course a hysterical text like this should not be confused with the positions of all defenders of French, but the general tone of the arguments put forward by the latter has troubling connotations. For direct state intervention into language with the intention of 'purifying' it took place not only in Turkey but also in the majority of Fascist countries. The defenders of French should realize that Mussolini suppressed the teaching of French in the Val d'Aoste in 1925[17] (an area until then officially bilingual), and that he then had all French-sounding place-names replaced by Italian names (even the question of Italianizing surnames was raised in 1939). From 1923 onwards, he penalized the use of foreign words on posters and shop-signs with fines.[18] In Franco's Spain, there was a succession of laws to prohibit the use of non-Castilian words for posters, trade-names, etc., and the use of non-Castilian patronyms in the registering of births, marriages, and deaths, these measures being primarily directed against the Catalan and Basque languages.[19] In Germany, non-Germanic place-names were systematically replaced by 'purer' names in Pomerania, Silesia, etc. In short, all these measures, similar to

[16] P. Bercis, 'Les Amers-looks', *Le Monde*, 10 Dec. 1985.
[17] Decree-law of 22 Nov. 1925, no. 2191.
[18] Decree-law of 11 Feb. 1923, no. 352.
[19] See e.g. F. Ferrer i Girones, *La persecucio politica de la llengua catalana* (Barcelona, 1985).

those taken in Turkey during the 'language revolution' are, at the same time, not very different from those which, as we have seen, have been taken in France in the last fifteen years.

Klaus Bochman, an East German linguist, has compared the language policies of the different Fascist states, and found four constant factors: a xenophobic purism at the level of the national language; an anti-dialectical centralism; a nationalist centralism directed against national minorities; and a linguistic colonialism or expansionism outside the country's frontiers.[20]

Now these four tendencies are found in many language policies, in particular, in France's policy, at different periods of its history. The ambiguity can be seen: it is because they have been taken by Fascist regimes that the linguistic measures listed above appear, a posteriori, open to criticism, but taken by a democratic regime they appear acceptable. Nevertheless the differences between Italian language policy under Mussolini, Spanish under Franco, German under Hitler, and the law 'relating to the use of French' passed in 1975 are differences of degree and not of kind.

Is this language policy Fascist, then? Surely not, but it is clearly chauvinistic and above all, alas, doomed to ineffectiveness since it is not based on a serious analysis of the situation. We shall see in fact, on the subject of the international status of the French language, that this situation is to be treated by an external approach, a sociolinguistic approach, and not by internal tinkering. The power of the Anglo-Saxon countries, in particular the United States, will not be changed by fighting against borrowings from English, any more than the status of women will be changed by giving feminine forms to the names of trades and professions.

French in the World

The preceding pages were about the defence of the French language and attempts at excluding recently borrowed foreign words, which some think a danger to the language. But there is another discourse on language, complementary to the one we have just discussed, according to which French might lose its international position, and give ground almost everywhere abroad; this corresponds with another branch of language policy, which intervenes not in the form of the language but in its functions.

[20] K. Bochman, 'Pour une étude comparée de la glottopolitique des fascismes', in *Problèmes de glottopolitique* (Université de Rouen, 1985), 119–29.

Here again, we must be precise. It is probable that in the course of its history French has never been spoken across the world as much as today, and this has come about as much through the natural increase in the population of native French-speakers as from the consequences of colonial expansion. Between France, Belgium, Switzerland, Luxembourg, and Canada there are around 70 million speakers for whom French is their first language, a number to which should be added the speakers of North and Black Africa, difficult to calculate, and those of Asia (former Indochina). There are about 40 million inhabitants in North Africa and a hundred million in so-called 'Francophone' Africa and Madagascar. If we start from the reasonable hypothesis that 10% of them speak French (but the question of what is meant by 'speak a language' still needs to be understood), that would give us an extra 14 million French-speakers. If we add to this the people across the world who have studied French at school and at university, and they are many (there are about 30,000 French teachers abroad, and 250,000 teachers of French in the world, 25 million pupils who study French in secondary schooling, 250,000 who take courses with Alliances Françaises, etc.) we reach a total of speakers of French as first or second language which would have astonished Rivarol when he wrote his *Discours sur l'universalité de la langue française*: being very prudent, about one hundred million. Certainly we are a long way from some very optimistic evaluation, like the 264 millions quoted by X. Deniau in his work of French-speaking countries,[21] but we have nonetheless evidence for a remarkable increase in the number of speakers.

We can add to this that, from the functional point of view, the situation of French has also developed positively. At the time when, so it is said, everyone spoke French in Europe, this 'everyone' meant, in a very elitist way, the nobles and the high bourgeoisie whose members were often educated in French, but did not really include the European population. It is quite obvious that the peoples of Europe spoke their respective languages and not French. From this point of view, French has been democratized, at the same time as it has spread across new continents and gone beyond the frontiers of Europe within which it was, according to Rivarol, 'universal'. From the social point of view as from the geographic point of view, the French language has acquired a stronger position than a century ago.

So where do these pessimistic discourses on the retreat of French come from? They result, of course, from a different analysis, which takes into

[21] Deniau, *La Francophonie*, 45.

account not the progress of French, but its retreat in relation to English. Once again, the 'illness' of French has a name, the name of another language. In fact, in the great majority of international organizations (UN, UNESCO, OAU) French coexists as official language with, as the case may be, English, Spanish, Russian, Arabic, and Chinese. A Belgian who has worked as an international official notes that more and more French has been spoken at the UN since the 1960s:

I experienced the French language's difficult times at the UN. We had a Secretary-General who was indifferent, if not hostile, to its use; a body of officials obliged to listen to each other in English, the only language that climbed the thirty-eight storeys of the centre. . . . But since this testing time a political upheaval has taken place with a miraculous effect for French: the emancipation of Africa. The mass admission into the UN of twenty-two new African states speaking French raised the number of delegations using our language to almost a third. From that moment everything changed: atmosphere, conditions of work, debates, votes, public relations. In the general debates of the Assembly there are now as many French speeches as English.[22]

It remains clear, however, that English everywhere exceeds French, not only in the number of native speakers, which is nearly four times larger, but also and above all through the extent of the economic, cultural, and political growth of countries speaking English, in particular the United States. Here we are at the heart of the problem, and it would be a mistake to consider only its linguistic aspect, since the roots lie elsewhere. At the time of the 'universality of the French language', the United States did not exist on a world scale, but today it is the leading economic power in the world. The massive borrowings from English which we discussed in the preceding section are also the result of this situation. If, to the annoyance of purists, the French use a 'walkman' and not a 'baladeur', to take only one example, this is quite simply because the 'walkman' has come from the United States, in the same way that the English have always spoken of fashion, art, and perfumes by using a vocabulary borrowed from French. The problem, then, is a sociolinguistic one or, to put it another way, it comes under what some call functional linguistics: the problem cannot be resolved by acting on language, but by acting on the situation is which the language is dying and for which it provides some evidence. This is what has to be kept in mind when evaluating the language policy of France and French-speaking countries.

[22] Robert Fenaux, *Discours sur la fonction internationale de la langue française* (Liege, n.d.), 63.

This leads us to the phenomenon of French-speaking and, more broadly, to organizations for the propagation and defence of French. The term 'francophonie' appeared in the last century with a sense very close to the present one. It was Onésime Reclus who created the word 'francophonie' while working out a typology of the populations of the world based on the languages they used. Born under the pen of a geologist, the word reappeared in 1962 under the pen of a statesman who was also a poet, Léopold Senghor. The notion slowly took political form through the foundation of different French or international organizations: here is a list for the Presidencies of Charles de Gaulle and Georges Pompidou.

- 1961, foundation of the Association des Universités Partiellement ou Entièrement de Langue Française (AUPELF).
- 1966, foundation of the Haut Comité pour la Défense et l'Expansion de la Langue Française, which in 1973 became the Haut Comité de la Langue Française.
- 1967, foundation of the Association Internationale des Parlementaires de Langue Française (AIPLF).
- 1967 again, foundation of the Conseil International de la Langue Française (CILF) and holding of the first 'Biennale de la langue française'.
- 1970, foundation of the Association de Coopération Culturelle et Technique (ACCT).
- 1973, foundation of the Comité de la Francophonie.
- 1974, foundation of the Comité Interministerial pour les Affaires Francophones, and so on.

To these official organizations can be added, for the same period, regular meetings of conferences of ministers from francophone countries (education, culture, youth, health) and the foundation of various professional francophone associations.

As the discourse on the dangers of penetration of French by English developed (see in particular the decrees on terminology listed above for the period 1973–85), we can see the development of an official effort to spread French outside France, through the foundation of different organizations and the provision of large sums of money for linguistic and pedagogical operations (for example, the production of school television programmes for abroad, help for the publication of textbooks, etc.).

Today (1986), then, the problem of the defence and propagation of the French language comes under a number of different authorities. The following list is incomplete: the Commissariat Général de la Langue Française, a Secretary of State responsible for the speaking of French, the Division Générale des Relations Scientifiques, Culturelles et Techniques

(DGRST, an organization of the Ministry for Foreign Affairs), the Haut Comité de la Langue Française, without forgetting, of course, the immortal Académie Française. Still, it may be feared that this profusion of organizations, energy, and sources of finance is not necessarily a guarantee of effectiveness and that this type of language policy misses the point. Since 1634, when Richelieu founded the Académie Française, there has been a tendency in France to think that language problems can be settled by applying standards and by state intervention. Linguists never stop saying the opposite, but in vain. Rather than take up this discussion again here, I would prefer, since we are dealing with the question of effectiveness, to compare what we have just seen of French language planning with what happens in the United States. If English is so widespread in the world, this is because they have an effective policy, surely?

The language problem arose at the time of the Declaration of Independence, in 1776. The North American population had come from different countries and spoke different languages, and the new state found itself faced with a problem of multilingualism very similar to the problem experienced today by developing countries. Shirley Brice Heath has devoted a long article to this question[23] from which it emerges that first of all, looking at the question internally, the 'founding fathers' refused to make English the official language, believing quite simply that it would establish itself, without official support: their language policy consisted in not having a policy. Accordingly, in the first years of the Union, Congress published some of its documents in French and German in order to spread them more effectively in some regions. Besides, Heath writes, the majority of American politicians identified the desire to standardize language with the practice of European monarchies, and the academies of France and Spain were a model they rejected out of anti-royalist sentiment.

The language debates at the beginnings of the history of the United States are a good illustration of this position. In 1780 John Adams, convinced by what he knew of Europe that a strong nation should have a strong language and that, for example, Holland lacked the international influence it deserved because its language had not spread beyond its borders, proposed to Congress the foundation of a public institution resembling an American Academy, an institution which the English had not founded and whose existence would bring honour to Americans. He increased the number of his speeches, varied his arguments, but his

[23] S. B. Heath, 'A National Language Academy? Debate in the New Nation', *International Journal of the Sociology of Language*, no. 11 (1976), 9–43.

proposals were finally buried in a commission of Congress: 'Adams himself was often termed a monarchist', Heath writes, 'and his proposal for a centralised language academy must have seemed to many republicans further "proof" of his monarchist leanings'.[24] All the same the debate was not over, and it crystallized around two opposing positions. One consisted in asserting the linguistic independence of the United States, that is, the right of Americans to make English a language different from the one spoken in Great Britain, to create new words, etc. This was, for example, the position of Noah Webster, proposing to establish an 'American dictionary', and also the position of John Adams proposing in 1812 to place a special tax on all dictionaries imported from Britain. Taking the opposite view, others called for the purity of the language to be protected; one of these was John Pickering, a member of the 'American Academy of Arts and Sciences' (a private society founded in Boston), who presented a paper in 1815 insisting on the need for urgent action to impose standards, in his eyes a patriotic duty to keep the United States from losing the English language.

It was in this context that a group of intellectuals founded the 'American Academy of Languages and Belles Lettres' in 1820 with the avowed aim of purifying and codifying the language and with the hope of transforming itself into an Academy for the national language (naturally John Adams belonged to the society and also, surprisingly, the Marquis de Lafayette). But the 'American Academy of Language and Belles Lettres' never obtained any official support nor any subsidy from Congress, and the project slowly faded away, dying a natural death. Thereafter, the United States never had an official language policy, never intervened directly in this field.

And yet . . .

And yet, Joshua Fishman rightly notes that, despite this absence of constitutional or legal definition of an official language, millions of emigrants and indigenous peoples speaking other languages have been anglicized.[25] But it remains the case that there is a constant factor of close to 20% of the population who do not have English as a first language: 22 million whites in 1940 (18.6% of the white population), 33 million in 1970 (16.3% of the total population), and 28 million of the population over the age of 14 in 1975 (17.8%).[26]

---

[24] Heath, 'A National Language Academy?', 22.

[25] J. Fishman, 'Language Policy: Past, Present and Future', in *Language in the USA* (Cambridge, 1981).

[26] Dorothy Waggoner, 'Statistics on Language Use', in *Language in the USA* (Cambridge, 1981), 486–515.

And yet, also, English is today the world language most spoken as a second language, even if the considerable increase in immigration from central America and Cuba should lead to Spanish one day being able to compete with it on American territory.

This situation might seem paradoxical, when compared to the result of the policy of promoting French. Of course, private organizations (like the Ford Foundation or the Summer Institute of Linguistics) have taken over from the state, but it remains the case that globally it does not seem to have ever been the primary objective of the United States to spread its culture (perhaps because it does not have its own culture, but that is another story) and its language; its imperialism has been principally political and economic. And language has followed.

There is an important lesson in this example: a language does not spread only because it is a medium for literature. This cultural factor has little weight in the face of economic and political factors. It certainly played a leading role in the growth of French up to the nineteenth century, but this growth, as we have said, only reached the elite minority, and is in no way comparable to what is taking place today between French and English. And when, with the rise of nationalism and the emergence of nations, national literatures have flourished in national languages, the status of French was largely destabilized. All official action in French-speaking countries since then seems to have completely neglected this fundamental fact in its analyses: cultural arguments cannot compete when the driving force behind the spread of a language is economic. Faced by the immense American machine, the defenders of French have begun trench warfare: while English was imposing itself in Canada as the language of commerce, French was recently being defended as the language of the Catholic religion; while today English spreads as the language of an economic hegemony, of a science and technology in continuous progress and, incidentally, as the language of the culture of rock and Coca-Cola, French is defended as the language of a cultural community. This contrast bears the stamp of two analyses of the world, of two ideologies. Perhaps it also indicates the conflict's final result.

17

The Pacificist Illusion and Esperanto

Faced by the myth of Babel and the reality of multilingualism, human-kind, as we have seen, has taken up the challenge *in vivo*; pidgins as well as lingua francas demonstrate that social practice has usually been able to provide itself with means of communication, despite the multiplicity of languages.

Historic Landmarks

In the seventeenth century, however, there appeared in Europe the notion that it might be possible to resolve the problems posed by multilingualism *in vitro*, by constructing a universal language. Evidence of this exists, for example, in the writings of Comenius (Jan Komensky), such as *La Porte ouverte sur les langues* (1631), but also in a long letter by René Descartes who kept up a large scientific correspondence from Amsterdam. On 20 November 1629 he devoted a letter to the plan that a correspondent, Martin Mersenne, had put forward, a plan for a new language in which there would only be 'one way of conjugating, declining and constructing words'. The philosopher showed his reservations from the very first sentence: 'This proposal for a new language seems more remarkable at first than I find it upon close examination.' The end of his letter is even more explicit: 'I believe that such a language is possible', he writes, continuing a little later: 'but do not expect ever to see it in use. For this to happen, there would have to be great changes in the order of things, and the earth would have to become a terrestrial paradise, which is only worth proposing in the world of fiction.'[1]

It is interesting to note that, even though Descartes suggests in passing that it would be simpler if everyone learnt Latin, this notion of a con-structed language emerges precisely at the time when Latin's function as a lingua franca was losing ground. There are many anecdotes from the end of the seventeenth century which show this, such as the long debate

[1] René Descartes, *Oeuvres et lettres*, Gallimard edition, Bibliothèque de la Pléiade (Paris, 1937), 698–702.

(1670–1681) concerning the language that should be used for the inscriptions on a triumphal arch for Louis XIV, or the scandal caused in 1660 by the publication of a missal in French by Voisin.[2] It is shown above all by the fact that French was gaining ground as a language for teaching, as well as for literary and scientific writings. Until then communication between people of different languages had been in Latin and now its effectiveness was being placed in doubt. Leibniz, a little later, took up the same idea with his 'characteristica universalis', in the desire to establish a symbolic system that would allow, in the sciences, communication that did not require natural languages. In both cases there was a sort of universal grammar for a written language, with the help of which everyone would understand each other from one end of the earth to the other: the reader can see that in this project we have the archetype of all artificial languages.

In the nineteenth century, the 'logothètes', to adopt a neologism from Roland Barthes, the inventors of language, changed direction. Until then they had argued primarily in terms of the classification of ideas, natural languages being considered by philosophers as misleading and imperfect; from now on they would actually construct languages. There was no shortage of schemes. Pierre Janton numbers them at nearly 500.[3] Without going this far, and without special research, it is easy to establish a list of about one hundred languages. The one that follows[4] is shorter because I stop at 1914, but it does show the intense 'logothetic' activity between 1879, the date of the invention of Volapük, and 1914. In particular, during the first fourteen years of this century, one can see from this list, which is certainly very incomplete, that there were two new 'languages' per year.

1858 Cosmoglossa
1868 Universalglot
1879 Volapük
1883 Weltsprache
1887 Balta
1887 Esperanto
1887 Spokil
1888 Spelin
1889 Anglo-franca
1890 Mundolingue
1893 Dil

[2] F. Brunot, *Histoire de la langue française*, v (Paris, 1917), 10–20, 25 et seq.
[3] P. Janton, *L'Espéranto* (Paris, 1973), 13.
[4] Simply drawn up from the work of Janton mentioned above and that of M. Yaguello, *Les Fous du langage* (Paris, 1984).

1896 Veltparl
1898 Dilpok
1900 Lingua komum
1902 Reformlatein
1902 Universal Latein
1902 Idiom neutral
1903 Latino sine flexione
1903 Interlingua
1904 Perio
1905 Lingua internacional
1906 Mondlingvo
1906 Ulla
1907 Ido
1907 Lingwo incernaciona
1907 Apolema
1907 Lingua european
1908 Mez-voio
1908 Romanizat
1908 Dutalingue
1909 Romanal
1910 Adjuvilo
1910 Nuv-esperanto
1910 Reform-esperanto
1910 Semi-Latin
1910 Perfect
1911 Latin-esperanto
1911 Latin-ido
1911 Lingw adelfenzal
1911 Simplo
1911 Novi Latine
1911 Molog
1912 Reform neutral
1914 Europeo

These facts call for a few remarks which will perhaps help us to make sense of the phenomenon of artificial languages.

First of all, it is interesting to note that an average knowledge of the languages of Western Europe (and especially of the Romance languages) enables us to understand the roots from which the names of these artificial languages were coined, and this is in turn evidence for the striking Eurocentrism of these creators of 'universal languages'.

Secondly, we should stress that the notion of a 'lingua universalis' appeared at the moment in history when the use of Latin as a lingua franca declined among the elites of Europe. It was then embodied in numerous projects at another historical moment, when French, which had taken the place of Latin, itself began to decline in that function. In both cases, we find the same temptation to resolve the problems of international communication *in vitro*, and in the second case we see a close link between the emergence of the 'Esperanto phenomenon' and of nation-states. The very idea of a universal language appears as a response to the national (and linguistic) division of Europe.

Lastly, the frequency of constructed languages seems to increase as the First World War approaches, as if these projects were attempts to avert the catastrophe appearing on the political horizon.

Volapük and Esperanto, the only languages in this long list that had any success, thus appeared as bearers of a particular message, which we shall analyse a little later, when we have completed this historical survey.

Volapük, the first artificial language to come off the drawing-board and reach the practical stage, experienced a popularity as remarkable as it was brief:

Ten years after its appearance, 25 journals were being printed in the language, 283 societies had been established, and there were textbooks in 25 languages. An academy was founded, which was not slow to discuss reforms. The intransigence of the inventor caused all of these to fail and provoked a schism then a crumbling away from 1889.[5]

It was Esperanto that profited from this failure to fulfil a function made necessary by circumstances and to occupy the place available. In 1887 L. L. Zamenhof, born in 1859, published his first pamphlet concerning what he called the 'international language'; the word 'esperanto' was the pseudonym under which he signed the text. Two years later, the first magazine appeared, *La esperantisto*, in 1894 Zamenhof published a dictionary, then a collection of exercises, and finally in 1905, the *Fundamento de Esperanto*, a work which summed up the grammar in sixteen rules.

Then the international congresses began: 1905 in Boulogne-sur-Mer, 1906 in Geneva, 1907 in Cambridge, 1908 in Dresden, 1909 in Barcelona, 1910 in Washington, 1911 in Anvers. There were 668 people at the first congress, 3,739 signed on for the one in Paris, in 1914 (which did not take place, because of the war); the number of Esperantists increased regularly, although it is difficult to evaluate exactly the extent of this diaspora. Today the Universal Association of Esperanto has between 30,000 and 40,000

[5] Janton, *L'Espéranto*, 21.

members, but some count the number of speakers of the language at 15 million.[6] Be that as it may, it is clear that Esperanto is the only artificial universal language to have survived, and what's more its name has become synonymous with artificial language in people's minds: this says it all.

The Ideology of Esperanto

If we wish to understand what animates the members of this diaspora, we should of course begin with Zamenhof's own personality. From this point of view, one of his letters is significant:

If I were not a Jew from the ghetto, the idea of uniting humanity would not have entered my mind, nor would it have obsessed me so obstinately throughout my life. No one can feel the misfortune of human division as strongly as a Jew of the ghetto. No one can feel the need for a humanly neutral and non-national language as strongly as a Jew, who is required to pray to God in a long dead language, who receives his education and instruction in the language of a people who reject it, and who has companions in suffering over the whole earth, with whom he cannot gain understanding. . . . Since my earliest childhood, my Jewishness has been the principal cause why I have devoted myself to one idea and one essential dream—the dream of uniting humanity.[7]

So, from one point of view, the idea of a universal language is Zamenhof's response to an unhappy situation which in others will give birth to the ideology of Zionism (*The Jewish state*, by T. Herzl, dates from 1886). His speeches at congresses, like his writings, reveal an almost religious conception of the community of Esperanto speakers. In the letter quoted above, he writes to his correspondent: 'Promoting the cause of Esperanto is only part of this idea' and he speaks of a plan 'which I shall call Hillelism and which consists in creating a moral bridge capable of linking all people and all religions in brotherhood. My plan consists in creating a religious unity which would embrace all existing religions in peace and reconcile them all.'

Hillelism (which owes its name to Rabbi Hillel, who inspired Zamenhof) was not very successful with Esperanto speakers, who preferred to appeal to the neutrality asserted during their congress in Geneva. But, at this same congress, Zamenhof declared:

The country of Esperanto is governed not only by the Esperanto language, but also by the internal idea of Esperanto. . . . The motto of the ideal Esperantist,

---

[6] Janton, *L'Espéranto*, 112–14.
[7] Letter to Michaux, dated 21 Feb. 1905, quoted in Janton, *L'Espéranto*, 30.

which has never precisely formulated until now, but always clearly felt, is this: we desire to lay down a neutral foundation, on which the different peoples of humanity can communicate in peace and fraternity . . .

Torn between neutrality and universality, the adherents of Esperanto experienced deep ideological debates which in part explain the schism of 1907 and the foundation of Ido, but which can also be seen in the constant conflicts between those who took an 'elitist' line and those who took a 'populist' line.[8] The one thing that is clear, apart from these details, which do not matter much here, is that the very idea of a universal language is inseparable from a certain pacifism which was interpreted differently, in different places, according to the ideology of the moment and affected the way in which Esperanto was treated. During the period when the ideas of Nikolai Marr[9] reigned in the USSR for example, when it was thought that the languages of the world must converge, with the appearance of world socialism, in a single proletarian language, Esperanto was widespread in the countries of the East, since its ideology corresponded with official ideology. Today, it is well thought of in China, being considered as a possible curb on linguistic imperialisms, for example.

Then there is the ideology of Esperantists themselves, their behaviour, insofar as this use of the plural can cover an ununified reality and we can speak of Esperantists as a whole. Let us say simply that in encountering them one meets earnest people, as all that we have said would lead one to suppose, whose convictions generate three kinds of behaviour.

First of all, there is a proselytism about language that is not to be found anywhere else. It is difficult to imagine even the most enthusiastic of French-speakers attempting to convince their neighbours of the benefits of speaking French. But it should be specified that on this point Esperantists are relatively discreet, that they are content to distribute pamphlets, texts, but hardly anything else.

Secondly, they have an approach to the spreading of Esperantist ideas which in recent years seems to be modelled on the spread of scientific ideas. Esperantists organize conferences, to which they invite non-Esperantist linguists or sociologists; they have close relations with

[8] See e.g. Marti Garcia-Ripoll Duran, 'Cent anys d'esperanto. Apunts per a una sociologia d'una llengua internacional minoritzasa', communication to the *IInd congrès internacional de la llengua catalana* (Girona, 1986).

[9] The Russian linguist Nikolai Marr proposed a monogenetic theory of language: all languages evolved from one original made up of four basic elements. Languages themselves were the products of the underlying socio–economic structure and were therefore class-related and not national phenomena.

UNESCO, and in these cases they pose the problem in terms of international communication, by referring to the MacBride report for example. At this level, to use political terms and without any desire for controversy, I would say that they tend to the practice of entryism, of infiltration.

Thirdly, this leads, as is normal with people who have strong convictions and share the same ideas, to a group attitude which is sometimes in contradiction with the desire, described above, for a scientific approach to the problem, and which can turn to sectarianism. I will give only one example, but a very significant one. Often quoted in Esperantist publications is this remark of the great linguist Antoine Meillet: 'All theoretical discussion is vain, Esperanto has worked.'[10] Now this sentence, taken from a book long since out of print and hard to find, is naturally quoted out of context, and the sentence that follows it in the original text, 'it has only failed to enter into practical usage'[11] throws a quite different light upon it. But the sentence that follows is never quoted. In fact, Meillet was not at all hostile to the idea of an artificial international language, and he wrote a few pages later: 'the practical utility of an international language is obvious. And, since this language is possible, it should be achievable'.[12] But the use of a quotation taken out of context for publicity purposes provides scientific support for an idea that Meillet surely did not have: that Esperanto is used more than it is in reality.

The Sociolinguistic Approach

Be that as it may, for me the problem is not to be posed in these terms. It is certainly useful, if we wish to understand the 'Esperanto phenomenon', to try to understand its origins and to examine the behaviour of Esperantists. On this level, it is clear that the idea of a universal language which everyone would learn as a second language is based on noble and respectable principles, and it is also clear that Esperanto 'militants' are not defending personal interests, which is not always the case with movements based on ideas.

But the real question lies elsewhere—it is to see whether what we have learnt from studying the history of languages makes the success of Espe-

---

[10] For example in Janton, *L'Espéranto*, 123, which does not give the source, or in *L'espéranto, un droit à la communication*, a pamphlet published by the l'Union Française pour l'Espéranto (n.d.), 13.

[11] Antoine Meillet, *Les Langues dans l'Europe nouvelle* (Paris, 1928), 278.

[12] Ibid. 282.

ranto's programmes plausible or, in other words, to examine it from the sociolinguistic point of view.

Throughout this book (cf. in particular Chapter 8) we have observed that the growth of a language in space and time is always the expression of another kind of growth, which could be military, economic, religious, cultural, etc., that it is evidence of deeper social changes. Now we have to ask, of what deep social change is Esperanto (or any other artificial language) the expression? I wrote in the introduction that the history of languages is the linguistic side of the history of societies, and that a language that gains ground is the linguistic sign of a human group gaining ground, to be precise, the speakers of that language. But the Esperanto community, insofar as they are a group of speakers, raises a theoretical problem for it is a diaspora, a dispersed community. Now there are no examples in history of a linguistic diaspora succeeding in imposing its language. The one example that might be thought of is the resurrection of Hebrew, but for this to happen the creation of Israel was required and it is to be doubted whether a language can be viable without a country of origin.

On the theoretical level, then, the Esperanto programme seems unrealizable, or at least corresponds to nothing that has been experienced, but this is not sufficient to disqualify it. More serious, though, are the results of all the studies which have been carried out on the way in which human communities manage multilingualism. On many occasions I have contrasted two types of approach to the problem, one *in vivo*, in the field, the other *in vitro*, in the laboratory. Now it is clear that Esperanto comes under the second approach and that, whenever a communication problem occurs, social practice will not be looking to Esperanto for a solution. In the second part of this book we have seen how lingua francas develop, how people manage to communicate in markets despite multilingualism, and how the practices of commercial transactions perhaps prefigure the language situation of tomorrow, in that markets reveal larger changes.

Esperanto has no part in any of this, which is quite natural; it comes under a different logic. But cold sociolinguistic analysis of the situation leads to only one conclusion: a pacificist, idealist solution to the war of languages seems unlikely. One may regret this, but personal feelings have nothing to do with it, and the figure of Zamenhof should be compared to Jean Jaurès, the indefatigable campaigner for peace on the brink of the Great War.

Conclusion

The world, which has been multilingual ever since its beginnings, is, because of this very multilingualism, the site of a vast semiotic conflict, of a permanent tension between the group and what is common to all, between the language of the home and of the market-place, between the languages of power and the languages of minorities. This tension is one of the driving forces of history, languages change as the world changes, and the development of the relations between them is evidence for the development of societies. We have encountered this 'war of languages' on different battlefields, in the family, in markets and on the routes along which lingua francas languages develop, but we have also seen that this war has been fought on another level, not by speakers but by their leaders, not along the routes which transcend frontiers but within the rigid frame of state frontiers. War is always an affair of state.

'A statesman, if he succeeds . . . in controlling the course of language at one of its decisive stages, adds to his power another power, which is both anonymous and effective',[1] writes Claude Hagège, and he adds, a little later: 'All language policies play the game of power by strengthening this power with one of its most loyal supports.' The title of an article by Glyn Williams echoes this remark: 'Language Planning or Language Expropriation?'[2] These two quotations are a good summary of the problem facing us at the end of this book.

Language planning can be considered as one of the techniques developed by sociolinguists, a technique that can be divided into two large fields, action on language (or internal action) and action on languages (or external action), since it is possible, in each of these fields, to subdivide further (neologisms, writing, unification of dialectical forms, etc.). As a technique, planning is part of the linguist's work, it is even the area in which his intervention most deeply concerns the future of our societies, for the destiny of languages is the destiny of their speakers. But, in these

[1] C. Hagège, *L'Homme de paroles* (Paris, 1985), 203.
[2] G. Williams, 'Language Planning or Language Expropriation?', *Journal of Multilingual and Multicultural Development*, 7: 6 (1986), 509–18.

different fields, we have also seen that intervention into language or languages is sometimes more of a military attack. For all planning presupposes a policy, the policy of those in power. And from that moment the linguist is confronted by a deontological problem: by intervening in languages, he becomes part of the power game.

This power, the power of the state, intervenes in what I have called the search for *in vitro* solutions but, there are, in contrast to bureaucratic solutions like these, the *in vivo* solutions achieved in social practice. My insistence on the fact that the history of languages is the language side of the history of societies has been too strong for the reader to think that the war of languages is a war on its own. Language conflicts speak to us of social conflicts, linguistic imperialism always indicates other kinds of imperialism and behind the war of languages can be seen another war— economic, cultural (we have seen many examples of this in our case studies), without the converse being necessarily true. The Japanese economy, for example, floods the world market with its products and yet the Japanese language has not followed this progress.

The 'planner', then, whether he likes it or not, is playing a role in these conflicts and imperialisms. In the face of the power that intervenes *in vitro*, it can be imagined that *in vivo* opposition will emerge. The war on the ground gives us more examples of this every day. But usually the linguist is to be found on the other side, the side of power, even if he only considers himself as a technician or adviser. If they are not careful, language officials, like all officials, risk becoming servants of the state. I have described the scientific paradox revealed by this situation, where the linguist is implicated in a planning operation that intervenes in a language, when he knows in fact that it has its own, autonomous life. But the linguist also knows that this life is the product of its speakers' activity, of their social practices, and that intervention by planning tends to dispossess speakers of their own language: all planning is carried out by a handful of planners possessing all the power over a people who are planned.

This does not mean that management of these problems has to be abandoned to those in power. On the contrary, if war is the continuation of politics by other means, then language policy is a civil war of languages. Once pacifist illusions are disposed of, it only remains for the linguist, in the course of carrying out his trade, to behave as a citizen and keep democratic watch on language policy at all times.

Bibliography

Agee, P. (1975), *Inside the Company: A CIA diary* (London: Allen Lane).

Albo, X. (1974), *Los mil rostros del quechua* (Lima).

Alioni, M. (1978), *La vida del pueblo shuar* (Sucua).

Allardice, R. (1984), 'Language Equilibrium in the Soviet Union', dissertation submitted in partial fulfilment of the degree of Master of Arts (University of York).

Ampère, J.-J. (1855), *Promenade en Amérique: États–Unis–Cuba–Mexique* (Paris).

Apte, Mahader (1976), 'Multilingualism and its Socio-Political Implications: An Overview', and 'Language Controversies in the Indian Parliament: 1952–1969', in W. O'Barr, J. O'Barry (eds.), *Language and Politics* (The Hague).

Asgurally, I. (1982), 'La Situation linguistique de l'île Maurice', postgraduate thesis under the supervision of L.-J. Calvet (Université Réné Descartes, Paris).

Avila, R. (1985), 'La Langue espagnole et son enseignement: Oppresseurs et opprimés', in *La Crise des langues* (Paris).

Balibar, R. (1985), *L'Institution du français* (Paris).

Barnes, D. (1983), 'The Implementation of Language Planning in China', in J. Cobarrubias and J. Fishman (eds.), *Progress in Language Planning*.

Barthes, R. (1957), *Mythologies* (Paris). Eng. translation by A. Lavers (London: Cape, 1972).

Bazin, L. (1985), 'La Réforme linguistique en Turquie', in *La Réforme des langues, histoire et avenir*, i (Hamburg: Buske Verlag).

Ben Jelloun, H. (1986), 'Pédagogie des jeunes sourds au Maroc, cas de Tetouan, problèmes linguistiques', postgraduate thesis under the supervision of Frederic François (Université Réné Descartes, Paris).

Benveniste, E. (1966), 'Communication animale et langage humain', *Diogène*, 1.

Bercis, P. (1985), 'Les Amers-looks', *Le Monde*, 10 Dec. 1985.

Bernus, S. (1969), *Particularismes ethniques en milieu urbain: L'Exemple de Niamey* (Paris: Institut d'ethnologie).

Bible, New English.

Blachère, R. (1959), *Introduction au Coran* (Paris).

Bochman, K. (1985), 'Pour une étude comparée de la glottopolitique des fascismes', in *Problèmes de glottopolitiques* (Université de Rouen).

Bounfour, A. (1976), 'Théories et méthodologies des grandes écoles de rhétorique arabe', thesis under the supervision of R. Barthes (Paris: Ecole pratique des hautes études, 6th section).

Bouthillier, G., and Meynaud, J. (1970), *Le Choc des langues au Québec, 1760–1970* (Montreal).

Brunot, F. (1905–1935), *Histoire de la langue française* (Paris).

Burney, P. (1966), *Les Langues internationales* (Paris).

Calvet, L.-J. (1969), 'Sur une conception fantaisiste de la langue: La Newspeak de George Orwell', *La Linguistique*, 1.

——(1974), *Linguistique et colonialisme* (Paris).

——(1977) (ed.), *Marxisme et linguistique* (Paris).

——(1980), 'La Route sel/or et l'expansion du manding', *Traces* no. 4 (Rabat).

——(1981), *Les Langues véhiculaires* (Paris).

——(1982), 'The Spread of Mandingo: Military, Commercial and Colonial Influence on a Linguistic Datum', in *Language Spread* (Bloomington: Indiana University Press).

——(1984), *La Tradition orale* (Paris).

——(1985), *Les Langues de marché* (Paris: Université Réné Descartes).

——(1985*a*), 'Le Plurilinguisme à l'école primaire', *Migrants formation*, no. 63.

——(1985*b*), 'Mehrsprachige Märkte und Vehikularsprachen: Geld und Sprache', *OBSt*, no. 31 (Bremen).

——(1986*a*), 'Trade Function and Lingua Francas', in *The Fergusonian impact*, ii. *Sociolinguistics and the Sociology of Language* (Berlin–New York–Amsterdam), 295–302.

——(1986*b*), 'L'Enjeu néologique et ses rapports à l'idéologie', paper given at 13th International Congress of Functional Linguistics, Corfu, 24–29 Aug.

Calvet, M., and Wioland, F. (1967), 'L'Expansion du wolof au Sénégal', *Bulletin de l'IFAN*, nos. 3–4.

——et al. (1985), *Rapport de mission à Ziguinchor* (Paris: CERPL).

Cheng, Chin-Chuan (1986), 'Contradictions in Chinese Language Reform', *International Journal of Sociology of Language*, no. 59.

Cieza de Leon, P. de (1967), *El senorio de los Incas* (Lima).

Cohen-Solal, A. (1985), *Sartre, 1905–1980* (Paris).

Colegio de etnologos y anthropologos sociales (1979), *El ILV en Mexico* (Mexico).

Comrie, B. (1981), *The Languages of the Soviet Union* (Cambridge).

Contenté, J. (1978), *L'Aigle des Caraïbes* (Paris).

Coyaud, M. (1969), *Questions de grammaire chinoise* (Paris).

Dalby, D. (1967–9), 'The Indigenous Script of West Africa', *African Languages Studies*, no. 8 (1967); no. 9 (1968); no. 10 (1969).

Das Gupta, J. (1970), *Language Conflict and National Development* (Berkeley).

——and Ferguson, C. (1977), 'Problems of Language Planning', in *Language Planning Processes* (The Hague: Mouton).

de Francis, J. (1977), 'Language and Script Reform in China', in *Advances in the Creation and Revision of Writing Systems* (The Hague).

de Heredia (1983), 'Les Parlers français des migrants', in *J'cause français, non?* (Paris).

Deniau, X. (1983), *La Francophonie* (Paris).

Descartes, R. (1937), *Oeuvres et lettres* (Paris: Gallimard).

Dieu, M., and Renaud, P. (1979), 'A propos d'une étude statistique du multilingualisme au Cameroun: Quelques problèmes métholodigiques', in P. Wald and G. Manessy, *Plurilinguisme* (Paris).

Delaforge (Captain) (n.d.), *Grammaire et méthode bambara* (Librairie militaire Charles-Lavauzelle).

Delafosse, M. (1912), *Haut-Sénégal Niger* (Paris).

Dorian, N. (1981), *Language Death: The Life-Cycle of a Scottish Gaelic Dialect* (Philadelphia).

Dressler, W. (1972), 'On the Phonology of Language Death', in *Papers of the 8th Regional Meeting, Chicago Linguistic Society* (Chicago).

Dubly, A. (1973), *Evaluacion de las escuelas radiofonicas de Sucua, 'Radio Federacion'* (Quito: INEDES).

Dubois, J., et al. (1973), *Dictionnaire de linguistique* (Paris).

Duboz, P. (1979), *Étude démographique de la ville de Brazzaville, 1974–1977* (Bangui: ORSTOM).

Fasold, R. (1984), *The Sociolinguistics of Society* (Oxford).

Federacion de centros Shuar (1976), *Solucion original a un problema actual* (Sucua).

Fenaux, R. (n.d.), *Discours sur la fonction internationale de la langue française* (Liege).

Ferguson, C. (1959), 'Diglossia', *Word*.

Fernandez-Garay, A. (1986), *La Mort des langues, bibliographie critique* (Paris: Université Réné Descartes).

Ferrer i Girones, F. (1985), *La persecucio politica de la llengua catalana* (Barcelona).

Fishman, J. (1967), 'Bilingualism with and without Diglossia, Diglossia with and without Bilingualism', *Journal of Social Issues*, no. 32.

—— (1970), *Sociolinguistics: A Brief Introduction* (Rowley, Mass.)

—— (1981), 'Language Policy: Past, Present and Future', in *Language in the USA* (Cambridge).

Fouts, R., and Rigby, R. (1976), 'Man-Chimpanzee Communication', in *How Animals Communicate* (Bloomington).

Galtier, G. (1980), 'Problèmes dialectologiques et phonographématiques des parlers mandingues', postgraduate thesis under the supervision of L. Guerre and S. Sauvageot (Université de Paris VII).

Garcia-Rippol Duran, M. (1986), 'Cent anys d'esperanto. Apunts per a una sociologia d'una llengua internacional minoritzada', paper given at Second International Congress of Catalan (Girona).

Gillian, A. (1984), 'Language and Development in Papua New Guinea', *Dialectical Anthropology*, 8.

Goudaillier, J.-P. (1982), 'Sprache und Macht: Wie ein Gesetz in Frankreich die Sprache reinigen will', *Dialect*, no. 6, 28–37.

Grandguillaume, G. (1983), *Arabisation et politique linguistique au Maghreb* (Paris).

Guitel, G. (1975), *Histoire comparée des numérotations écrites* (Paris).

Hagège, C. (1978), 'Babel, du temps mythique au temps de langage', *Revue philosophique*, no. 4.

——(1985), *L'Homme de paroles* (Paris).

Haugen, E. (1959), 'Planning for a Standard Language in Modern Norway', *Anthropological Linguistics*, 1 Mar. 1959.

——(1966), *Language Conflict and Language Planning: The Case of Modern Norwegian* (Cambridge: Harvard University Press).

Heath, S. B. (1976), 'A National Language Academy? Debate in the New Nation', *International Journal of the Sociology of Language*, no. 11, 9–43.

Hvalkof and Aaby (1981), *Is God an American? An Anthropological Perspective on the Missionary Work of the Summer Institute of Linguistics* (Denmark).

Janton, P. (1973), *L'Esperanto* (Paris).

Jespersen, O. (1922), *Language: Its Nature, Development and Origin* (London: Allen & Unwin).

Knappert, J. (1968), 'Language in a Political Situation', *Linguistics*, 39.

Koelle, S. W. (1854), *Grammar of the Vai Language* (London).

Koran (1964 edn.), translated by A. J. Arberry (Oxford: Oxford University Press).

Labrousse, P. (1985), 'Réformes et discours sur la réforme, le cas indonésien', in *La Réforme des langues* (Hamburg).

Le Palec, A. (1981), 'Brazzaville, note sur la situation linguistique de deux quartiers', paper given at the fifth round table of AUPELF, Yaoundé.

Lehmann, W. (1975) (ed.), *Language and Linguistics in the People's Republic of China* (University of Texas).

Leroi-Gourhan, A. (1964), *Le Geste et la parole* (Paris).

Lévy-Bruhl, L. (1951), *Les Fonctions mentales dans les sociétés inférieures* (Paris).

Lewis, G. (1972), *Multilingualism in the Soviet Union* (The Hague).

Martinet, A. (1986), *Des steppes aux océans* (Paris).

Mashinkiash, R. (1976), *La Educacion entre los Shuar* (Sucua).

Maurais, J. (1985) (ed.), *La Crise des langues* (Paris).

Meillet, A. (1905–1908), 'Comment les mots changent de sens', *L'année sociologique*.

——(1928), *Les Langues dans l'Europe nouvelle* (Paris).

Michenot, E. (1983), 'Parler-pouvoir: Études des caractéristiques du quechua et des conséquences de la situation de contact avec la langue officielle: Cochabamba, Bolivie', postgraduate thesis under the supervision of D. François (Paris: Université Réné Descartes).

Milner, J.-C. (1978), *L'Amour de la langage* (Paris). Translated by Ann Banfield as *For the Love of Language* (London: Macmillan, 1990).

Mistral, F. (n.d.), *Lou tresor dou felibrige*.

Muysken, P. (1975), *Pidginization in the Quechua of Lowlands of Eastern Ecuador* (Instituto inter-andino de desarollo, University of Amsterdam).

Rojas, I. (1980), *Expansion del Quechua* (Lima).

Rygaloff, A. (1973), *Grammaire élémentaire du chinois* (Paris).

Saint-Robert, P. de (1985), preface to *Guide des mots nouveaux* (Paris).

Schläpfer, R. (1985), *La Suisse aux quatre langues* (Geneva).

Schlieben-Lange, B. (1977), 'The Language Situation in Southern France', *Linguistics*, 191.

Schoell, F. (1936), *La Langue française dans le monde* (Paris).

Sidikou, A. (1980), 'Niamey: Étude de géographie socio-urbaine', 2 vols., doctoral thesis (Rouen).

Summer Institute of Linguistics (1959), *Estudios acerca de la lenguas Huarani (Aucua), Shimigae y Zapata* (Quito).

Swadesh, M. (1986), *Le Langage et la vie humaine* (Paris).

Takdir Alisjahbana, S. (1976), *Language Planning for Modernization: The Case of Indonesian and Malaysian* (The Hague: Mouton).

Torero, A. (1972), 'Linguistica e historia de los Andes del Peru y Bolivia', in *El reto del multilingismo en el Peru* (Lima).

——(1974), *El quechua y la historia social andina* (Lima).

Von Frisch, K. (1974), 'Decoding the Language of the Bee', *Science*, no. 185.

Waggoner, D. (1981), 'Statistics on Language Use', in *Language in the USA* (Cambridge).

Westermann, D. (1970), *Les Peuples et les civilisations d'Afrique* (Paris).

Williams, G. (1986), 'Language Planning or Language Expropriation?', *Journal of Multilingual and Multicultural Development*, 7: 6, 509–18.

Yaguello, M. (1984), *Les Fous du langage* (Paris).

Yanco, J. (1983), 'Niamey, une communauté bilingue', unpublished (Niamey).

Yang Jian (1985), 'Problèmes de chinois contemporain', in Maurais (1985).

Zhou Youguang (1986), 'Modernization of the Chinese Language', *International Journal of Sociology of Language*, no. 59.

Index

'Africa' alphabet 154
Aasen, I. 138–9, 142, 144
Académie Française 49, 191
Adam, J. 191–2
Albo, X. 94, 104
Algeria 33–4, 39–40, 145
Alliance Française pour la propagation de la langue française 178
Ampère, J.-J. 181
animal communication 3–4
Apte, M. 125, 128n
Arabic xiii, 33–4, 39, 40, 97, 126, 171, 189; classical Arabic 5, 12, 26,100–1; in France 73–5; in Mauritius 61–2; in the Koran 20–2, 24–5; in Turkey 140–3
artificial languages 77, 194–201 see also Esperanto; Volapük
Aru 91
Assam 128
Atahualpa 94
Aymara 91–3, 114

Babel, myth of 17–19, 22–4, 113, 194
Balibar, R. 64–5
Bambara 29–30, 35, 38, 40, 67–70, 97, 153–5, 167–9, 172
barbarism 41–2
Barnes, D. 122
Barthes, R. 60, 195
Basari 132
Basque 150, 176, 186
Bassa 153
Bazin, L. 140n, 141
bees, see animal communication
Belgium 31, 37–8, 188
Ben Jelloun, H. 169
Bengali 128
Benveniste, E. 4

Berber 33–4, 75, 104
Bercis, P. 186
Bhojpuri 62
Bible 17–20, 22–5
bilingualism, see diglossia
Bislama 95
Bjerke, A. 139–40
Bochman, K. 187
borrowing 166–70, 174
Breton 32, 40, 55, 114, 176
Broca, P. 6,11
Brunot, F. 46, 48, 64, 175
Burkina Faso 34–5, 38, 153–4, 170
Burundi 34–5

Canada 177, 179–82, 188, 193
Cantonese 79–80
Castilian 42, 92–4, 97, 114, 147–50
Catalan 101, 104, 176, 186
Central African Republic 34–5
Chad 34–5
Chardonnet, Abbé 182
Charles I of Spain (Holy Roman Emperor Charles V) 92, 114
Charles IX 182
chimpanzees, see animal communication
China 77–80, 88–9, 119–25, 134–6, 158–65, 199
Chinese 12, 57, 77–80, 119–25, 158–65, 189; see also Cantonese; Putonghua
Chomsky, N. 109
Cieza de Leon 91
Comenius 194
Congo 80–4, 88
Corsican 55, 75, 176
Coyaud, M. 119
Creole 36, 61–2, 177
Cyrillic alphabet 156–8, 184

Danish 137–40, 142–4
de Gaulle 128, 190
Delafosse, M. 76
Deniau, X. 183, 188
Descartes, R. 194
Devanagari 126, 163
dialect 115, 145
diglossia 26–38
Dogon 69–70
Dominici, G. 59–61, 65
Dravidian languages 126–7
Drummond case 59–61
du Bellay 44–7

Ecuador, *see* Shuar
edict of Villars-Cotterêt 46, 182
Engels, F. 11
English 6, 13, 29–30, 99, 152; in India
    126–8, 134–5; in Mauritius 62–3; in
    relation to French 49, 180–4, 187, 189,
    193; in the USA 191–2
Esperanto 77, 114, 178, 194–201

Fang 86
Ferguson, C. 26–30, 40, 117
Fishman, J. 27–30, 114, 192
France 31–8, 45, 175–93
Franco, General 186–7
francophonie 189
French 6, 13, 29, 107, 128, 155, 167, 169,
    175–93; and diglossia 31–40; as
    descendent of Latin 100–2, 104; as
    lingua franca 55, 99, 128, 152, 175–93;
    du Bellay's defence of 45–7; in Congo
    82–4; in Guinea 132–3; in Mauritius
    61–3; Rivarol on 47–50; Strasbourg
    Oaths 64–5
Frisch, K. von 3
Fulani 69–71, 75, 86, 104, 131, 154, 171–2

Galtier, G. 154
Gambia 154
Gandhi, M. 127, 136
German 49, 65, 99, 171, 191
Goudaillier, J. P. 183
Gourmantche 86
Grégoire, Abbé 47–8

Greek 5, 16, 26, 40, 41–2, 100–1
Guadeloupe 65
Guinea 34–5, 128, 131–5, 149, 153–5
Guinea Bissau 154
Gujerati 62, 126, 128

Hagège, C. 19, 202
Haiti 26–7, 36
Haugen, E. 113, 116–17, 137, 138n, 139,
    140n
Hausa 70–1, 84–7, 98, 154
Haut Conseil International de la
    Francophonie 186
Heath, S. B. 191
Hebrew 5, 19, 97, 100, 201
Heredia, C. de 175
Hindi 61–2, 126–8, 134, 136, 164, 171
Hindustani 127
Hiri-motu 95

Ido 178
India 125–8, 134–6
Indo-European 50
Indonesia 115, 163–4, 171
International Africa Institute 154
Italian 37, 44, 49
Ivory Coast 38, 154

Janton, P. 195
Jespersen, O. 5, 13
Jivaro, *see* Shuar

Kanté, S. 154
Kashmiri 126
Kemal, M. 140–4, 185
Knappert, J. 157
Knudsen, K. 138–9, 142
Koelle, S. 153
Koniaigi 132
Koran 17, 20–2, 24–5, 44
Kotocoli 86

Labov, W. x
Lacan, J. 109
Lambert, J. 180
Lançon, G. 183
language death 100–10

language origin 3–16
langue 109
Lari 81–4, 88
Latin xiii, xiv, 5, 12, 46, 97, 100–4, 176,
    194–5, 197
Leibniz, G. 195
Leroi-Gourhan, A. 6
Lewis, G. 157
lexis 115, 144, 166–74
Liberia 154
Lingala 81–4, 95, 97, 99
lingua francas 17, 55–66, 77, 90–9, 194
linguistic cannibalism ix, 174
linguistic purity 141–2
Luxembourg 188

Mahgreb 33–4
Malay 95, 98, 99, 115, 164, 167
Malaysia 163–4
Mali 29–30, 39–40, 69–70, 88, 153–5,
    167–70
Malinke 69, 131, 153, 155
Mandingo 96, 99, 153–5, 163–4
Marathi 128
markets 76–89
Marr, N. 199
Martinet, A. 101
Mauritius 61–3
Meillet, A. xiv, 200
Michenot, E. 105–7
Milner, J.-C. 109
Mistral, F. 58
Monokutuba 81–4
Montesquieu, C. 47
Morocco 33–4
mother tongues 72–3
Mussolini, B. 186–7
My Fair Lady (film) 59, 61, 139

Nehru, J. 127, 136
neologisms 166–74
Neo-Melanesian 95
Niger 70–1, 84–8
Nigeria 87
Norwegian 137–40, 142–5, 163–4
Noum 153
Nsibidi 153

Ophuysen, C. van 164
Oriyu 128
Orwell, G. 118

Pa Kin 160
Pakistan 127
Panet, J. A. 179
parole 109
Persian 126, 140–3, 171
Pickering, J. 192
pidgin English 56–7
pidgins 77, 194
Pinyin 125–8, 161–5
Plato 42–3
Polo, Marco 175
Provençal 32, 40, 57–8
Puquina 91–3
Putonghua 79–80, 121–5, 134, 161, 163
Pygmalion (play) 59, 61, 65, 139

Quechua 38, 90–9, 104–10, 114, 148,
    150

Ramulu, P. S. 127
Reclus, O. 190
Rivarol, A. 47–50, 188
Romansch 37
Rousillon Ordonance 182
Russian 99, 152, 155–8, 171, 189
Rygaloff, A. 122

Saint, Robert, P. de 184
Sango 95
Sanskrit 97, 100, 126, 171
Sartre, J.-P. 56
Saussure, F. de 43
Schoell, F. 176n, 177
Senegal 29, 67–9, 88, 95–6, 149, 153–4
Senghor, L. 190
Serer 104
shibboleth 23–4
Shuar 146–52
Sierra Leone 154
Sociolinguistics x, xiv-v, 109–10, 173–4,
    202–3
Solomon Islands pidgin 95
Songhai 69–71, 85–6, 154

Spanish 49, 99, 100, 104–7, 152, 189; *see also* Castilian
Speroni, S. 44
Stalin, J. 124, 173
Strasbourg Oaths 64–5, 175
Susu 131
Swadesh, M. 13–15, 91
Swahili 29–30, 95–6, 98–9
Sweden 137
Switzerland 31, 37–8, 188

Takdir Alisjahbana 170
Tamasheq 154
Tamil 62, 126, 128
Tanzania 29–30
Telegu 126, 128
Tibetan 114, 120, 125
Tocqueville 179–80
Torero, A. 90–3
Touré, S. 128, 133
Tunisia 34
Turkey 137, 140–4, 185, 186, 187
Turkish 140–4, 163

UNESCO 131, 147, 154, 189, 200
United Nations 189

United States 187, 189, 191–2
universal languages 194–201
Urdu 126–8, 136, 163–4, 171

Vai 153
vernaculars 17, 55–66
Volapük 178, 195, 197
Voltaire 47

Webster, N. 192
Westermann, D. 153
Whitney, W. xiii
Williams, G. 202
Wobe 86
Wolof 35, 67–71, 75, 95–6, 104
Writing 38–40, 115, 139, 141, 144, 145, 153–65; of Chinese 158–65; of Russian 156–8

Yang Jian 161
Yoruba 86

Zaire 34–5, 170
Zamenhof, L. 197–8, 201
Zarma 70–1, 84–7
Zhou Yougang 158